Ecological Security

Ecological Security

The Foundation of Sustainable Development

Edited by

SAMAR SINGH

SHIPRA

INDIA INTERNATIONAL CENTRE, NEW DELHI

ISBN: 85-7541-321-2

First Published in India in 2007

Ecological Security: The Foundation of Sustainable Development

Published by:
SHIPRA PUBLICATIONS
115-A, Vikas Marg, Shakarpur
Delhi-110092, INDIA
Phone: 91-11-65277210, 91-11-22500954
Fax: 91-11-22458662
E-mail: info@shiprapublications.com
www.shiprapublications.com

Preface

Since its inception, the India International Centre has been inviting eminent thinkers to join in holding lectures, discussions and symposia on the significant problems of our times. The Centre's founding principles embody 'a dedication to the life of ideas', and as Prime Minister Jawaharlal Nehru said at the inauguration of the IIC in 1962, the Centre wants to associate with 'effective people who get tied up with the problems of the day, emotionally and intellectually, and who want to solve them, solve them, no doubt, as far as they can objectively…'

Today, the Centre is in a highly privileged and unique position of being able to bring together people and ideas on serious issues concerning the problems of the day, issues concerning life and death. And what could be more serious than the greening of the earth, conservation of scarce natural resources and securing a healthier environment for the future generations?

The essential principles that inspire 'ecological security' are undoubtedly grave issues. Instead of invading armies, the world must secure against large-scale and mind-less depletion of scarce natural resources, 'invading' deserts, pollution, rising sea levels, increased ultra violet radiation, that are no less threatening than conventional warfare.

Ecological Security raises a broader set of concerns not yet commonly addressed in policy forums. In the wake of the escalation in public concern over environmental degradation in the previous decades, it is not surprising to find that the environment has also found its way on to the expanded security agenda. The growing appreciation of global ecological interdependence has engendered the daring hope that not only a 'peace dividend' but also an 'ecological dividend' might accrue to a global community conceived as citizens whose allegiances are 'planetary' as well as national, ethnic and racial.

In the year 2001 the Centre had, in collaboration with the Foundation for Ecological Security, which is based at Anand (Gujarat), co-sponsored a series of lectures on the subject of Ecological Security, organized by Mr Samar Singh, who is a Member of the Centre. There were twenty lectures (of which eighteen are included in this volume) in the series, spread over two years, starting in October 2001 and ending in August 2003. The lectures were delivered as well as chaired by eminent persons.

Mr Samar Singh's initiative to bring together eminent public figures in India to deliberate on this vital issue and to raise consciousness about the policy implications deserves special thanks. The present publication, planned while the series was being organized, was long over-due. The credit for its prompt publication goes to Mr. D. Kumar of Shipra Publications.

India International Centre
New Delhi

Bela Butalia
Editor

Contents

Introduction

The Foundation for Ecological Security (FES) was established in 2001. In the process of finalizing the name for the new organization, there was considerable discussion among the founding members and it was realized that the term 'ecological security' was not well known or understood. Hence, it was considered necessary to do something concrete to make the concept better known and understood, especially among the policy planners and decision makers. Thus arose the idea of instituting a lecture series on the subject at the national capital and the responsibility was entrusted to me. I felt that the India International Centre (IIC) would make an excellent venue for the lecture series. So I approached the then Director IIC Shri NN Vohra with the proposal and was very happy to get his instant and positive response. It was quickly agreed that the lecture series would be jointly organized by the IIC and FES. This is the short background leading up to the eighteen lectures presented in this publication.

The term 'ecological security' is derived by a fusion of two meaningful words: *ecology* and *security*. *Ecology* is the science concerned with the relationships among and between organisms and all aspects—living as well as non-living—of their environment. *Security* stands for that which is safe, sure and guaranteed. Linking these two substantive words connotes an ecological condition in safekeeping, firmly fastened and guaranteed against minimum loss or damage. This is both the basis and raison d'être of the concept of 'ecological security'.

The German scientist Ernst Heinrich Haeckel (1834-1919) is credited with having coined the word *ecology* in 1866, deriving it from the Greek word *oikos*, which means a house or dwelling place. In fact, the German word for household (*haushalt*) goes well beyond the English meaning, implying the place where an organism is at home and the interactions of the organism with its fellow occupants, as well as the budgeting of resources and other such aspects of home economics. These aspects are not only biological but also physical and chemical. Haeckel's description was so well thought out that it is still valid, after more than a hundred years. Here, it is noteworthy that some ecologists, especially in Germany, have been referring to this discipline as 'the science of the balance of nature'.

This is quite justified too. After all, present-day ecologists recognize that it is only by extensive consideration of all natural phenomena as well as all relevant aspects of civilization that one can possibly come to a proper understanding of the conditions for the existence of an organism in its habitat. Thus, ecology is always more than just a discipline of the natural sciences. Besides, botany, zoology, physics, chemistry, meteorology, applied technology, and even the history of civilization, are simply aids, to be used as needed, in understanding a section of nature in its entirety. The immense diversity of plant or animal life leads the botanist or zoologist to focus on individual species. But, from an ecological standpoint, each species is at best a component of a much larger web of influence and dependence, environment and adaptation, which—in the final analysis—encompass the whole biosphere.

During more than three billion years of evolution, the various ecosystems of our planet have organized themselves in very subtle and complex ways, so as to maximize productivity linked to sustainability. Here, sustainability stands for ecological sustainability, a concept put forward forcefully more than twenty years ago by Lester Brown, President of the Worldwatch Institute in Washington DC. He defined a sustainable society as one that is able to satisfy its needs without diminishing the chances of future generations. However, this definition does not provide clues about how to actually build a sustainable society. Hence it is necessary to have an operational explanation of the term ecological sustainability. For this, the key lies in the realization that nature provides enough models for this purpose. After all, nature's ecosystems are essentially sustainable communities of plants, animals and microorganisms. The most outstanding characteristic of the biosphere is its inherent ability to sustain life in all its myriad forms. So, a sustainable human community must be designed in such manner that its ways of life, its physical structures, businesses, economy, polity, etc., *do not interfere with nature's inherent ability to sustain life*.

For a clearer understanding, it is necessary to know about the basic principles of organization that natural ecosystems have developed to sustain the web of life. These include certain fundamentals: that matter cycles continually; that the energy driving the ecological cycles flows from the sun; that diversity assures resilience; that one species' waste is another species' food; that it is through very subtle networking that life has evolved from the very start more than three billion years ago; that the world, as a whole, is a living, self-regulating system based on a network of inseparable patterns of relationships. In essence, it is all about contexts, connections and relationships. Ecology is, first and foremost, a science of relationships among members of ecosystem communities. Moreover, ecology is inherently multi-disciplinary, because ecosystems connect the living and non-living worlds. In other words, ecology is grounded not only in biology, but also in chemistry, geology and other branches of science. When the human dimensions get added, several other disciplines come into play, including economics and politics. Thus, ecology and ecological sustainability necessarily involve systemic and multi-disciplinary approaches.

The basic principles of ecology are all closely inter-related. They are just different aspects of a single fundamental pattern of organization that has enabled nature to evolve and sustain life on earth for billions of years. In this process, no individual organism can exist by itself. Thus, the animals depend on the photosynthesis of plants for their energy needs, while the plants depend on the carbon dioxide produced by animals and the nitrogen fixed by the bacteria at their roots; and together the plants, animals and micro-organisms regulate and maintain the conditions conducive to life. Sustainability is, therefore, not any form of individual property, but a state of being with an entire web of relationships and implies community acting in concert. The most profound lesson that nature provides is that the way to sustain life is to build and nurture community living.

The lesson for humankind, caught up in the present day web of economics, is quite obvious. Basically, the clash between economics and ecology arises from the fact that whereas nature is cyclical, the industrial and commercial systems fuelling our present-day economy are entirely linear. Human businesses take resources, transform them into products plus waste, and sell the products to consumers, who generate more waste in the act of consuming the products. Corporate entities treat natural resources such as air, water and soil as free commodities and also disregard the delicate web of social factors. Private profit is then made at public cost, especially in terms of deterioration of the environment and the general quality of life, which is also at the expense of the future generations. Such a set up cannot possibly be sustainable. Sustainability requires patterns of production and consumption that are cyclical, imitating the processes of nature. This is possible only through changed human perceptions and by redesigning human businesses and the economy as such. In effect, human survival depends on our ability to understand properly the basic principles of ecology and to live accordingly.

Here, it is pertinent to quote Norman Myers, a leading ecologist of our time. He has been talking and writing on 'environmental security', which is the same as ecological security. In his fascinating book titled, *Ultimate Security: The Environmental Basis of Political Stability*, Myers raises the question: What is this thing called Security? He then explains it as follows:

'Just as health is more than the absence of disease, so security—let alone peace—is more than the absence of hostilities. Yet while a nation knows what insecurity is, it cannot say so readily what it means by security—just as disease is more readily recognizable than health in the full and proper sense of the term. We need a clear-cut idea of what security is: what it amounts to, where we get it, and, most of all, what it means to *feel secure*, whether on the part of governments, global society, communities, or individuals. At the same time, we need to determine how we can gain security without resorting to force.

'In essence, and little though this is generally recognized by governments, security applies most at the level of the individual citizen. It amounts to human well-being: not only protection from harm and injury but also access to water, food, shelter, health, employment, and other basic requisites that are the due of every person on Earth. It is the collectivity of these citizen needs—overall safety and quality of life—that should figure prominently in the nation's view of security.

'As conventionally understood, a nation's view of security entails ensuring its territorial integrity and maintaining its position in the world beyond its borders. So a nation must enjoy assured access to raw materials and energy, to trading opportunities wherever available, and to scope for its government, enterprises and other institutions to pursue activities without let or hindrance. In addition, a nation needs to foster its political ideals and its cultural outlook, both within its own land and further a field. Without these essentials, a nation has no security.

'So, too, the entire community of nations, indeed all humankind, needs to enjoy security in the form of acceptably clean (unpolluted) environments, supplies of environmental goods such as water and food, and a stable atmosphere and climate. In short, all nations need a planetary habitat that is secure in every down-to-earth respect—which means, in turn, that "we" are only as safe as "they" are.'

It is significant that Norman Myers uses the term 'Ultimate Security'. Fritjof Capra, another well-known ecologist, has called this 'True Security'.

Following from the above discussion, it is obvious that ecological issues pervade and shape all facets of human existence and endeavour. Viewed in totality in terms of an ecological condition of safekeeping, as implied by 'ecological security', there are necessarily several dimensions, including the multiple factors that are involved and the manner in which all these affect the lives and well-being of the people as well as national economy and security. The Lecture Series presented in this volume attempts to deal with various aspects of this rather wide-ranging and complex subject. This would be clear from the choice of lecture topics.

However, the central focus throughout has been on the overarching theme of ecological security, which was introduced appropriately in the first lecture titled 'Ecological Security, Issues and Challenges' by Dr. Amrita Patel, Chairman, Foundation for Ecological Security. Introducing the central theme of the lecture series, she emphasized that economic progress, indeed sustainable development in any and every aspect of our nation's socio-economic endeavours, is possible only if this rests on secure ecological foundations. She explained that, in essence, ecological security is about maintaining the natural integrity, the optimum functioning of the vital processes of the natural systems which sustain all life forms as well as the matrix of interlocking biotic and a biotic forms, in their totality, that constitutes the critical biological foundations of life on earth. She also highlighted the very complex nature of the problem of how to go about reaching a state of ecological security and suggested some approaches in that direction.

The following seventeen lectures included herein continue to focus on the central theme of ecological security, while dealing with various related aspects. These include topics such as the dimensions of ecological security, the role of Faiths, the Political Process and the Media, the Earth Charter, Governance, Policy and Planning, Institutional Framework, Gender, Livelihoods, Lifestyles, Human Rights, Education, National Food Security, Natural Resources Management, Globalisation and Accounting. It is unfortunate that due to unavoidable reasons, it has not been possible to include herein two other lectures on the legal aspects and human health issues.

In any case, I am deeply beholden to all the eminent speakers who have graciously contributed their valuable time and effort to enrich the lecture series and thereby helped in generating greater awareness and understanding of the ecological issues that are so central to human welfare as well as the national economy and well-being. Likewise, the contributions made by all the distinguished chairpersons for various sessions, namely, late Dr T. N. Khoshoo, Dr P. C. Joshi, Justice Shri. M. N. Venkatachaliah, Dr Ajit Mozoomdar, Mr. P. V. Jayakrishnan, late Dr Kamla Chowdhry, Mr V. B. Eswaran, Ms Maneka Gandhi, Dr V. R. Panchamukhi, Dr S. C. Jain, Ms Sunita Narain, Shri Som Pal, Prof. Yashpal, Mr. Manmohan Malhoutra, and Mr. B.G Verghese, have to be acknowledged. I am equally grateful to the FES Chairperson, Dr Amrita Patel, and the India International Centre Directors, Shri N. N. Vohra and Shri P. C. Sen, for asking me to coordinate this whole effort on behalf of both the organizations and for all the help and support provided to make this possible.

Finally, it is necessary to recall here the following words of the former Prime Minister Indira Gandhi:

> One cannot be truly human and civilised unless one looks upon not only all fellow men but all creation with the eyes of a friend. Modern man must re-establish an unbroken link with Nature and with life. He must again learn to invoke the energy of growing things and to recognise, as did the ancients in India centuries ago, that one can take from the earth and the atmosphere only so much as one puts back into them.

The ecological wisdom contained in the above statement arises from the intuitive feeling of the oneness of all life, which is best expressed in the Atharva Veda, compiled about four thousand years ago, as follows:

> We are birds of the same nest,
> We may wear different skins,
> We may speak different languages,
> We may believe in different religions,
> We may belong to different cultures,
> Yet we share the same home — Our Earth.
> For man can live individually,
> But can survive only collectively.
> Born on the same planet,
> Covered by the same skies,
> Gazing at the same stars,
> Breathing the same air,
> We must learn to happily progress together,
> Or miserably perish together.

Samar Singh

1

Ecological Security, Issues and Challenges

AMRITA PATEL

The all-embracing nature of the concept of Ecological Security is humbling, considering the enormity of its dimensions. However, practical field experience leaves no doubt that the need for ecological security is of overriding importance to the future well-being of India and its economic development.

The rapidly growing destruction of the ecological foundations, not only of our country, but also of the Indian sub-continent—indeed of the world as a whole—is seriously worrying an increasing number of persons as it is placing the livelihoods, particularly of the least privileged and of the future generations, in the gravest jeopardy.

The Foundation for Ecological Security has emerged from the chrysalis of an earlier organization set up by the National Dairy Development Board, in response to a request from the then National Wastelands Development Board of the Government of India, to support the Board's efforts to meet the fodder, fuel and timber needs of our villagers. The organization the NDDB set up was the National Tree Growers Co-operative Federation (NTGCF). This continues to exist, but many of its primary responsibilities have now been assumed by the Foundation. The Foundation for Ecological Security works directly with village communities, to partner and assist them in revitalizing their natural resource base, the village commons and the institutions that support them. The physical work involves the restoration of biomass productivity, moisture regimes, protecting and enriching local biodiversity and generally sustaining and strengthening the livelihood and cultural base of village communities.

The institutional framework of Foundation's activities embraces the revitalizing of collective action for the governance of common property natural resources at the local level, as well as participating in the framing or reforming of relevant government policy and legislation at the state and federal levels.

In the fifteen years of NTGCF's existence, we have learned a great deal. Perhaps the most important lesson is that to achieve our objectives we needed to look at the problems that confronted us at the micro level more holistically. In doing so we have come to realise that there were more fundamental multi-dimensional problems of the surrounding region as a whole that had to be addressed if we were to enhance biomass productivity and achieve sustainable development of the rural areas in which we are working.

I believe it is an incontrovertible fact that economic progress, indeed sustainable development in any and every aspect of our nation's socio-economic endeavours is possible today, more so than ever before, only, and I emphasize, only, if this rests on secure ecological foundations. It is such foundations, which are the most fundamental and important basic infrastructure we need. This is far more important than any other human-conceived forms of infrastructure that are so frequently insisted upon by our leaders of commerce and industry, our economists and development planners, as being essential for the economic progress of our country. The types of infrastructure I refer to are power supply, roadways, railways, telecommunication systems, etc., all of which are geared to economic development. While such man-made infrastructure is certainly required, without secure ecological foundations it is only a question of time before these could become infructuous and accelerate the erosion of what remains today of our present ecological foundations. It is the infrastructure required to sustain our ecological foundations that we must above all else put into place and securely protect, if there is to be any hope of achieving sustainable economic development. By this, I refer especially to forests which are vital to protect and enrich our soil, ensure the availability of water, stabilize our atmosphere, etc., but most of all ensure our long-term food security.

Let me attempt to explain what we in the Foundation believe to be the meaning of the term 'Ecological Security', the major focus of our concerns. In essence, Ecological Security is maintaining the natural integrity, and in a state of stability, as far as present circumstances can possibly permit, the optimum functioning of the vital processes of

Nature's Biological Systems that sustain the myriad life forms—plant and animal, both macro and micro, which through their symbiotic relationship, complementary interaction and adaptation to their abiotic environment over millions of years, have thus far supported the evolution of all life on earth, and not the least human. It is this matrix of interlocking biotic and abiotic forms, in their totality, that constitutes the critical biological foundations of life on earth.

One may now well ask, how on earth do we commence achieving and sustaining a state of ecological security? The initial and greatest challenge will be to build a consensus and a common perspective on how we use our land and our water 'resources'. To commence with, we need to determine a Landuse Policy and Strategy that not only takes into account the fundamental principles of how Nature functions, and in determining this, take into account the critical livelihood needs, rather than market provoked wants, of the poorest of our people, and do so in ways that are both equitable and enduring. A tall order you will say, both politically as well as in the face of the global consumeristic onslaught to which I refer below. But I see no alternative. Any broadbased, consensual process of landuse planning would inevitably be a highly political and contentious process. Inversely, the lack of such planning, or exclusive and arbitrary decisions taken in this regard, are in themselves highly political and even more dangerous. I must admit that I am daunted by this prospect, but not without hope.

At this juncture it is impossible to visualise the solutions to every conceivable aspect, but the basic imperatives are discernible and provide leads to the directions in which we should proceed. Given enlightened political and social leadership and will, and the realisation by the more responsible elements in society in general and the business and industrial community in particular, that what is proposed is not merely simple common sense but is the only way to ensure that their enterprises continue to survive, even flourish, we can set ourselves firmly on the path to long term sustainable development in the truest sense of the term.

A coherent and comprehensive perspective Landuse Plan, covering the whole geographical area of the country, with the various eco-systems and eco-zones clearly demarcated, whether they include one or more states or only a portion of a single one, and highlighting the major watersheds, down to the micro-watersheds at the village-cluster level, is required. The technology required to do this is available. It is only when we have such a unified holistic perspective, can we begin to plan our landuse at the different geographical and ecological levels, and structure our development plans and budgets accordingly. I believe that in the present scenario of state governments in competition and conflict with one another and with varying political ideologies and development trajectories, this would present a most important, though difficult challenge but it is the basic essential master plan for ecologically relevant development. The FES has been invited by the state government of the newly formed state of Uttaranchal to undertake a preliminary landuse study, hopefully a precursor to a state-wide landuse planning exercise. I am told that a similar initiative is being undertaken in the state of Orissa. We hope to learn the complexities such processes involve, and contribute to a meaningful and positive outcome. Perhaps, after we have done our bit in Uttaranchal we may be able, with this valuable experience behind us, to demonstrate to the central government how crucial it is for a similar exercise to be carried out for the whole country. Thereafter, in some small but important way, we may perhaps be able to assist whichever agency is entrusted with this marathon but all important national task.

At the national level, perhaps one of the most critical landuse decisions will involve identifying our present and prospective ecologically critical areas which must carry forest cover. We believe that today, the most threatened and the most critical of the ecological processes, or life-support systems, to which the nation must give the highest priority and therefore its immediate attention, is what we in FES term as the country's hydrological regime, what some scientists have very appropriately called 'the blood stream of the biosphere'. To do so we must strengthen and sustain our primary sources of fresh water supplies, which are today so seriously threatened. Given what we consider the particularly favourable geo-physical location and features of the Indian sub-continent and consequently the favourable agro-climatic conditions that prevail, a particularly valuable characteristic of which is the monsoon, restoring and sustaining the hydrological regime is not an insuperable problem. Through the fifteen years of experience we have gained in NTGCF we believe that the approach that has the greatest and most promising ecological spin-off benefits is one based on restoring the forest and vegetative cover on our country's 'Uplands'—our mountains, hills and plateaus, which constitute 40 per cent of the 328.7 million ha. that is the geographical area of our country. It is these Uplands that are today the least populated and by and large the most degraded. These consequently now suffer the least human-caused adverse biotic pressures. Restoring forest and vegetative cover to these Uplands primarily through a process of natural regeneration, aided to the extent necessary, by sensitively conceived and nature-complimentary measures can, we believe, accelerate the restoration of forest cover over the Uplands of our country in a relatively short space of time, at a modest cost, and thereby contribute a wide range of ecological benefits. I make a distinction between forest and vegetative cover since a number of our Uplands do not carry forests but are natural grasslands of long standing.

I venture here to suggest what some of us believe should be the true definition of the word 'forests'. Forests are a multi-storied stand of diverse endemic plant and tree growth with its complement of fauna. Tree plantations alone, as many would have us believe, are not true forests any more than are other perennial plantations of tea, coffee, rubber, horticultural fruit groves, etc.

With such forest cover there will be a major reduction in the loss of top soil which had, not long ago, been estimated by our Ministry of Agriculture to be over 6 billion tonnes per annum, placing in serious jeopardy the long-term food security of our country. Since the maximum precipitation of rainfall takes place on our Uplands, given adequate forest and vegetative cover a much greater proportion of this water will be retained in our Uplands for long periods thereby enhancing the purity and duration of flow of our rivers, recharging the sub-soil water table and, over time, the deeper aquifers. This would lead to restoring the output of innumerable tubewells that have gone dry due mainly to the drastic fall in sub-soil water tables throughout the country in the last few decades from overuse and because of the wholesale felling and clearing of forests. A particularly important benefit from establishing forest cover over our Uplands is that such areas will provide refuge to a substantial proportion of our bio-diversity—our plant and animal life and thereby help secure the crucial biological foundations of our existence. It is important to note that forests are the richest repository of our bio-diversity, representing, as bio-diversity does, the most valuable component of our national heritage. Without such forests, which must be fully protected, much of our bio-diversity will soon be lost forever.

We need to realize that our National Parks and Sanctuaries, particularly those in the more fertile areas of our Plains, are already under intense and increasing pressure from a growing human population with rapidly rising material aspirations stimulated by a market driven economy. This is leading inexorably to the increasing conversion into cash of our finite and living natural resources. These areas are becoming islands in a surrounding sea of frenetic so-called 'developmental' activity. Fortunately ecosystems by their very nature are dynamic, and by and large move to where there is the least disturbance. If there is to be any hope of saving a reasonable proportion of our bio-diversity—our macro and micro forms of wildlife, both plant and animal—we believe it is in this approach that lie our greatest hope and promise.

India's national forest policies have successively mandated, and very sensibly, that $33^1/_3$ per cent of its land area should be under tree and forest cover. From an ecological point of view this should be under forest cover rather than mere tree plantations. Given the looming ecological crisis with which we are now confronted, this $33^1/_3$ per cent forest cover, preferably more, should be re-established in our Uplands. We believe that this will secure for us the maximum ecological and consequently economic benefits and contribute thereby, more than any other approach, to long-term sustainable development. Because of the crucial role of such forests to the country as a whole, the re-afforested Uplands should, I urge most fervently, be declared inviolate and designated as National Forests. In the national interest these forests must be placed under the direct jurisdiction and protection of the central government. In these National Forests all forms of 'development', as currently understood, must be restricted to the absolute minimum, preferably avoided altogether. I realise that many of you will have the gravest doubts as to whether, without a strong central government that not only understands the importance of Ecological Security but is convinced of the ecological imperatives that will determine our future, areas of such National Forests can be established.

I confess I share the doubts that many of you will have about the success of pursuing such an approach. But we see this as the best and only long-term means of mitigating the looming ecological crisis. Our hope lies in gaining the support of a critical mass of committed articulate and influential people to support this approach to enable us to collectively persuade government at the central and state levels to initiate and pursue such a course of action.

In the FES we are in the process of mounting a media campaign which we hope will not merely contribute to creating an awareness but stimulate the degree of concern necessary to persuade our governments to take effective action. One can but pray that this will not prove to be a vain hope. It is our belief that it is still possible to initiate a process of ecological restoration leading to ecological security. But I fear time is rapidly running out. In a few years from now, the difficulty of doing so will be infinitely greater, indeed it will require more effort than ever to achieve the required results; that is, if by then it is already not too late.

Worldwide economic integration, referred to now as globalization and liberalisation, is also enfolding humankind in a frightening and perhaps inescapable grasp that portends grave environmental consequences. Economic integration, as we are witnessing in some of our remoter project areas in the Himalaya and in Orissa, is resulting all too often, and quite suddenly, in 'commodifying' nature, by focusing the demands of people of far off countries upon our limited areas of supply. These areas, often sparsely populated, are remote frontiers where human pressures have so far been light, and where systems of control and restraint upon such rapacity are limited. The resulting avaricious extraction we are seeing today is the rapid over-exploitation of natural resources, and consequently the local ecosystems are beginning to come apart. Anything that can be extracted is sold, from wildlife to valuable medicinal and aromatic plants, trees of valuable timber, and in many landscapes which carry valuable minerals, large areas are mined for export to distant markets leading to serious adverse ecological and environmental consequences to areas where these resources are exploited. The penetration of the global market to the very remotest corners of our country is now firmly underway with inevitable and tragic repercussions, more often than not to our poorest communities.

In tandem with world economic integration are the phenomena of the disruption and disenfranchising of common property regimes, which for centuries have served to stem rapid environmental degradation. Water bodies, forests, productive fishing streams and rivers, and once rich pastures were, as some still are in places, governed by communities whose rules of access allowed rational and renewable use of the living natural resources, but are now subject to overuse and exhaustion. Today, we are witnessing a growing struggle over the commons where the power of money, both foreign and Indian, prevails regardless of the consequences to those unable to protect themselves, much less their rights.

The struggle is staged on multiple fronts, and most of them ironically in the name of 'development', in the name of 'decentralisation', and in the name of the 'people'. Today the commons have become a central metaphor for ecological politics, especially what policy makers worldwide call the 'global commons'. In this context let us look at 'global' here for a moment. Good governance of a local commons does have a positive effect on more than just the local community. Similarly, any ecological disturbance also has its downstream or downwind consequences. The Western inspired advocates of global-commons are quick to urge that 'global' experts or global managers are required to understand the trans-boundary problems involved. They even insist that global institutions and global policy is necessary to manage them and we mindlessly and irresponsibly accede!

Let me attempt to put this into a global context and add the essential ethical dimension to Ecological Security since it is contemporary extravagant life-styles that are, in the final analysis, responsible for undermining the means of achieving Ecological Security.

The human race has grown in physical numbers far beyond the carrying capacity of its natural environment. If this continues, as it is, to grow by geometrical progression to calamitous proportions, if it has not already done so, we shall irretrievably undermine the self-sustaining and restorative capabilities of the life support systems and the natural resource base that have hitherto sustained all life on earth. Frightening evidence of the progressive breakdown of the natural life support systems is now becoming all too apparent. Evidence of this is in fact now so all-pervading as to escape the discerning capabilities of both the majority of the average urban raised intellectual and the urban communities at large who are regrettably the decision-makers of today.

We in India appear to be rapidly losing the moorings of our ancient traditions and forgetting the teachings and example of the Father of our Nation. We are being swept off our cultural bearings by the tidal wave of today's modes of market economy which promotes crass and totally unsustainable consumerism that is wrecking our ecology and progressively our economy.

In talking about our cultural roots and the ethics of ecology, I am reminded of Rabindranath Tagore's words, quoted below:

> The civilisation of ancient Greece (which, may I add is the foundation of Western civilisation) was nurtured in the city walls. In India it was in the forests that our civilisation had its birth, and

took a distinct character from this origin and environment. It was surrounded by the vast life of Nature, was fed and clothed by her, and had the closest and most constant inter-course with her varying aspects.

Man, in particular Western technological man, whom we are thoughtlessly aping instead of being able to persuade him to adopt the value systems of our ancient culture which has enabled us to live in symbiotic harmony with our natural environment, has accumulated wealth by denying the rights of others to share in Nature's bounty. These 'others' include marginal communities (tribal and landless peasants), and non-human species. Inequality, non-sustainability and ecological instability all arise from the selfish and arrogant assumption that Nature's gifts are for private exploitation, not for sharing. In contrast to this rapaciousness, diverse ancient cultures of the world have based their relationship with Nature on the foundation that man is a member of the earth family and must respect the rights of other members of the family. The importance of trees and plants, of rivers, of mountains has created the ethical constraints on human use of the environment. Prudence was the outcome of the respect of the rights of other living beings.

In its concepts of material progress and development, mankind is conditioned by aspirations, mental processes and systems of functioning (management systems), rooted so deeply and inexorably in its primordial struggle for survival through the subjugation of Nature that it seems conditioned irrevocably to continue to apply its patchwork knowledge of science and technology to the increasingly efficient destruction of natural phenomena and processes. In its early history and until comparatively recent times, humanity's capacity in this respect limited it to micro-level changes from which Nature could quickly recover. But as scientific power and capability increased, the mega distortions and destruction of natural processes humanity is bringing about is resulting in undermining the very matrix of the systems of Nature on which all life on earth depends.

There is a vast area of research and development that lies ahead in this field. But it will need to be based on a different philosophy than the one that usually informs our modern R & D establishments. Our scientists and administrators will need to assume a degree of innate modesty in the role they perform as participants in a total system of relationships. I stress that one of the basic postulates of this is that the only appropriate model and philosophy of development is to treat life as a whole and not in fragments. I believe that this calls for a perspective on science that is oriental rather than occidental, feminist rather than macho, rural rather than urban, drawing on the accumulated wisdom of centuries of our ancestors (each succeeding century and generation refining the inherited pool) rather than turning one's back on all that is 'past' and 'traditional'.

All these shifts to an alternative and sustainable development are primarily ethical shifts. They are not a new technological quick fix, nor a matter of new financial investment. They are a shift in values such that Nature is valued in herself, for her life support functions, not merely for how she can be converted into resources, 'raw materials' and commodities to feed the engine of economic growth. The respect for Nature's diversity, and the responsibility to conserve that diversity, becomes the basis of sustainable development. And out of this ethics of respect for Nature flows a respect for cultures. If Nature is to be conserved in all her diversity, the cultures, which must necessarily include the culture of the non-human species that preserve themselves through an evolutionary process that maintains that diversity, are naturally preserved. Respect for the rights of Nature and other cultures becomes the basis not just of sustainability, but also of justice and equity, because it conserves a diversity of livelihoods and the means of sustaining these livelihoods. The ecological crisis is in large part a process of having laid waste large parts of Nature—through pollution, or erosion of vital resources like soil, water and genetic resources, or forms of colonisation by humans that have made so many vital life forms endangered or rendered them extinct. The dispensability of Nature and of a large variety of non-human forms of life has gone hand in hand with the dispensability of a large portion of the human race.

The scenario laid out above with globalization and liberalisation added to it is already acutely evident in India. It is increasingly apparent that the poor and defenceless are increasingly being pushed to the brink of survival. We know that the landed interests are exploiting the landless and if the latter dare to oppose, they are rewarded with oppression and atrocities. We know that the urban rich are getting richer by encroaching on the rural hinterlands and the wilderness beyond and appropriating both land and other means of livelihood of the poor and the defenceless. We know that forests are being allowed by the politician/bureaucrat nexus to be cut wantonly and illegally by contractors on a scale hitherto unknown. We know that there is growing greed and hunger for agricultural land and hundreds of thousands of villagers and tribals are being deprived of their land, displaced and forced to migrate out of their original habitats. We know all this but we hesitate to act in the certain knowledge that the governments (national and state) that we have elected to power are deliberately doing all this. We tend instead to place most of the blame on established 'vested interests'—the landlord, the financier, the capitalist class, multinationals—'the foreign hand' but too little on the politician. We do not give sufficient credence to the fact that it is they who are primarily responsible with their growing ties with government bureaucrats and narrow vested interests.

This apart, through the media there is a series of policy pronouncements, attractive declarations of principle and bold commitments usually in the form of slogans and metaphors that have a highly populist ring. Poverty alleviation programmes are announced and are given high priority and large schemes for providing basic needs to the people are launched. Publicity campaigns are mounted to project the belief that the environment is being protected, the rivers are being cleaned up and—the worst of all fallacies—that the forests are being replanted on a massive scale, bringing a so-called 'management focus' to bear and utilising the latest technology for this and imploring the people to co-operate in these new ventures to recover lost ground. Information Technology, while being a tool of great potential, is not being used for the benefit of the people as a whole but today is largely making the rich richer by improving 'efficiency' in the exploitation of natural resources.

Perhaps the most diabolical attempt has been to ascribe the worst possible motives and denigrate as anti-people, those frail cries in the wilderness protesting against the growing ravaging of Nature despite its all-pervading beneficence, and their desperate appeals for ecological sanity and restitution, claiming as they do that this is the only path to long-term economic salvation, particularly for the poorest in the country. The impoverished can no longer be left to suffer the ignominies increasingly inflicted on them by the predatory proclivities of an unjust society. An awakened public conscience and a genuine national desire to establish a new and truly just social order must now be manifested to protect the under privileged from total destitution to which they are being reduced.

I have tried to sketch with a few broad strokes a tentative outline of a canvas that depicts what I believe represents the Ecological Security of this wonderful but endangered country of ours. I hope I have been able to illustrate some of the major links that connect the micro to the macro factors of what constitutes Ecological Security, that I have come to recognise from my years of field observation of the rural and urban areas, and to lesser degree of the wilderness areas of our country, the importance of which very few of us recognize. This has been followed by much reflection and analysis that has preceded my attempts here to articulate the broadest dimensions of Ecological Security. I sincerely hope that my attempts to do so carry conviction with at least some, if not all.

2

Faiths and Ecological Security

Karan Singh

According to the great philosopher, Sri Aurobindo, man is an evolving being and is in a transitional phase halfway between the animal and the divine. Sri Aurobindo held that the evolutionary process will continue till man reaches a higher level of consciousness. In sharp contradistinction, Arthur Koestler, the celebrated European author, maintained that man is programmed for self-destruction because of a bio-engineering defect in the human cortex whereby the neurological linkages between the thinking and the feeling elements in a human being are inadequate. As a result, sooner or later, emotions will overcome the rational mind and the human race will destroy itself. These are two vastly differing prognoses and the jury is still out. Only time can tell what the future holds for the human race. Meanwhile, all that we can do is to pray.

However, one thing is clear. Humanity, in its long and tortuous history, is now at a crucial crossroads on planet Earth. The twentieth century, through which most of us have lived, has been the most astounding. On the one hand, there has been tremendous and unbelievable progress and breakthroughs. Science and technology have achieved feats that appear to be miraculous. We have broken the space barrier and are reaching into extra-galactic cosmology. We are looking into the heart of the atom, the electron, the neutron and the neutrino, and unraveling the mysteries of the human genome. It is absolutely astounding what science and technology have been able to achieve.

The other side of the picture is that three major threats to the future of the human race have emerged in the last century. The first is the threat of nuclear disaster. Let us not underestimate it. With the end of the Cold War, most people assume that the threat of nuclear conflict has disappeared. One wishes it had. There are thousands of nuclear weapons in this world and each one of them is capable of destroying a hundred times as many people as were killed in Hiroshima and Nagasaki. Taken together, these can destroy all life on Earth many times over. The nuclear threat is not something that arose only because of ideological rivalry between two super powers. Today, it is at our very threshold. And it is one danger that still haunts us. Major General Vinod Saighal, in his book, *The Third Millennium Equipoise*, has provided a prescription for overcoming this disturbing problem that is dogging our footsteps for the past half century. This is the first threat and it still persists.

The second major threat is the population explosion, about which something more is mentioned below. The third one is the threat of ecological destruction. Of the three, ecological destruction is probably the most lethal in the long run. The depredation caused to the ecological systems and the environment in the last century is unbelievable. The earth has been contaminated with dangerous pesticides; the entire food chain has been poisoned. In Auroville, which the Mother started as an experiment in international living, considerable experimentation is going on to grow food organically and to green the countryside. But the fact is that, with the excessive use of chemical pesticides and fertilizers, the earth, the *prithvi* that supports all life forms on this planet, *bhavani vasundara* in our scriptures and *gaia* in Greek iconography, has become dangerously poisoned.

The air has become polluted. I will not go into the detail of green houses gases that have a disturbing impact on human beings and ecological systems. However, the atmospheric pollution levels in many places around the world are reaching lethal levels. The city of Delhi had also almost reached a lethal level; fortunately, it is now abating gradually. The tragic aspect of the campaign against atmospheric pollution is that the Kyoto Protocol that was signed by many nations has been denounced by the United States, one of the most retrogressive steps that we have witnessed recently. The Rio Earth Summit in 1992, then the Rio+5 and now the Rio+10 scheduled in 2002 in Johannesburg are all attempts to contain, if not reverse, the trend of increasing air pollution.

Of the three *tattvas* that support life on Earth, two, *prithvi* and *vayu*, are badly polluted. The third one is the *jal*, water. The water resources have been very seriously depleted and contaminated. The rivers, which are worshipped throughout the country, are heavily polluted. The Yamuna in Delhi has virtually become a sewer, the Ganga, the *param pavini Ganga*, which was traditionally considered to purify everybody and everything, we have succeeded in polluting it. This must rank as one of the great negative achievements of the human race because from time immemorial the Ganga has been looked upon as the source of purity.

How do we move towards ecological security and what role can faiths play in this? The great religions of the world have had a role in ecological conservation. There are, of course, many theological and ideological differences between various religions of the world. But despite these divergences, there are some striking areas of convergence between them, and one of them is ecological security. On the twenty-fifth anniversary of the World Wide Fund (WWF) for Nature in 1986, a unique and path-breaking conference was held in Assisi, a small town in Italy which is the birthplace of the great saint, St. Francis of Assisi. Legend has it that his consciousness was so highly evolved that he could communicate with animals and birds, and that they used to come to listen to his sermons. This is also the tradition of our ancient *rishis*, that they were able to talk to the animals.

At this unique Interfaith gathering in Assisi in 1986, five religions were represented—Buddhism, Christianity, Hinduism, Islam and Judaism. A series of declarations on Man and Nature came out of this conference, the celebrated Assisi Declarations. I had the privilege of being one of the five authors as I composed the Hindu Declaration. At the end of the meeting, there was a remarkable event in Assisi's magnificent Basilica, the Jewish representative blew his traditional ram's horn; the Muslim representative went up the church tower to give *azaan*, the call to prayer; the celebrated Indian danseuse, Yamini Krishnamurthy, gave a dance performance choreographed on the Rig Vedic Hymn of Creation; and the Buddhist priest played sonorously on his traditional long horn. Subsequently other religions—Sikhism, Jainism, Baha'i and Zoroastrianism—also came out with their respective declarations. The WWF-India publication, *Religion and Conservation* contains the text of all the nine declarations.

The Atharvaveda, written thousands of years ago, has the great Hymn to Earth, the 'Bhumisuktam', whose 63 *shlokas* are probably the most comprehensive testament of environmental values to be found in any faith. In it, the close and symbiotic nexus between religion and ecology comes out most tellingly and eloquently. A few examples are:

High truth, unyielding Order, Consecration,
Ardor and Prayer and Holy Ritual
Uphold the Earth; may she, the ruling Mistress
Of what has been and what will come to be,
For us spread wide limitless domain.

On whom the flowing Waters, ever the same,
Course without cease or failure nigh and day,
May she yield milk, this Earth of many streams,
And shed on us her splendour copiously!

Whatever I dig up of you, O Earth,
May you of that have quick replenishment!
O purifying One, may my thrust never
Reach right unto your vital points, your heart!

This most beautiful hymn shows the deep understanding that our seers and sages had of man's abiding relationship with nature. Unlike the Greek civilisation, Indian civilisation was born amidst nature. Greek civilisation had its origin in the city-states of Greece and is therefore an urban-oriented civilisation. Ours was an *aranyaka* civilisation, born in forests, mountains and verdant river valleys. The great utterances of our ancient sages, the Vedas and the Upanishads, were particularly a source of tremendous inspiration. Poet Kalidasa in his epic, *Kumarasambhava*, describes the Himalayas as *devatatma*, a divine presence, and Sri Kishna in the Gita says, 'Among the immovables I am the Himalays,' For us, the Himalayas are not a mere geographical feature but the *devatatma*. A very vital and key concept in our ancient tradition is the concept of nature, being suffused with divinity, representing the divine.

Speaking of the Himalayas, Kalidasa in *Kumarasambhava* says 'There in the northern direction is a great spiritual presence stretching from the west to the eastern sea, standing like a measuring rod.' If the greatness of human civilisation is to be measured, the only yardstick that can do justice to it are the Himalayas. That is the poet's concept of this towering mountain range. Our civilisation arose among great natural beauty and it infuses nature with a divine aura and makes it one of the civilisation elements of great significance.

In this context, the World Charter for Nature is an important document. Unfortunately, people seem to have forgotten it. The United Nations adopted it in 1982. I am glad that the publication, *The World*

Charter for Nature, includes it in several Indian languages. It is a document of utmost significance. It is not legally binding but represents a series of 'directive principles' for people to follow. There is a paragraph in it that says, 'civilisation is rooted in nature which has shaped human culture and influenced all artistic and scientific achievements, and living in harmony with nature gives man the best opportunities for the development of his creativity, and for rest and recreation.' This is entirely true. All of us, from time to time, want to break out of the cities and go up into the mountains to rejuvenate ourselves. In a city like Delhi, because of atmospheric pollution, you can hardly see a few stars. When you go up into the mountains, you are overwhelmed by the glorious panorama of the stars in the night sky. There is nothing more moving, dramatic and impressive than the sight of millions and millions of stars wheeling across the intensely dark blue sky. It reminds us of what our seers have said of '*ananta koti Brahmand'*, millions of galaxies surrounding us. It makes us realize two things; first, how tiny our earth is compared to the tremendously vast outer space; second, that the light that illuminates the Cosmos glows also in our own hearts.

This is the secret of Indian culture. It teaches us that the light that illuminates the universe is the same light that lights up our consciousness. One is often asked what is the definition of God in Hinduism. The definition of the Divine, as given in our scriptures, is 'that which, shining, causes everything else to shine'. As the word 'God' has a rather schematic connotation, the term 'Divine', is preferable. Francis Thompson, in his poem, says:

> Not where the wheeling systems darken
> And our benumbed conceiving soars!
> The drift of pinions, would we hearken,
> Beats at our own clay-shuttered doors.
> The angels keep their ancient places;
> Turn but a stone, and start a wing!
> 'Tis ye, 'tis your estranged faces,
> That miss the many-splendoured thing.

The many-splendoured light of the *atman*, the *Noor-e-Illahi* of the Sufis, *Ek Omkar* of the Sikh gurus, and what the Bible calls 'the light that lighteth every man who cometh into this world,' is the light that is within us and illumines the universe as well. These are the insights that our seers had. If we can get away from cities, go into mountains and be in communion with nature, we may rediscover these truths.

There is another document which requires attention and that is the Earth Charter. It is an important document as it contains an integrated ethical vision of humanity's future. On of its sections deals specifically with ecological integrity. There is no lack of idea, no lack of excellent articulation of ecological values. The problem is how to translate these ideas into practice. While we try to find ways to do that, things seem to be slipping out of our control. The population of the planet is growing apace, and has now crossed the 6 billion mark. Viewed from space, our planet looks like a tiny speck of light and life against the silent vastness of Outer Space. Its carrying capacity is finite and it cannot support an infinite number of people.

Out of 6 billion people, we have the privilege of contributing 1 billion. When I was Union Health Minister in the mid-seventies, we worked out three population projections for the year 2000. The optimistic one was 900 million, the median projection was 950 million and the Doomsday projection was 1 billion. Believe it or not, India hit the 1 billion mark on 13 May 2000. The population growth is creating a host of problems, be it ecological, desertification, deforestation or slumification of cities. All these problems are contributing to the uglification of India, the towns are turning into vast slums. Delhi may be clean and green, but if one visits any other town with the exception of Auroville, it is a total disaster. The people are being forced to migrate from villages to cities in search of better opportunities. As a result, urban slums are proliferating at an alarming rate, and they are aggravating the existing social tensions creating enormous psychosomatic stress. There is no denying that, insofar as environment is concerned, the growing population is one of the major problems that we face.

The point that needs serious thought is whether the faiths of the world are able to exert any demonstrable influence on our thinking on ecological matters. Our scriptures set two goals before us, to work for the liberation of our souls as well as for the welfare of the world at large. Faiths usually emphasis the individual, but it is now becoming increasingly clear that if they neglect the external environment, then humanity is likely to fall between two stools. We would neither be able to attain salvation nor save the world for the posterity. If the religious teachers and leaders were to direct their attention specifically towards protecting the environment and safeguarding ecological integrity, it would be an extremely valuable step forward.

Every one throngs their respective places of worship. In the Hindu religion, there is the custom of making offering to the deity and the supplicant carrying away a part of it as '*prasad*'. One of the ways of instilling ecological values could be giving a sapling, instead of *prasad*, when a devotee visits a temple. It would go a long way in creating public awareness. A creative linkage between religion and the environment is essential. If that linkage is firmly established then we can be somewhat assured of ecological security. Along with that linkage, the great religions of the world also need to propagate the small family norm. Here I tread on dangerous grounds because I know that very important religious leaders have come out strongly against family planning. I submit that, by opposing family limitation, a great disservice is being done to the human race and its survival on this planet. The way the population situation is developing, some effective steps have to be taken sooner than later. Apart from teaching the way to salvation and performing the rituals, it is absolutely necessary for the leaders of all the religions to take concrete step towards population stabilisation.

Let me say in closing that while the faiths by themselves may not be enough to ensure ecological security, they can play a major role in motivating people to work towards sustainable development and concomitantly ecological sanity. We need to have faith not only in our religion but also in ourselves. We must have faith in the ultimate destiny of humanity. At the outset, I spoke of two very divergent views, one put forward by Sri Aurobindo and the other by Arthur Koestler. Two roads are opening before us all the time. The poem, 'The Road Not Taken' by American poet, Robert Frost, eloquently speaks of the dilemma of two roads opening before man. He says:

> Two roads diverged in a yellow wood,
> And sorry I could not travel both
> And be one traveler, long I stood
> And looked down one as far as I could
> To where it bent in the undergrowth;
>
> Then took the other, just as fair,
> And having perhaps the better claim,
> Because it was grassy and wanted wear;
> Though as for that the passing there
> Had worn them really about the same,

And both that morning equally lay
In leaves no step had trodden black.
Oh, I kept the first one for another day!
Yet knowing how way leads on to way,
I doubted if I should ever come back.

I shall be telling this with a sigh
Somewhere ages and ages hence:
Two roads diverged in a wood, and I
I took the one less traveled by,
And that has made all the difference.

The *Kathopnishad* also tells us of two roads, the *Shreya* and the *Preya*. It is for each of us to choose the one that will lead us to spiritual security. In the final analysis, only if we are able to attain spiritual security will we be able to ensure ecological security.

3

Dimensions of Ecological Security

L.M. Singhvi

I was requested to speak on constitutional dimensions of ecological security. But we have to understand that there are many dimensions of ecological security. Before we get to the constitutional dimensions, we must understand the multitudinal dimensions in which the issues related to ecological security are rooted. It is important therefore, first, to understand and to enumerate the many dimensions of ecological security. Of course, one may say that these dimensions of ecological security are of a long-term security, but what about the short-term, the immediate question of the other security, physical security? Lord Cannes once jokingly and light-heartedly said that, in the short term, we must be depressed because, in the long term, we are all to die. So, the physical security issues are important but then equally, if not more important, are the ecological security issues, which could involve us all in a greater tragedy, in a greater possibility of a dangerous parallel situation.

There are two schools of thought on what has been described as the cornucopian vision of limitless advances in science. First, a 'no problems' syndrome in our life-style or in our consumption patterns; and second, based on what is being described as a Malthusian concept, that is, that there are finite resources in the world and that we are already experiencing crises after crises in all respects. But there is a third aspect and that is an aspect which we are rooted in, which is our ancient outlook on life. The ancient outlook on life is best demonstrated by the principle of what you may call austerity or the principle of restraint and moderation.

I remember when I presented a declaration of nature to Prince Philip of Britain, he asked me why the ancestors of present-day Indians had been concerned with these issues in times when there was no green house effect, when there were no problems similar to the kind of ecological crises that we face at present? Why did they bother so much about moderation and restraint and putting some limit on one's wants? I told him, equally light-heartedly, that perhaps those ancestors opined and believed that they should not begin digging the wells when they are thirsty but start digging the wells for posterity. They had hence given us some wisdom for the future. Perhaps they anticipated what would happen to our world. But the problem is that the perspective, which I call the moral perspective, is one which I can describe in six different ways—the theological, the cosmological, the philosophical, the teleological, the ontological and the ethical dimension. That perspective, in a sense, revolves around a concept of the sanctity of the sacredness, of the sense of the sacred, and that sense of the sacred is fundamental because that is then not a merely utilitarian concept. What we have today is the concern of ecology because of the apprehensions we have of the finite resources of the earth, because an American feels the nightmare of all petrol having run out, and he wonders, 'What will we do?' and 'How do we run our car?' It is a perspective rooted in apprehensions, in fear, in what may happen but not in a moral perspective of the universe, moral perspective of consumption, a moral outlook on how life should be lived, and that, I think, is the point of departure.

I would like to emphasize that among the many dimensions of ecological security, the legal and the constitutional dimension is one such dimension, but that is more a normative dimension. Then there is the realistic dimension, the scientific and technological dimension of the understanding of the biosphere. The understanding of the biosphere is very important before a normative programme can really be made, because we really do not know enough about the biosphere and its many interconnections. It is these interconnections which make for the science of ecology. So the scientific and technological dimensions of the understanding of our biosphere seems to be one of the most important and one through which we are trying still to find out the whole reality of this universe and how it works. There is the issue then of the relationship of the basic elements of nature, because in that you have the whole relationship of man and the biosphere. That is where you have to understand whether our pattern of life is so extravagant, it is so wasteful that it cannot last., The cornucopian school of thought says there are limitless ways in which humanity will march from one scientific progress to another and there will never be a problem of the kind that we, who think in Malthusian and more limited terms, envisage. We believed, we have always believed in our country, as have most other civilizations, in the relationship between land and water and air. These are considered as fundamental. But in modern life people think that because they have been able to pay for air conditioning they do not have to bother about the quality of air and that obviously is a short-sighted view of the earth on which we live.

What is ecology, and what is ecological security? Simply stated, ecological security only means what has come to be a popular term—sustainable development or sustainable life, or that which will not undermine and impair the balance of nature. What then leads to greater ecological security and lesser ecological security? What endangers it and what protects it? In a sense, security is really a fortress, a defence system that guards its security, that which guarantees its security. But ecological security, therefore, must take into account those factors which have come to endanger our quality of life and also endanger the way in which we may hope to live (when I say 'we' I mean the future generations). Security of our common whole or planet earth is then what is implied by ecological security and when we speak of the earth, we do not speak merely of the human population on earth. We speak of the planet earth with all life on it, with different forms on it, with different vegetations on it. All kinds of insects are on this earth and even outside. Thomas Berry, a great philosopher, I think one of the greatest ecologists, posed a very interesting and very simple question. He asked, 'Is the human a viable species on an endangered planet?' If the planet is endangered, then can the human species survive and if the planet is endangered, as it seems to be, the human species are equally endangered. Now we have to therefore understand these different dimensions, the scientific and technological dimensions and their limits. We have to understand the dimension which is cosmological.

We have the concept of 'shristhividhan', the constitution of the cosmos and before I go to the more mundane constitutional and legal aspects and into the dimensions of ecology, it is 'shristhividhan' I would like to describe, as I see it. There is a concept in the ancient Vedic tradition of *r̄ta*. *R̄ta* is the concept of balance and harmony, *r̄ta* is the concept of discharge of functions by every component of the universe—that is what is called *'shrishtividhan'*, and this *shristhividhan*, based on *r̄ta,* is also based on a harmonious relationship between all that is on planet earth and in the cosmos. Planet earth alone is not capable of survival. The cosmos itself is to survive and in that cosmos we relate to it by the sense of the sacred. The philosophers of India thought of many different ways of relating to the cosmos. The other traditions equally thought of how to relate to the cosmos. An author has described in a book on the *Gathas of Zarathustra* a very telling episode. The episode is of a cow or a bull going around and complaining about what is happening and that is the symbol of earth, the earth going around and complaining of what is happening to it and thus the boon of a great seer and saint is granted. But that is a metaphor also. The world today, planet earth today is crying and it cannot be a cry in the wilderness as to what is happening to it today in terms of pollution, in terms of the quality of life, in terms of our relationships, in terms of the reciprocities of life. That is one thing that in a sense is to be found at the essence of the chant of the sacred in all the different traditions of the world, whether it is the Hindu tradition, the Vedic Hindu tradition, the Jain, Buddhist, or Confucian, whether it is Judaism, Zarathustrianism or Christianity. In all these traditions was embedded the fundamental concept of the sense of the sacred and I believe that dimension, which I call the cosmological, philosophical and ethical dimensions of ecological security, postulates most importantly this sense of the sacred and the consequences of the loss of the sense of the sacred.

The consequence of the loss of the sense of the scared is moral un-relatedness, moral irresponsibility and moral chaos in society. It is from that point of view that the sense of the sacred may still regard ethics as the overriding principle of life. Ontology, the understanding of the being–what am I, who am I, from where have I come, why do I relate to others–this is what gives one a sense of responsibility. So ethics is the science of responsibility... From the theological and cosmological to the ethical, these are dimensions of ecology and understanding of ecology, of creating ecological responsibility. Now ecological responsibility is, I believe, the most important dimension.

Some years ago, a body called the Interaction Council, a very important body with a very elitist membership confined only to former Heads of State and former Heads of Government, who had assembled in Vienna in 1997 asked me to share with them my ideas on what I thought was the most important thing for the world to address, the most important item on the world's agenda? As a representative of my country I decided to share with them some of the thoughts which arise from our tradition. I told them that the most important thing is the moral agenda of humankind and the most important thing on the moral agenda of humankind is to put equal emphasis on responsibility as we put on rights. I put before them the Gandhian thought that without responsibility you cannot fulfill rights either for yourself or for others and, in this sense, the combination of rights and responsibilities becomes extremely important when we are thinking of ecological security. There are no ecological rights without ecological responsibilities; no ecological rights can be fulfilled without ecological responsibilities, of individuals, of societies, of groups, of people, of nations. But we have a situation where, even after the great conference in Rio, the attitude is generally speaking of the enjoyment of life without ecological responsibility, without respecting the ecological rights of others and without performing our ecological duties towards others. Now this is what has resulted in what I call ecological insecurity. You cannot have ecological security unless you have a combination of rights and responsibilities. I do not wish to give figures on this, but the kind of consumption and the kind of production of pollution that is taking place in certain countries of the world is highly out of proportion to the number of people who live there. The life-style, if it does not change, imposes a heavy burden on the universe as a whole. The extent of pollution cannot be justified by saying my life, my way of life, my American way of life, my Canadian way of life. It has to be a human way of life, it has to be a responsible way of life, and that is why I would like to put forward the first principle that the moral agenda for ecological security, first and foremost, is an understanding of ecological rights and ecological responsibilities.

In a lecture I gave some time back I had said that one particular new covenant needs to be made in the world. I called it the Third Covenant. We have the covenant on civil and political rights, we have the covenant on social and cultural rights and I advocated, as I had advocated about fifteen years ago, a third covenant against ecocide, because ecology is getting destroyed. We did put in an international statute, the law against genocide, but at that time we did not (although now we need to) create a law against ecocide because ecocide is worse than genocide and ecocide is happening all the time. The destruction of diversity, the bio-diversity of the world and its destruction is something phenomenal. Every minute, every hour of the day we are destroying the biological diversity of the world and that destruction will lead us to a destruction which would irreversible, of that there is no doubt whatever the cornucopian theorists may say in terms of the limitless possibilities of human ingenuity and innovation. One thing is certain, the destruction of biodiversity in this world will imperil the human future as well, it will imperil the future of the world and it will imperil the future of the human race also. That is why I put the question that Thomas Berry had put: 'Is the human a viable species on an endangered planet?' Therefore, ecological security must address the question of what endangers the planet, what destroys its balance.

According to some estimates, in the next twenty-five years we will be facing a water crisis, the magnitude of which we are unable to imagine. In a few more years we will be told that the salt water of the oceans can be converted. What will you do when you have also consumed much of the salt water of the ocean after converting it for potable purposes? There is a limit. Therefore, you have to consider the moral agenda and in that context you have to consider the demographic dimensions, as somebody might say that this planet was not designed for the number of people that have come to inhabit it. One might say you have a train going somewhere and that train has so many compartments and so many berths and so many seats and it can take maybe 20, 40, 100, 200, 500 persons, but can it suddenly take 50,000 persons? So the difference between the capacity of the earth and its resources and the population that consumes the resources, that disproportion, that imbalance, is creating a demographic crisis for the world, a demographic crisis leading to an ecological crisis, and those are dimensions which too have to be addressed. The problem with ecological crisis and ecological security is that it has many dimensions; it does not have just one dimension. Those dimensions have to be addressed by a common plan, by a blueprint of concerns and a blueprint of solutions but, most importantly, I believe by addressing the question in moral terms. Without it we are doomed to failure.

There is the problem of the biosphere. The UNESCO has had a project on biosphere studies for many years now. They publish their studies. They have come to the theory of ecotones. It is just another word for getting a better relationship between the elements with which we have to live. They call it ecotones. Now be it ecotones or ecology, there is no longer any logic in the way we function. There is the whole issue of coming to a definite approach to life and that approach, if it misses the sacred dimensions, if it misses the moral dimensions, if it misses the dimension of responsibility, then it would have failed to achieve whatever it can achieve. I have this feeling that the crisis may sometimes frighten us into inaction. Somebody said it is already too late to do anything about it and therefore we might as well live as we have been living, irresponsibly and chaotically. That, in my opinion, is an irresponsible answer because ecology is a science of organizing knowledge and unifying it. It is a unified organization of knowledge. It is, at best, a multi-dimensional discipline, a multi-disciplinary approach to problems. It seeks to establish, in my opinion, the laws of nature and I believe it's the laws of nature which we must hark back to. The laws of human beings have been too greedy, have been too selfish, have been too egocentric and, therefore, we must resort to making the laws of man more compatible with the laws of nature. A holistic approach to life has to be evolved. It will not be evolved in a day, not in a year, nor in ten years, but I think the moment has come to start with a proposition which develops the faith of ecological responsibility.

R̄ta, the concept of cosmic balance, is the concept from which the law of *dharma* is derived. Dharma is that which sustains. We speak of sustainable development as if it is our own invention of the twenty-first or twentieth century, but in the very roots of that term is that which sustains. Dharma and ecology is that which sustains. Ecological security can best be defined as the dharma of life because that is what sustains. And, the very literal meaning of dharma is that which sustains, it is not religion at all. Therefore, ecological security has to be routed in a life-style that is sustainable, in developments which are sustainable, in an approach to each other which is sustainable. Why is terrorism so angular and so wholly deserving of rejection? It is so because it is not an approach which sustains, there is no reciprocity in the way in which the behaviour patterns of terrorism function. Terrorism is one form of lack of consideration for others, a form of fanaticism, egocentric fanaticism or ethnocentric fanaticism, due to the resort to violence. I developed the theory that in the kind of world in which we live moral irresponsibility is also violence, lack of moral responsibility is violence, and waste is violence.

In the society in which we live, resources seem to be limited. The truth of the matter is that we are today a peculiar society of human beings many of whom are suffering from food insecurity, many others are suffering from other kinds of insecurity, but in material things, in the very basic material things, you have to make a philosophy of responding to the human needs, human rights and human responsibilities. This trinity of concept of human needs, human responsibility and human rights gives to us a philosophy of responsibility. By itself, human rights will not give you a feeling of responsibility. In fact, after having spent almost three and a half decades thinking about human rights, I have come to the conclusion that the dimension of responsibility cannot possibly be ignored, human rights will not succeed if you overlook the dimension of human responsibilities; human responsibility and human rights will not create a stable society unless you address human needs. So this is something which leads us to ecological security because human society must find an answer to the problem of the depletion of many resources of our world, of a situation where many species are becoming extinct, of a situation where the resources are being depleted and a situation where we can see, twenty-five years hence, a total scarcity of the essentials of life. What does it matter if you have lots of goods–whatever goods you have–if you do not have water to drink? Already in the last 10-15 years we are facing a situation where many of us are drinking water out of bottles. We can no longer drink water out of taps or out of a normal supply. Even the water of the Ganges is polluted, the water what we thought is the purest is no longer as pure as we thought it should be. We have, therefore, the whole question of going back and going forward at the same time and, when I speak of going back and going forward, I would like to emphasize that the spiritual resources of humanity must be harnessed to the new movement for ecological preservation, ecological security, ecological rights and responsibilities. How do we do that? I believe that all disciplines have to contribute to this.

I think we have to understand that the future of the world, despite the cornucopian vision of the possibility of many new innovations, is something that is not the plaything of this generation. There has to be an intergenerational dimension of responsibility. It is not solely that we are able to earn a comfortable living, in a house which has all the comforts of life. We have to have a sense, a dimension, of intergenerational responsibility. This is something which cannot be brought about merely by writing a chapter in the Constitution on fundamental duties. That we have done so is very good. It is a reminder, but what if we do not heed the reminder in the Constitution, in the laws? The legal and the constitutional dimensions of ecological security, therefore, become important. The Supreme Court rendered great service to the whole cause of ecological security, when it ruled by interpretation that in the concept of life is included ecological security.

Ecological security is embedded in the concept of life and the right to life is guaranteed by the Constitution of India and because the right to life–I do not mean liberty now, but right to life–is guaranteed by the Constitution of India, the right to ecological security is guaranteed by the Constitution of India, as interpreted by the Supreme Court.

There were days when there was a more limited meaning given to it. The Supreme Court had said that law has also to answer to certain norms. It has to be a reasonable law. Therefore, the right to ecological security was established as a principle, as a fundamental principle of our constitutional jurisprudence. The right to ecological security was established by an international law at the Rio Conference, when they adopted a declaration and an encapsulation of the fundamentals of international law. So, it has now become a part of the jurisprudence of humankind. But, the question is, how do we implement it, how do we bring it into action? To bring it into action, we need to have an approach by which we can make it happen and, in my view, having spent almost forty-nine plus years in law, that law is not an adequate instrument unless there is a culture of law. Law is rooted in ethics and unless the social ethics, unless social choices are informed and enlightened, the 'do's and don'ts' of the law are generally violated, they do not become the warp and woof of life as it is lived and unless it becomes a part of life as it is lived, it does not have the resonance of something real. It then appears to be words which may have constituted the rock of the constitution but which have no meaning in our lives. It is important, therefore, that the constitutional ethos of ecological security, the international laws of ecological security is translated into a way of life. We often say about Hinduism, that it is not a religion but a way of life. Why? Because, unless it becomes a way of life, it remains imprisoned in a book. A whole movement for ecological security has to be built in the minds of men, women and children where it will find ground to grow or not grow that is where the battle is.

The other day I was reading *Confucianism and Ecology,* an extraordinary book which brings to us an ethical aspect. But what is ethics unless it is a set of norms which have become internalised in the life of a society, unless it expresses itself in social choices. Many principles of Indian thought are relevant. The first is '*vasudhaiv kutumbakam*'. Ecological security is not a matter which can be confined to the frontiers of one or the other country. All countries have to have a sense of relatedness if we want ecological security. We are all interdependent and related. This universal interdependence and relatedness is a fundamental, spiritual, intellectual, scientific and social concept. This interdependence and relatedness has to be accepted as a fundamental principle.

The principle found in almost all traditions of the world is 'do not do unto others what you would not have done unto yourself'. This is one of the most fundamental principles, which emancipates us from an egocentric view of life towards a view of life where we are accommodating and considerate. So that is the third principle of ecological security, as between nations, as between people, as between the communities. There has to be a way of life in which wants are reduced by the practice of moderation and restraint. Unless we know and learn that we will not be governed and ruled and controlled by our wants only, we will not be able to overcome the type of consumerism in which we are engulfed. There have to be limits on consumerism and those limits have to be defined by a sense of a moral responsibility and by a movement, which makes conspicuous consumption as something ugly and obscene, which makes wastefulness ugly and obscene, which makes moral irresponsibility a crime in the eyes of humanity. I am not speaking of something very utopian. I have been a lawyer all my life. I am treading the hard ground of reality. But this ground of reality cannot be created unless we have a cultural movement, an ethical movement, a movement which makes a religion of ecological responsibility and ecological rights.

4

Governance for Ecological Security

ASHOK KHOSLA

Almost anything of any importance in the life of our country and in the lives of its people has its roots and its consequences in some form or another of ecological security. A very large part of the daily existence of some three out of four of our fellow citizens depends, day-to-day, directly on the processes of nature and the products they make possible. For the rest of us, even those living in the largest cities, the impacts may be more indirect, but there are many and they are pervasive. All of us face them, no less than villagers do, in our daily lives: from how much clean water we have to drink or how much dust there is in the air we breathe to the numbers of villagers that crowd our urban slums—eco-refugees from a rapidly degenerating resource base—and to the price we pay for onions.

While the resilience of ecological processes in certain types of biomes and climates might well be greater than in others, the human impact on the environment and its resources is widely acknowledged to be reaching a stage where it is beginning to limit the opportunities for people everywhere. Left alone, nature has its own sources of resilience, but in the face of growing human intrusion into its processes, any ecosystem can become fragile and die. Nowhere is this more apparent than in many parts of our country.

While ecological security is, by its very nature, a holistic concept, the devil lies in the detail. And, of course, so do the angels. If we are to establish a secure ecological basis for our economy, as Amrita Patel showed in the lecture with which she inaugurated this lecture series, we must get to the root causes and deal with the fundamental barriers to achieving it. It is crucial to keep in mind the whole picture and also to understand the little elements, the pixels, that combine together to make it what it is.

One of these elements, the importance of which is often not fully appreciated, is governance.

By 'governance' I mean the institutional frameworks through which we make decisions in society and how we allocate the resources among its different constituents. The term 'governance' covers not only the agencies of formal government; it also includes all those policies, laws, rules, and institutions in government, civil society and other sectors that have an influence on the individual's access to the resources of a society. The nature of governance in any society has a deep and often quite direct impact on its natural resource base and on how sustainably it is managed.

Governance for ecological security is an area that very few people seem to have given thought to. My colleagues in People First, particularly S.K. Sharma, who is with us here, and I have spent a great deal of time over the last decade trying to see how the institutions of governance are impacted by ecological security and how, in turn, they impact it. I would like to share with you some of the lessons that we have learned. But before I do so, it might help to look at some aspects of the current state of affairs in our country.

Over the last fifty years, India has undeniably made considerable progress on several fronts. Look at food production, for example. We have increased grain production by a factor of four, from 50 million tonnes in 1950 to some 200 million tonnes today. This is truly a remarkable achievement. No country in the world—not even the US—has ever made such an enormous expansion in grain production in such a short period of time. Or, take energy production, which has grown by leaps and bounds since independence: electricity use is now more than a hundred times what it was in 1947. The employment in industry has doubled several times. The government will proudly tell you that the literacy rate in our country has grown from 17 per cent then to some 55 per cent now. Many of these achievements went hand in hand with a massive investment in not only infrastructure but also science and higher education. As a result, India is known for having one of the largest workforces of scientists and engineers.

Yes, we have made a lot of progress. But one must also ask for whose benefit? It would be hard to deny that most of the benefits have gone to a very small number of people—most of them living in the towns and cities of our country.

One must further ask: at what cost? The cost of the pattern of development we have chosen has been huge: sprawling slums everywhere, squandered natural resources, devastation of land and forests, half the population without clean drinking water and three quarters without proper sanitation. Some three quarters of our fellow citizens have, more or less, been left out of the so-called 'mainstream' economy. Take a look at nutrition—perhaps the saddest story of all. The average consumption of pulses, which provide the bulk of the protein for our poor, has steadily gone down. It is now some 15 per cent below what it used to be at independence. Are we raising successive generations of under proteinised children? I am sure all of you know what the implications of this would be.

When we look at the flip side of the development coin, things are not so pretty. We may have multiplied the literacy *rate* by a factor of four, but the total number of *illiterates*, the absolute number of people who still cannot read or write, has actually doubled since 1947. While we have increased the workforce in our formal industrial sector to some ten million, the number of people unemployed has gone up to well over 200 million! That means twenty additional unemployed people for every job created. Few people, least among them our decision makers, recognize this rapid downward slide. Government, official sources of information and thus the media continuously feed us the positive picture, ignoring how the other side of the coin is deteriorating.

Did you know that there are twice as many illiterate people today as there were when we became independent? If those who govern us do not know such things, how can they possibly come up with the right policies?

The standard response to this deteriorating situation is that, over this period, the population has grown. And that is, of course, a good part of the reason why we have more illiterates, more people unemployed and more hungry people. Population growth, however, is not an independent variable that just happens on its own. It is the result of how well the benefits of development reach the poor—itself a result of our development policies. The population has not only grown but it has also built up a momentum for the future: the number of people under 15 years—the parents of tomorrow—is larger than it has ever been.

Look at the forests in India. From some 70 million ha. in 1947, we are now down to some 30-odd million ha. If we continue to go on this way, the date for a completely tree-less India is somewhere between 2025 and 2030. Of course, by then we will have seen the light and changed our ways. But the present trends are not good. Wastelands, that euphemism for the deserts we have created, have nearly doubled during the same period from some 65 millions hectares to some 110 million hectares.

So, after five decades of so-called development, what we have is more poverty, more pollution, more people and more marginalized people. There are many who find all this very inconvenient and will say that I am looking at the wrong side of the coin. After all, the story of independent India is the story of progress. Yes, for the 25 per cent or so of us who are rich enough to take advantage of this progress. But what about the other three quarters, more than 700 million of them? These are real people; each one of them has a name, a family, dreams and aspirations. Each one is a human being—though often not treated as one and totally left behind by the mainstream economy.

To make matters worse, we have created a massive dependency all around, based on the promise that government will take care of everything. Some *sarkar* or some *mai-baap* will basically be responsible.

The champagne glass on UNDP's Human Development Report describes very graphically the distribution of income in our country. The top 20 per cent of India's people basically get 85 per cent of the nation's income. The bottom 20 per cent get about 1.5 per cent. The richest fifth gets 60 or 70 times as much as the poorest. Economists hide behind statistics, which constantly change, as they change the definition of the poverty line. But, no matter how you look at it, the disparities in the country are unacceptably high. Whether the number of poor is 300 million, as defined in one way by some of our planners, or it is more than 500 million, as defined by the World Bank, it is too many. They live in some half a million villages spread throughout the remotest parts of our country. This is a huge numbers game.

It is also a matter of extreme emergency. We are talking about a country in which every year we lose some four million children unnecessarily because of hunger and disease. In the same year, about two million hectares of forests just disappear; hundreds, maybe thousands, of plants and animal species vanish, never to come back, and millions of eco-refugees migrate to city slums. These are major threats to our life support systems: our oxygen-producing forests, our water-regenerating rivers, our life-giving soils. Those of you who have been to the countryside recently will have seen that our rivers are now almost gone. Sabarmati, the mighty river on whose banks Gandhiji built his ashram some eighty years ago, is now a dry bed for much of the year. So are the myriads of rivers and streams which were the life-blood of this proverbially rich land of ours. The genetic resources, the bio-geochemical cycles, the local climate are all suffering massive perturbation, threatening the basis of life itself, the productivity of our eco-systems.

I believe that the development strategies we have been pursuing over the past fifty years will neither eliminate poverty nor bring us ecological security. There is a basic and urgent need for change and the change we need is now generally known by the term 'sustainable development'. There are two simple pre-requisites for sustainable development: first, we must meet the basic needs of all, of every single person in our country; and second, we must maintain the resource base for future generations to be able to live on it.

Sustainable development means a more equitable development, a more socially just development, a more ecologically secure development; it is a form of development that uses its resources—whether human, natural or financial—more efficiently. The driving force for such a development has necessarily to come from within, from within the genius of our people and their aspirations. It depends deeply on the understanding they have of their resource base and on the control they have over their own future. I believe all these four factors—equity, ecological security, efficiency and empowerment—are very closely tied to each other. So when I refer to ecological security, I include the other three factors since we cannot have any one of them without the other three at the same time. To get ecological security, we must have equity and social justice, efficient use of resources and an empowered public. Greater ecological security then means that we must convert the champagne glass of income distribution into something that looks more like an ordinary glass of water. In any society, there will, of course, be some rich and some poor people, so the glass could possibly become more like a tall flower vase.

As Amrita Patel says, ecological security is the primary foundation on which the future of India rests. She has compared it in importance to the other kinds of security, whether it is defense security or security of the economy. And she suggests that ecology provides a kind of infrastructure that is at least as important as the physical infrastructure that we make. In fact, if either is neglected, loss of the one can undermine the other and make it more expensive to maintain. It is also meaningless, she said, to talk about economic development unless the future is assured through the foundations of ecological health. The specific issues she identified as needing urgent attention include land use and how it affects the sustenance of nature's biological systems. She also called for simpler and better consumption patterns and food production systems that are much less wasteful than those that are being imposed on us by the processes of globalization and liberalisation. So she was talking, basically, about the need for adopting sustainable lifestyles and sustainable livelihoods, though these were not the exact words she used.

I believe that making India more efficient and livable is going to need a fuller understanding of our aspirations, our resource endowments and of how to innovate and how to develop our institutions, our technologies and our solutions through our own enterprise. Few people can doubt that Indians have enterprise. On the contrary, it seems to be in their very genes. They run a very large part of the rest of the world—from North America all the way across the Pacific, from East Africa, all the way through to the Caribbean; there are whole economies that are run by Indian entrepreneurs. Yet, at home we seem to have failed on so many fronts. If we are not genetically deficient in entrepreneurship, then what is it that holds us back? The only cause one can reasonably pin our lack of performance on is the faulty system of governance we have adopted. What it has created is not a healthier, growing and self-reliant economy but a massive dependency of all its citizens on government, foreigners and established mindsets.

We now have to bring about a fundamental change in our society—to create a nation that is truly empowered, self-reliant and sustainable. But how do we get from here to there?

The type of technology we choose for our production systems is a major intervention that can help us on to the new path. It is one of the easier and more immediate instruments of change. Its impacts are visible quite quickly but do not necessarily last very long. The technology needed by India, because of the many different epochs in which our people live, side by side, and the many different geographies they inhabit, is a mix of very big technologies—big dams, big steel mills, big refineries—together with small and very small industries for creating jobs in villages. Appropriate technologies, which are technologies with a human face, will continue to be necessary for a very large part of our country.

The second type of intervention is the set of fiscal policies, incentives and reward systems that mould our economy. The third group of interventions, the institutions of governance—making policies and allocating the benefits and costs of development—are even more important and have a deep and pervasive impact on our behaviour as well as on our surroundings. Planning systems are needed that are geared not simply to creating economic growth, but for equity and ecological harmony as well. New kinds of institutional systems are needed for innovation and for delivery of the goods and services people need. These include, for example, little industries that can be set up with very small capital investment in villages which can provide not only goods and services that people need in the local villages, but jobs and the purchasing power to buy those goods and services. This was, in fact, the vision of Mahatma Gandhi who had understood many of the problems of ecological security almost a century back.

Then, more fundamental in scope but also getting harder to change are the knowledge structures by which we understand the world around us. In particular, it is the way we compartmentalize our knowledge—a factor that varies widely from society to society—that determines how well we can relate to nature. And finally there is the whole system of values that determines our relationships with each other, with machines, with the rest of creation. These values influence how we deal with waste and, more generally, our understanding of what is a good life.

All these interventions are important and necessary if we are to create a more sustainable India. As we progress from technology and economic policies through governance and knowledge structures to value systems, the potential for causing change grows bigger and bigger, becomes longer and longer lasting, but is more and more difficult to bring about. But each of us must work on the ones for which we have the skills. Religious leaders and statespersons like Gandhi are needed for changing value systems. Academics and philosophers normally bring about changes in knowledge structures. Technology and economic policies, being the easiest, are where Development Alternatives does most of its work. But some of our attention, in collaboration with our sister advocacy organization, People First, is devoted to the important issues of governance and the institutions of society.

Our work in the field of governance, carried out over the past ten years, shows that among all the interventions that impact our ecological security, governance may well be the most profound and yet the least understood.

What is governance? As I understand it, governance is the whole fabric of decision-making systems that affects our lives. Governance is not the responsibility of just the institutions of government alone, though they are very important parts of it. It also includes civil society, the family, the whole community, not to leave out business and, of course, religion and faith organizations. These are all bodies whose decisions impinge on our lives deeply in one way or another. And what they do is called governance. Government is, of course, one of the primary factors that determines the quality of governance. But governance has to be seen as a much richer concept: it is the entire social environment that enables or prevents citizens and communities from fulfilling their lives and destinies.

In essence, governance is about leadership—leadership in every sector of society.

I believe that the best systems of governance are those that enable people to create sustainable livelihoods for themselves, that encourage adoption of sustainable lifestyles, that facilitate fulfilment of basic needs and that promote the attitude of self reliance. These are essentially the jobs of a good system of governance and, if carried out well, they lead people and their communities to acquire a sense of 'ownership'—ownership of problems, of solutions and of responsibility for one's resources. This sense of ownership—which is not synonymous with formal private ownership of land or other assets, and can effectively exist where resources are owned collectively by villages or communities—is crucial and possibly the most fundamental requirement for ecological security. Without it, people have no incentive to protect their natural heritage.

What we need to do is to generate that sense of ownership as a way of mobilising the latent energy of our country. I have been to innumerable places in India where the local people say that the reason they allowed their hills to be denuded and their water resources to be depleted was simply that outsiders (often government agencies, sometimes private parties, with no commitment to the local community) were responsible for them and why should the local people take the trouble to protect them? Everyone, particularly the women, fully understand that the disappearance of forests and drinking water supplies, and the gradual deterioration in living conditions, results from the massive destruction of the eco-system around them. When you ask why they let this happen, they say, 'Well, we don't own it. But if somebody else is going to come and do a hit and run on it, we might as well get there first.' So whether they do it themselves, or they let the Forest Department do it, or the Forest Department lets the contractor do it—whoever does it—basically the root cause lies in this enormous sense of alienation, the feeling that if neither they nor their future generations will benefit, why take the trouble? Such thinking is a very large part of the reason why our communities have not been able to protect their resources.

Good governance is simply a matter of defining clearly who does what. And it has well formulated answers to the questions: What is the mandate of each actor in society? What are their roles and responsibilities? What are the competencies and skills needed? How will they be held accountable?

How effective governance is depends on the ability of the leaders to make good decisions reflecting the interests of the community or society as a whole, their capacity to implement these decisions and to ensure compliance by those who have to abide by those decisions and the existence of appropriate systems of monitoring, accountability and rewards or punishment.

The key to effective governance lies in establishing institutional frameworks in which the different responsibilities are separate and distinct, particularly between the branches of government, the levels of government and the sectors of economy. In doing so, the systems of accountability—including legislative bodies, oversight agencies, watch dogs, ombudsmen, or whoever is formally charged to audit performance on a day-to-day basis, must ultimately recognize that it is the people who have to be overall in-charge. They must, whenever necessary, be involved directly in monitoring the functioning of government.

To make the argument more specific, let us look at the branches of government. There are essentially three branches of government: the legislature, to make laws; the executive to implement them; and the judiciary to enforce them. Now, in any good management system, these are three separate bodies that function independently and act as checks and balances on each other. Each has clearly defined functions and is expected to focus entirely on its own mandate. Unfortunately, in our country everything is mixed up. The judiciary is doing the work of the executive, the executive is doing the work of the legislature and the legislature is doing no work at all. They are just shouting at each other, or arguing about local issues or private interests, but hardly making any laws. That is why we have ad hoc decisions and resulting crises, like sudden evacuation of industries or equally sudden prohibition of diesel-fueled buses. We have the Supreme Court making decisions on issues that it has no business to be making, but it is forced to do so because of the vacuum of decision making in the government.

Everyone in our country, it would seem, wants to do other people's work—anyone else's except one's own. And this problem is not simply between the branches of government; it is even worse between the different levels—central, state and local. Prime Ministers and Ministers often spend their time on the most trivial of issues and have little scope left for matters of state. Decisions on what kinds of houses are appropriate in the villages of Andhra Pradesh are decided in the exalted corridors of New Delhi instead of by those who should know best—the villagers of Andhra Pradesh. Grand programmes are designed at the Centre for eradicating poverty without any consultation with the people most affected—the poor. The central level, the state level and the local level should all be distinct and separate governments, with their own domains for governing and without interference from higher levels. In actual fact, they are all mixed up. Hence, nothing much can happen.

Look, on the other hand, at the example of Washington, DC. There is a big man over there, who is, on any scale of measurement, quite powerful: the President of US. He is capable of pushing people around all over the world. But so far as Washington is concerned, he has not the slightest say whatsoever—running that jurisdiction is the prerogative of the city's mayor. Democracy can only work if there is adequate discipline—in setting up systems where every job is assigned to someone and in insisting that every one sticks to the job that is assigned. Today, in our country every MP is angling to run the town councils or local village bodies; that seems to be how our political leaders perceive the basis of power.

Under the principle of subsidiarity, every public decision or action should be made at the lowest level of government at which it can meaningfully be made. Subsidiarity has been made famous in the past decade by the highly centralized European Union, which has been under tremendous pressure from member countries to devolve political powers to the lowest possible level. The interesting irony is that the word 'subsidiarity' was actually invented in India some two hundred years ago by the British, who needed to run their colony with the least possible people and realized that this could only be done by a thoroughgoing devolution of power. The British, in turn, learnt the concept from an age old system of governance that had prevailed for centuries in many parts of India. Regrettably, at independence the concept of subsidiarity simply vanished. We set up a highly centralized form of government that believes in making decisions at the *highest* possible level.

For the citizen, the most important interactions with the state are almost entirely with the local government. Perhaps 80 to 90 per cent of the considerable time and effort they have to devote to dealing with government at one level or another is with local and district agencies, not the state or central ones. So, we need to set up a system of governance which is the exact opposite of the one we have: the bulk of the decision making would take place at the bottom and only those issues that require higher level attention (because they cross jurisdictions or need to be standardized on a larger scale) would be passed on to higher levels. In particular, it would be the local governments which would have responsibility for maintaining the natural resource base and thus ecological security. I would call this bottom up approach to governance by the somewhat ungainly but more accurate term "supersidiarity". At one level, supersidiarity and subsidiarity are very similar: the results are often the same. At another level, the two concepts are diametrically opposite: the process to devolve decision-making starts from the bottom in one case and from the top in the other; the results can sometimes be very different. Supersidiarity means that the real government is the government with which the citizen has the bulk of his or her contact: the local government. And it is this level, of course, at which the citizen can exert the fullest possible watchdog authority. Since it is the local government that is elected in a democracy to serve the citizen, the main functionaries—the people who have the responsibility to maintain law and order (police chief), protect and manage the forests, water sources and other public services (the forest officer, those in charge of water and sanitation, etc) must be answerable to the local community, not to some far away department at the state or central level.

Support to science is another way in which governance can impact ecological security. Since the days of Pandit Nehru, our country has made a commitment to science that is truly remarkable. For much of the period since independence India's scientific research and development budget was running close to one percent. This is more than most countries other than Japan, the US and a few European nations devote to science. Today, our science budget is close to 0.65 percent of GNP, which still amounts to more than twelve thousand crores. That is a lot of money going into science. But if you ask how much of that twelve thousand crores is going to science that has any relevance to the poorer half of our country, few people will be able to tell you. Based on information supplied by the science departments of the Government of India and its scientific agencies, it comes to much less than 100 crores, i.e., not even 0.1 per cent of the money spent on science that has relevance to those 700 million people. If science is so important in solving problems that it merits 2 per cent of the GNP, as the Prime Minister recently promised, how is it that we as a nation see no role for it in improving the lives of the poor?

As long as the decisions come from the top, it is unlikely that we will get the right answers. All we have to do is to look at any of the many large so-called "development" projects that have been designed without consulting local people, and you can get a pretty good picture. We have innumerable housing programmes of thousands of crores which are used as cattle sheds because the so called "beneficiaries" are not prepared to live in them. And empty cattle stalls because the project designers forgot that highly bred cows could not survive on the fodder that can grow locally.

So, I think it would not be exaggeration to say that our economy is somewhat mismanaged. And the mismanagement has led to all these basic issues, poverty, pollution, population, alienation, violence, corruption, destruction and this attitude of hit-and-run which has permeated our whole society. This short term, get-rich-quick mentality is the greatest threat to our ecological security because we treat nature as just another thing to be mined and left behind.

But it is even worse than that. These are actually the symptoms and not the causes of our problem. This is actually the end result and not the source of the predicament. The roots of mismanaging our nation lie in the priorities that we have chosen. The nation's priorities are set by the few who control the systems of governance, with very little regard for their impact on the majority. It starts with the simple premise that the majority are ignorant and live not much better than animals. Therefore, it is the job of the *mai-baap* of government, which is all-knowing and beneficent, to take care of them and decide for them. With such an attitude, it is only natural that we end up by creating the dependencies and the results that we have got. Particularly, we have set up huge, centralised systems for planning and administration that bring forth many promises but very little performance. The overbearing bureaucracy, subject to virtually no real accountability, is quite possibly the greatest threat to ecological security.

Digging even further, we come to the ultimate root causes, but they are very deeply embedded in our systems and culture. It is hard to recognize or understand them because they are unfamiliar and often very inconvenient. Most of us would rather brush them under the rug and not deal with them at all. They are very difficult to sort out and most of the time we don't even try, which is why we have been called a 'soft state'. But the term 'soft' has several meanings, and, unfortunately they all apply.

The first meaning is soft, as opposed to hard, in the sense of difficult. Our decision-makers have rarely been prepared to do the difficult things that are needed to build a nation. Allocate sufficient funds to ensure high quality education for all our children, for example. Or, introduce the land reform that everyone agrees is necessary.

The second meaning of soft is as the opposite of hard in the sense of solid, as in a pillow. This implies that decisions must be implemented and we as a nation are notoriously bad at doing that. To everything there are numerous exceptions.

Soft is also the opposite of hard as in harsh or cruel. Our country is notoriously harsh to its underprivileged sections and cruel to its animals. But when it comes to making and implementing decisions that require firmness in the face of resistance from vested interests deserving harsh treatment, we rarely have the nerve to make them stick

The opposite of the fourth meaning of soft is hard as in hard science, for example physics or chemistry. It implies lack of rigour or deep analysis. In that sense, our planning systems are certainly soft, heavily weighted towards simplistic economic concepts without looking adequately at the issues of technology or physical planning. One part of the bureaucracy frequently negates the work of another for lack of concern of the bigger picture. High level government committees spend their entire time deliberating the cause of one failure or another and finding that lack of coordination among agencies and lack of the bigger picture in each one is the primary cause.

Soft is also the opposite of hard meaning firm or durable. There is no policy in India that seems to stick for long. After a few years, it disappears, to be replaced by one formulated to respond to another emergency. Establishing ecological security needs long term commitments.

And, finally, soft is the opposite of powerful and intense, as in a soft light. Our nation's leadership is definitely soft in this sense.

So we lose out on all fronts because it is true: we are, today, a soft nation—in all the senses of soft—and as long as we are, there can be no hope for our forests, our soils, our waters or any of the other resources that form the basis of our ecological security. We need to take much harder, more rigorous and firmer decisions to hold the line on our ecological security. These solutions will need a different kind of leadership, a very genuine and selfless leadership and a leadership that is capable of taking hard decisions. We need a leadership that does not have to keep watching and looking back over its shoulders to see whether it might lose an election because it does the right thing. We need a leadership that says 'this is our country and we have got to make it work for everyone'. Since we cannot afford to wait for the next Mahatma Gandhi to come along, we also need to support that leadership with a citizens' movement. Community organizations, civil societies, religions, schools all these essentially have to play a role in being able to create and support that leadership and make it work.

It is becoming clear that no small tinkering with our systems of governance, a tweaking here, a fine-tuning there, is going to produce the results we need. Poverty is growing, corruption is galloping and nature is rapidly dying. Change is needed urgently and that change must be quite fundamental. The issue right now is how can we bring about such change? For normal people like us, it is very difficult to question certain basic assumptions and institutions that make up our society. Just as it is hard for a Hindu to question the Bhagavat Gita or for a Muslim to question the Koran or for a Christian to question the Bible, it is no less easy for a citizen to question his or her nation's constitution. However, after more than a decade of initial denial and subsequent deep analysis, my colleagues and I do not see any alternative, but to recognize that the present constitution—which admittedly was a truly remarkable document for its time and purpose—can no longer serve the needs of our country. I refer not to the profoundly important directive principles which guarantee the rights of citizens and the integrity of the country but to the systems of governance it has established: centralized, top-down decision-making, lack of proper checks and balances implied in the Westminster model of government and the marginalisation of the citizen in the decision process.

Can this system of government which has been established under the constitution take us where want to go? The 1950 Constitution of India is basically anti people. It is largely a replica of a colonial instrument (the Government of India Act of Westminster) whose purpose was basically to enable a colonial power to run a large, sprawling, remote colony in the most efficient manner possible. Many of its institutions are based on exploitative colonial requirements, and at independence these were adopted, often without any change, lock, stock and barrel. As a result, the government of independent India simply continued the colonial tradition of being a Ruler that is highly centralized, top down, insensitive, non-participative and non-transparent. Such a system of governance simply cannot deliver equity or ecological security.

While the Westminster system has certain flaws in it from a management theory perspective, it has evolved over a period of almost a thousand years to suit the particular genius and circumstances of its country of origin, Britain. It is not working in India which has yet to build up the institutions of accountability and the systems of checks and balances needed to ensure that government functions in the best interest of everybody. The mixing up of powers between the branches of government, the centralisation of decision structures at the federal and state level and the peripheralisation of the citizen lie at the heart of the political, economic and ecological problems of our country.

Gandhiji understood all this and suggested a totally different form of government, in which local communities would have been autonomous and where the executive and legislature at each level would have been completely distinct and separate. With transparency, citizen's rights to information, and an administrative system that would nurture professional excellence and responsibility, such a system would have produced a very different outcome for our country. I believe that it is an excellent model for universal democracy. Gandhiji had a fairly detailed idea of how such a government should work, which for lack of time I will not try to get into. However, a few examples might help. The upper house, which was supposed to protect the interests of the States but today has become an appendage with little independent meaning, could more appropriately have been a forum for all the major stakeholders to be represented. The Rajya Sabha or the State Legislative Councils need housewives, scientists, jhuggi dwellers, business persons and others to represent their interests as stakeholders of society. Such a second chamber would enable stakeholders to bring their professional and personal insights into the legislature as well as the audit process, as distinct from elected representatives who have a separate and distinct point of view and responsibility.

How can the Constitution be changed? Not very easily. As a nation, we have too much of our national ego invested in it. It can probably only be changed by the will of the people, as expressed through a referendum. Referendum is not allowed for in the Constitution, but it is an intrinsic right in any democracy. The sovereign people should be able to express their will at any time—in elections or between elections. And, we believe that we would need a mechanism to administer it because referendums can run away with themselves, as they sometimes have in such places as California or Switzerland. To ensure that referendums are held only for significant issues and are properly formulated, and that they do not touch the issues of fundamental rights or national integrity, People First has proposed the setting up of a 'Sovereign Rights Commission', which would act as the conscience keeper of the country.

How can such changes be brought about? Clearly, we cannot expect our politicians or parliamentarians or even bureaucrats to initiate such changes. They have their fingers in the current pie. There is no way that any of them would be prepared to lose all the great things they have been getting out of the system over the last fifty years by changing it. So, it would seem to be an impossible situation. That is where all of us come in. It becomes the individual responsibility of everyone who believes that this country needs a change—and some of us feel it is needed rather urgently and fundamentally—to take that responsibility. The time has now come when we need to prioritize, we need to talk a lot less and act a lot more in our country.

I can suggest a three point agenda for India. The first priority simply has to be to eradicate poverty in our country. And that does not have to take anywhere near as long as we have been taking since independence—since when poverty has grown, not reduced, in any case. Second, in parallel with that, to empower people to stand on their own feet. And third, to regenerate the environment and to bring about the ecological security that we are talking about.

Those are the three essential things that this country needs immediately. We have, collectively, to find ways to do it. There are probably no short cuts and no soft solutions that can get us there. But if you ask for the most effective intervention that could take us a long way towards a more effective system of governance and higher ecological security, I believe that it is eliminating the three most egregious perpetuators of poverty: government schemes for alleviating poverty, non-accountable bureaucracies and development economics.

If, as individuals we believe that this country is not heading in the right direction, a large part of our work is cut out for us. Each one of us has the responsibility to pitch in and work to re-orient the direction our country is taking. People First is one such effort and the Foundation for Ecological Security is another. We need many more.

5

Policy and Planning for Ecological Security

SHEKHAR SINGH

When we talk about policy and planning for ecological security, the first question we need to ask is: what is meant by ecological security? When I looked up the term 'security' in a dictionary, it had a very interesting meaning. Security was defined as 'meeting obligations and fulfilling pledges', and I thought this very appropriate for the topic, because one way of understanding whether our policy and planning is adequate to meet the imperatives of ecological security is to ask: do our policies and plans allow us to meet our obligations and fulfil our pledge to the people of India and to the people of the World to conserve nature. This is the sense in which I want to look at this broad topic.

Towards whom do we have such an obligation and to whom have we made such a pledge? I will try to highlight the three groups that need our most focused attention. The first is, of course, the future generations, to whom we have to provide what we would call inter-generational security. This, I think, is well understood. When talking about sustainable development, the crucial issue is how the consumption patterns of the present generation are not to be allowed to compromise the options and opportunities of future generations.

The trouble is that sustainable development is the most uttered phrase across the world in conferences and workshops and it means different things to different people. In many Western countries, it is not so much development or nature that they want to sustain, what they want to sustain are their exorbitant lifestyles. But, of course, it is very difficult for them to tell us to curb our consumption because they want to sustain their lifestyle. Therefore, the whole thing gets covered under the amorphous term 'sustainable development'. Hence, it is important that when we talk about sustainable development, it is in the context of India and of countries like India, rather than in a global context, where it means something quite different.

Second, we talk about ecological security for the disempowered and the oppressed, within our country and within the world, and how to ensure that our obligations towards them are met. This is intra-generational ecological security for people in our own generation who are disempowered, who are oppressed: the tribals, women, the rural poor, urban poor and many others. And here, I think, we have relatively weak policies and plans. For example, there is no rehabilitation policy in our country, yet we continue to displace people for development projects. This is despite the fact that, barring China, there is no other country in the world that has displaced as many people as India has for development projects. We do an environmental impact assessment of our projects, we do cost benefit analysis of our project, but we do not do a 'class benefit' analysis. We do not ask the question: who benefits and who pays?

As many of you would know, there is a requirement that a project, in order to be approved, must have a 1:1.5 cost benefit ratio. So, if the cost is Rs. 1.00, the profits or benefits must be at least Rs. 1..50, for the project to qualify. But, if we brought in a class-benefit analysis, then this would become rubbish. For example, you might want to support a project that costs Rs. 2.00 and the benefit is only Rs. 1.00 if the cost is being paid by the rich and the benefits are going to the poor. Similarly, you might not want to support a project that costs Rs. 1.00 and the benefit is Rs. 4.00, if it is the other way round. But we do not have a system by which we do a distribution analysis or class-benefit analysis of our projects.

Interestingly, India is considered globally to be one of those countries that is fighting very hard for equity, especially when it comes to climate change and ozone depletion, and we are a leading voice among the global community, demanding that we the poorer countries, we the underdeveloped, we the developing, we the countries of the south, must get a fair deal. But that same principle of justice is rarely applied internally to issues of national equity. So, we fight to bring about global equity, but we do not fight to bring about national equity. This is a very weak area of our policies and plans.

The third sort of ecological security is the ecological security for other species. I know this is not a very popular point of view and very often I have been told that this is unnecessarily making the whole debate too abstract. But, the fact is that the earth was not created just for human beings and we should be sensitive to our responsibility and obligations towards other species who share this world with us. In fact, people who are familiar with the legal system would know that if there is a piece of disputed property, the person who came and first occupied that property has an advantage in law. If you take that principle, most of these other creatures came to earth much before we did, and yet we have assumed that this earth belongs to us and that they have no rights except what we feel inclined to grant them.

Unfortunately, this is also a very weak aspect of our policy and though we have an Act for the Prevention of Cruelty to Animals, I have yet to see a plan for a dam that, apart from talking about human beings being submerged and therefore the need to shift them out, sheds even one tear for all the animals that are drowned when the water rises.

These, to my mind, are the three groups that we must keep in front of us, when we look at ecological security. There are others, but these are the ones that demand and deserve most concern for ecological security.

The plans and policies that we make and the strategies we adopt, must be such that they are *scientifically valid.* A large number of environmental issues inevitably involve science, all sorts of science, not just the biological sciences or chemistry, but also social sciences. All plans, policies and strategies must be scientifically evaluated. But this is problematic. There are three types of problems. First, in some area, science is weak in this country. For example, we have a protected areas network, but we do not yet have a scientific understanding of the minimum viable populations of various species of animals that we need to maintain, in order to ensure their long term genetic viability. Therefore, we also do not know what is the minimum size that a protected area needs to be. The views of scientists on this issue differ widely. In fact, one view is that whether the tiger gets poached or not, it is already doomed because there is not a single viable population of tigers remaining in the country.

Part of the reason why we do not have good answers to these questions is that this is not such a critical issue in countries of the West. Therefore, they don't research it. However, though this is a critical issue for us, we also don't think too much about it. As we have huge human population pressures, we need to justify every inch of area that we include in a protected area.

The second problem is the weak application of science. In India there is a deep divide between science and administration and the two rarely interact. There are problems on both sides. While the administrators do not think there is much in science that could be of use to them, the scientists, by and large, are not geared to meet the demands, time-frames, issues and questions that the administrators have to deal with. When I was in the Planning Commission, I decided that I would not approve a single project without consulting the concerned scientists. I found that it was very difficult to get the scientists to give an opinion in the five days that one typically had to assess a project. The usual thing was that they needed time for study, but the file had to be cleared and the bosses were not going to wait, even if I had no opinion. The main problem is a lack of interaction. Scientists are not called upon often enough to deal with administrative decisions and administrators don't often find scientists helpful enough in what they are trying to do.

The third problem, to my mind, is very poor levels of applied research. It is the business of universities to do pure research and it is the business of ministries to sponsor applied research. Ministries should have a clear idea of the problems being faced in the field and the solutions they are looking for. That is the sort of research that should be encouraged. In my own experience, we have not only haphazard research but also poorly focused research. I am tempted to share an experience when we were reviewing the Seventh Plan, in the process of formulating the Eighth Plan. Looking at the research projects that had been funded by the Ministry of Environment and Forests, I found that there was one project that had been approved, with quite a large amount of money, to study the ant-eaters in a particular place. The project report stated that when the particular place was visited to study the ant-eaters, they did not find any, so they decided to study the birds instead, and they therefore listed the birds that were found in that area! The attention and priority that research gets in India, especially applied research, leaves much to be desired.

Apart from being scientifically valid, the second point about what our plans and strategies need to be is that they have to be technologically sound. Technology is a double-edged weapon. You can use technology to protect nature or to destroy it. The socio-economic and political environment influences the development and choice of technology. It doesn't grow in a vacuum. Unfortunately, in our world, the technology to use and exploit nature has grown much faster than the technology to conserve and re-generate it. The reasons are obvious. Initial technological development took place mainly in the West, where private profits were the main fuel for technological development. The use of technology to exploit nature led to private profits, but nature was a public good and there were no profits to be made out of its conservation and regeneration. There was no internalizing of the costs of environmental degradation, and therefore you had this schism, this divide. Unfortunately that divide still continues. We still find that we are discovering newer and newer ways of using natural resources, an of misusing them, but very few ways of protecting or re-generating resources, and this has become a big problem.

We also need cost effective and innovative mechanisms to protect nature. This is a particular need in India. We are a poor country with many demands on our financial resources. We also have many constraints, some of them peculiar to our country. Therefore, what we need are little things that might work, things that take into consideration the political and social reality and are yet able to deliver the goods that you want.

Finally, we have to have strategies which are functionally harmonious. This is our weakest card. An activist friend of mine once described the Government of India as an organization with vertical loyalty and horizontal animosity! This is a pretty good description, because we have different Departments of different Ministries pursuing their own agendas without any effort at trying to interface with each other.

Here, imagine the Government of India as an orchestra. Right in front you have the Finance Ministry, which has huge big drums, which are deafening out everybody, saying 'GDP, GDP, GDP'. You also have, in prominent positions and with large trumpets and horns, the Water Resources Ministry insisting on 'dams', 'dams', 'dams', and the Power Ministry, the Ministry of Industry and the Department of Mines, all saying 'produce', 'produce, 'produce'. You have the Environment Ministry and the Welfare Ministry in one corner, with a flute each, trying very hard to be heard over all this din, but of course nobody is hearing them. You have the Prime Minister, who is the conductor of this orchestra, and one would have thought he would bring in some harmony, but he has in front of him not one music score, but twenty music scores. There is the Environment Ministry score, as there is a separate score for every other ministry and department. So the conductor does not know what to do because he does not have one consolidated score.

You have next the Planning Commission facing the other way and conducting some other orchestra that we do not know anything about. I am reminded of the experience when formulating the Eighth Plan in the Planning Commission. The way the plans were formulated in those days was that the senior people, the Members, all got busy writing the approach paper and the chapters and we, the advisors, got busy working out the financial allocations. The day before the Planning Commission meeting, the chapters and allocations were put together, bound in one volume and presented as a draft plan. I remember the very idealistic approach paper, which talked about transforming society, being applauded by the Members and the Deputy Chairman of the Planning Commission. The Secretary of the Planning Commission, in a very timid voice, said 'The approach paper does not match the allocations, because the approach paper talks about all sorts of new things but the financial allocations are for the same old things that we have been funding for the last 30 years'. The response was, 'You can't stop projects mid-term. After all, they are half completed and therefore you have to make allocations for them'. The Secretary then said, 'If you don't make the required changes in the Eighth Plan, its going to be more difficult in the Ninth Plan and even more difficult in the Tenth Plan'. But the matter was left at that.

Of course, this symphony orchestra has other disharmonies. It is not enough that the so-called 'development ministries' have loud instruments, they also have megaphones, provided by the World Bank, the IMF, and by industry and contractor lobbies, which further drown out all sounds of sanity.

The Environment Ministry and the Social Welfare Ministry are not without external support and NGOs, the Press and even the courts offer them a megaphone. But there is a wall around them, a wall of secrecy, of distrust and sometimes of careerism, and this wall stops them from accepting these megaphones. Of course, the courts have a 'bulldozer' call: the 'Contempt of Court,' which can breach this wall and come across. However, such legal intervention is, I think, creating a very strange and unhappy situation, not only in the Ministry of Environment but in the Government in general. For example, in the face of the very proactive attitude of the Supreme Court, there appears to be a hesitation in the Government to at on its own. The best way to describe this hesitation is to use the example of the three monkeys that were made popular by Gandhiji. The Government seems more and more to be behaving like these monkeys. There is one monkey who sits with his hands over his eyes saying 'see no violation of the law till the Supreme Court points it out to you,' there is one sitting with his hands over his ears saying 'hear no complaint till the Supreme Court tells you to', and there is one sitting with his hands on his mouth saying 'give no information till the Supreme Court asks for it'. There is also a fourth monkey, who is mostly asleep but jumps up and down and pretends to be very active every time there is a Supreme Court order.

I am sometimes happy with the orders that the Supreme Court passes regarding the environment, but I do not think the courts can run a democracy. Unfortunately, this is what is increasingly happening.

Then, there is the issue of administrative and political feasibility. Are our plans feasible? Are they the sorts of plans that we can actually implement? In 1985 Prime Minister Rajiv Gandhi announced the formation of the National Wastelands Development Board and said that he wanted to make forestry a people's movement. He announced that the NWDB would plant 5 million hectares of forests each year. That was a remarkable target; however the fact is that in the previous thirty years we had planted a total of 4 million hectares only. Therefore, to suddenly go from planting 4 million hectares in 30 years to 5 million hectares per year was a monumental task. That promise was never made good, for we had neither the financial nor the human and material resources to get anywhere near that target. Was this, then, a feasible plan? Would it not have been better to set realistic targets that could actually be achieved?

The Chairman mentioned in his opening remarks that the Planning Commission has now planned to afforest all the area requiring tree cover by 2012. Given the fact that our Forest Policy stipulates a forest cover of 33 per cent for the country and that our current forest cover, even if we include degraded forest areas, is less that 20 per cent, the total area to be afforested by 2012 would be in excess of 40 million hectares. I suspect that this would also go the way of other previous targets, because it is all very well to set a target without the calculation of what it is going to cost, how much land it is going to take out of other uses, how this is going to be done, what human and material resources are required and where are they going to come from.

There are some other issues that need to be considered in examining the adequacy of our planning process. First of all, in India we have no strategic impact assessment. We assess specific projects or programmes, but we don't assess our policies and strategies for their environmental impacts. No one, for example, says: 'Okay, this is your energy policy. But before it is sent out, let us look at what sorts of environment implications it has and whether they are acceptable.' For instance, the 1987 Water Policy of the Government of India lists all the uses that water in our rivers and lakes should be put to, in order of priority, and starts with provision of drinking water, then irrigation, and so on. But, the conservation of the ecological functions of lakes and rivers is mentioned nowhere. So, according to the water policy, you can drain a river or a lake of 100 per cent of the water and as long as you give first preference to drinking water and second to irrigation, etc., you are in conformity with the policy. What happens to the ecological functions?

Second, we do not have a system of natural resource accounting and budgeting. In most developing countries, and India is no exception, the governments are preoccupied with economic growth and development. Therefore, if the Ministry of Environment wants to be heard, they have to at least partly speak the language of economists, which happens to be the dominant language. They have to be able to say that environmental degradation and neglect also has significant economic costs. It is not just a matter of pretty trees and tigers. Yet, we have no system by which the economic and financial costs of environmental degradation and neglect are reflected in the national planning process.

Some years back the Ministry of Environment produced a white paper on natural resource accounting. It was almost entirely based on work done by the World Bank. This paper calculated that lack of action on the environment was costing the nation between 6 per cent and 9 per cent of our GDP. And, this was without taking into consideration many aspects like the loss of biodiversity, for which no good data was available.

This would imply that if our annual growth rate was between 5 per cent and 6 per cent, when one took into consideration the cost of environmental degradation, our real growth rate would be between–1 per cent and–3 per cent. Interestingly, in the National Conservation Strategy and Policy Statement on Environment and Development, brought out by the Ministry of Environment in June 1992, there is a very interesting clause which says that the government will prepare, each year, a natural resources budget which will reflect the state and availability of resources like land, forest, water, etc., and which will rationally allocate the resources in keeping with the principles of conservation and sustainable development. This was declared in 1992, yet no such budget has ever been prepared. What we need is a system that realistically calculates the economic cost o environmental degradation and incorporates this into the planning process.

It is not being suggested that environmental resources must be allocated on the basis of their economic or financial value alone. Here, I am remained of the Narmada case. Sometime in the 1980s, Mr. T.N. Seshan, then the Secretary, Ministry of Environment and Forests, referred the Narmada Sagar Project to the Forest Research Institute, asking it to calculate the cost of the forests that were to be submerged. At that point, the project roughly cost Rs. 2,000 crores and the benefits were expected to be around Rs. 3,000 crores, so it had a 1:1.5 cost-benefit ratio. The Forest Research Institute came back with the estimated cost of the forests to be submerged at around Rs. 35,000 crores. I was then, as I am now, on the Environmental Sub-Group of the Narmada Control Authority and I was delighted because if the cost of forests was Rs. 35,000 crores and the benefits were only Rs. 3,000 crores, the project was not viable. I remember the then Vice-Chairman of the NVDA, whom I shall not name, asked for one month and came back with a revised estimate where the benefits of the project had been re-calculated to Rs. 60,000 crores!

You can always add on backward and forward linkages, ad infinitum, and show them as project benefits. It is like the old principle, that if you run over a chicken that belongs to a non-economist, then it is only a chicken and all you have to pay for is the cost of a chicken. But if it belongs to an economist, then you have had it, because the cost of the chicken would include the cost of all the eggs it would have laid in its lifetime, each one of which would have hatched into another chicken, who would then each have laid so many eggs, ad infinitum. Therefore I am not suggesting that all decisions about the environment must finally be taken on financial or economic considerations. However, it is important that these be an input into the decision making process.

Hopefully in the Tenth Plan such a system might get activated because there was a working group set up by the Planning Commission to design an appropriate system of natural resource budgeting and accounting. This, to my mind, a very, very important agenda, which we need to urgently focus on.

The next point is that even when we do environment impact assessments, there is so much pressure that it is almost impossible to do a proper assessment or be able to get a fair decision. I had the privilege of serving as Chairman of the Environmental Appraisal Committee for Thermal Power and as Member of the Committee for River Valley Projects of the Ministry of Environment and Forests. That's when I learnt what really happens in the system. We would get a huge amount of pressure from various quarters for various projects. There were several examples, like the two well-known projects, the Tehri Project and the Sardar Sarovar Narmada Project. Neither one of them was initially cleared by the Ministry of Environment and Forests. In fact, the then Secretary to the Ministry of Environment and Forests went on record, in 1997, to say that the Ministry did not clear the Tehri Project, but that it was cleared by 'higher authorities', who ever that might be! Similarly, in the documents on the Narmada Sagar and Sardar Sarovar projects it is clearly written that the Ministry did not think that they should be cleared.

I remember also the case of the Kayamkulam super thermal power project in Kerala. When it came for environmental appraisal, I was the Chairman of the Committee. We went to have a look at the site and I then learnt the unfortunate truth that many of these large and controversial projects were located in the political constituencies of big shots. This project was in the constituency of a Union Minister, who also arrived at the site while the committee was there. He told me that the last man who stood for elections from there lost the elections because he could not get clearance for the project. Therefore, the Minister was going to ensure that the project was cleared this time, so that he didn't lose his elections. I laughingly told him that he had made the task of the committee more difficult, for now they had to not only assess the project, but also had to decide whether or not they wanted him to win the next elections! Though the committee finally decided not to accord clearance to the Kayamkullam project, the Environment Minister had a special meeting with the concerned Minister and the State Chief Minister and recorded in the minutes that thought the project did not merit environmental clearance, however the project was being cleared!

I must here say that my own experience has been that the Secretary, Ministry of Environment and Forests, has often put up a valiant fight for the environment. I remember that during my stint at the Planning Commission, I often attended the meetings of the Committee of

Secretaries as a representative of the Planning Commission. In these meetings, usually the Environment Secretary would be isolated and all the Secretaries would say 'you are anti-development, you are stopping the progress of the nation'. I was often the only other voice in support of the Environment Ministry. However, very often the pressure is unfortunately too much for the Ministry. So, it is not a system that is working well.

The Environment Ministry gives conditional clearance to many projects. The Tehri Project has conditional clearance, the Narmada Sagar has conditional clearance, Sardar Sarovar has conditional clearance. Very often the conditions stipulated include the *pari passu* implementation of the environmental safeguards, which means that environmental and social action plans should be implemented concurrently with the engineering works. However, many project authorities treat—'pari passu' to mean co-terminus rather than concurrent, so that only when the engineering works are about to be completed, they start worrying about the environment or about social considerations. The Environment Ministry has little ability to enforce the conditions of clearance, because once having given clearance, it has no teeth and is not in a position to withdraw clearance if the conditions are not being met.

It has been suggested that the Ministry of Environment should give clearance for two years only and that the onus should be on the project authorities to come back after two years and prove that they have fulfilled all the conditions of clearance. Only then, the clearance should be renewed. I do not know if such a system is ever going to come through. Therefore, there remains a huge problem of enforcement.

There are also other issues. There is an over-dependence on what one would call a regulatory approach, and this has limited use in India. The rich get away because the courts are slow, good lawyers can be hired, and the system can be subverted. When I was on the monitoring committee of the Ganga Action Plan, hundreds of cases had been filed against industry and all of them were bogged down in courts of law. Years would pass without any enforcement and industries would happily carry on because of the delays in dealing with the cases. In fact, I remember that every time they had a monitoring committee meeting they would produce statistics that would suggest that despite the hundreds of crores that were being spent, the Ganga water was getting dirtier. When I asked the person incharge of the plan the basis for giving more money, as the river was getting dirtier and dirtier, he said 'If we did not have the Ganga Action Plan, the river would get dirtier at a faster rate'.

Recently I was told that since 1997 they had given up monitoring the water quality! This revelation provoked one of the Members of the Planning Commission to recount a true story about 18th century London. Apparently pick-pocketing had become a serious problem then and the police were not being able to effectively control it. When this was brought to the notice of the Lord Mayor, he reportedly said 'If that's that problem, lets by law abolish pockets.' In the same way, if you have a problem about controlling pollution, lets just abolish monitoring!

We also have problems of enforcement among the poor, because they have few real options. For instance, they need resources from the forest for their survival. They do not have the option to sit back and watch wild animals ruin their crops or kill their livestock. If they have to survive, they have to have access to natural resources. They also have a very tough life and it is difficult to deter them through the threat of punishment.

I remember one of the NGOs working with street children telling me that one day some of these children decided to go for a holiday to Shimla. When asked how they were going to find the money to get to Shimla and back, they were frank enough to admit that they were going to travel ticket-less by train. They had even made a little song that explained their logic: 'Jana free, aana free, pakre gaye to khana free' (going was free and return was free, and if they got caught, even their food would be free!).

We have a system where a lot of people are already so desperately poor that you can't scare them by the threat of the jail. Many of them would be better off in jail, where they would at least have a bed to sleep on, a roof over their hear, three meals a day and basic medical care.

Therefore, just the threat of prosecution does not work. It does not work for the rich because they have ways of getting around the law. It does not work for the poor because they don't have any real options.

There is also the over-arching problem of corruption, though this is not peculiar to the Ministry of Environment and Forests, but a general malaise in the government and the society. This, however, makes regulation all the more difficult, because the system depends on individuals functioning as regulators. However, where the regulators themselves are corrupt, every new law just opens up new avenues for corruption. There is a very interesting story about Maharashtra, where the forest encroachers used to bribe the forest guards so that they were not recorded as encroachers. Then the Government changed its policy and the holdings of all those who had encroached before a certain date were to be regularized. Then the same forest guards started getting bribes to record these people as encroachers, so that they could also get the benefit of the new policy. The point is that we can keep changing the system but the rent-seeking behaviour does not seem to change.

So the regulatory approach has many drawbacks and we need to think of other ways of getting around the problem. What are these other ways? Let me end up by mentioning a few of them.

One approach that the Environment Ministry has been pushing is what is called 'eco-development'. This requires the development of alternate sources of livelihoods for those communities living in and around forests, national parks and sanctuaries and dependent on their resources to an extent, or in a manner, that is unsustainable.

I also feel that we have to focus far more on fiscal measures for conservation. The Finance Minister, before finalizing the budget, must consult the Environment Minister and see what fiscal measures can be put into position to help conserve natural resources, whether it is electricity, water, forests, soils, etc.

Then, it is necessary also to integrate environmental concerns into the policy and plans of all sectors, departments and ministries. Today the relationship of many of these ministries and departments is mutually antagonistic.

The N.D. Tiwari Committee Report in 1980, on the basis of which the Department of Environment was set up, had recommended that in each Ministry, like there is an internal financial advisor, there should also be an internal environmental advisor and, further, that this internal environment advisor should be, in some sense, under the control of the Ministry of Environment and Forests. The idea was that at the earliest stages of a project, or plan, or policy, i.e. at the stage of formulation, the environmental concerns should get attention. This was especially important for projects because, very often, by the time a project comes to the Ministry of Environment for appraisal, a large amount of money gets spent and project construction gets started. This leads to pressure to give post-facto clearance as, otherwise, there would be a 'national loss'. There are numerous cases where this has happened and there are many dams, including the infamous Tehri Dam, where construction was started many years before the environmental clearance was accorded.

There needs, therefore, to be a system where there is both an internal and a subsequent external review of the environmental impacts of proposed projects. The Ministry of Environment and Forests also needs to be more pro-active. It must tell the concerned ministries how better to design their projects, so that the environment is not destroyed. The Environment Ministry should enable the other ministries to meet their own obligations while meeting the environmental ones. They need to be helped to design better and safer projects, for you can't ask the Power Ministry not to produce power, or the Water Resources Ministry not to build dams.

We also need to immunize our system of environmental clearances from political interference. Even though this may not be easy, a serious effort must be made and some sort of statutory structures that cannot be subjected to day-to-day pressures can be set up.

At present, appraisal of projects is done by committees of the Environment Ministry which, in any case, are advisory in nature and the final decision is taken by the Ministry itself. Initially, when this mechanism was set up, the appraisal committees were mostly headed by people from outside the government. But over the years, perhaps because these committees were too independent, there was a change in the trend. The point is that in terms of public credibility, it is necessary to have some people who are independent of the government and who can be above suspicion. Unfortunately, that is not happening today.

We need to develop a land use plan for the country. A land use planning board was set up in the 1980s. It was chaired by the prime minister and had, as members, all the chief ministers and various central ministers. But in the last 20-25 years it has met twice only and we are certainly no closer to having a land use plan today than we were in the 1980s. But we do need such a plan. We also need to be able to take decisions dispassionately and in advance of project formulation. We need rational land use guidelines and we need to make all decisions regarding land use transparent to the public.

One advantage of a land use plan is that you can then apply the 'Judo principle'. Given the fact that the government is often slow and sometimes corrupt, let us offer industrialists a chance to set up in 'compliance zones', which are already identified. They can be told that if they opt for a compliance zone, then they do not have to go through the elaborate process of environmental clearances, which may save three or four years. For an industrialists a saving of three or four years is an important matter. If he wants to go to a non-compliance area, then he has to go through all the elaborate assessment processes. Thus, use the slowness and tediousness of government procedures as an advantage by enticing people to set up in pre-assessed areas and thereby save themselves the time and bother of procuring a special environmental clearance.

Another critical need is for the governments to be more transparent in functioning. There is now pending, in Parliament, a Freedom of Information Bill. When it is finally passed, hopefully many of these things will become easier. Unless we can be open, unless we can share information, unless we can tell people the basis on which clearances have been given, it is not going to work. Transparency would help in minimizing the suspicion and distrust that arises when citizens are kept in the dark.

Finally, I believe that ultimately human society will survive and progress. However, wise people can ensure that progress is achieved without heavy costs being paid, especially by the weak, the oppressed and the marginalized. To put it in another way, society evolves, and if we try and stop evolution or come in the way of the process of evolution, then pressure builds up and there is a revolution. And revolutions are messy things. They are costly, there are uncertain, and nobody finally wins. For the process of evolution to succeed, there is a need to forge new partnerships, especially between governments and community institutions.

Admittedly, there are people outside the government as there are within it, who have their own vested interests. There are unreliable NGOs, there are people who want publicity, people whose sole purpose is to run down the government. But there are others who have a genuine concern for the environment, an appreciation of the constraints that government systems impose, and a will to be constructive. It is only through constant interactions with such people that a real partnership for ecological security can be built.

6

Gender and Ecological Security

VANDANA SHIVA

Writers intellectuals and scientists perform their public role by throwing their weight behind those who are excluded and marginalised. That usually means throwing weight behind movements and activists at the grassroots. However, supporting the excluded is being interpreted as 'contempt' by the justice institutions, which have a certain leaning towards the more privileged sections of our society. This is the kind of situation into which Arundhati Roy got locked.[1] The judgement in her case was very interesting. I never heard such a long order read out in a court and I have done Public Interest Litigation for two decades.

I think the same Court had given the judgement to close the mines in Dehradun. In 1983, the Court had said that if commercial activity starts to undermine life support, it must be stopped as Article 21 of the Constitution guarantees the right to life. The right to life means the right to ecological security. In the same room, for the case relating to Arundhati Roy, the judgement was that any criticism of the Hon'ble Court is an affront to the Court, that a harsh judgement has to be passed to let the people know that they cannot cause affront to the dignity of the Court, but because Arundhati is a woman, she will be treated leniently with a one day imprisonment and Rs. 2000/- fine, which, if she had not paid, would have led to three months imprisonment. She was put in a police van and taken to the prison. In a way, one could read in the text behind the judgement the kind of issues that are thrown up when you think of how, on the one hand, our

1. On 6 March 2002, I had spent my time in the Supreme Court with Arundhati Roy. It was the day of the final judgement. This issue is linked very much to the subject of my paper.

dominant patterns of economic growth and development and globalization relate to our resource or survival base, and, on the other, how society is re-defining itself in terms of who decides to represent all of society. We have witnessed one part of society (representing all of India) in Gujarat redefining Hinduism as Hindutva and deciding for all of us what that religion is. The religion through which we were taught non-violence, through which we drew ecological inspiration, is being redefined as the practice of violence and the promotion of non-sustainable consumerism. That philosophy of compassion, of inclusion, of more than tolerance, is today being justified as reason for burning people alive, not in ones or twos but in thousands, in the state of Gandhi, the state of Jainism, the state of non-violence.

Actually, what is happening are two mutations: one mutation is in terms of our relationship with the earth and the second is in terms of our relationship with each other. Both these mutations are disrupting the ecological fabric of our security and both are connected. I have watched communities change from being rooted in their region, their rivers, their forests, and therefore having diversity in terms of cultural form, and also rootedness in terms of their ecological culture. So, the Gujarati Muslim and the Gujarati Hindu is a Gujarati first, eating the same food and speaking the same language. The Bengali was a Bengali first, till the partition happened. The fragmentation of our cultural identity is linked to the rupture of our ecological relationships. What is happening with society, I believe, is the same process that started to change our relationship with the earth two centuries ago.

We think of the earth as living, as dynamic, as self organising and therefore the earth had to be turned to dead matter. 'Terra Mater', the sacred earth, was mutated into dead matter. To do that, all kinds of issues, all kinds of philosophies, had to be created. Some years ago, I wrote *Staying Alive*, in which I addressed how I was brought up as a physicist. I did my Ph.D. in Physics, but we never read the philosophies of the 'great men' we learnt from. We never learnt the philosophy of Newton, the philosophy of Descartes, but we learnt Cartesian coordinates and Newton's law of motion. The inspiration behind the work of these founding fathers of reductionist science is all about fear of a living nature, a fear of a female nature, in fact, of a gendered nature, and that fear is dealt in two ways. One is violence and the other is escape. The violence comes from Francis Bacon, who said let us rape nature in ways that we can contain her because that is the way she will give us the real answers. The escape comes from the brilliance of Descartes, who said that the body is so unreliable that we can't really know if I am seeing you and if you are listening to me, so we need to have objective quantities and those measurable quantities are the ones we should then base a reliable science on. Everything that in ecological reality gives us a sense of the state of the earth and the state of our bodies—that the air stinks and that the water tastes foul—all are reduced to subjective belief. The fact that the water tastes toxic could now be treated as just a figment of your imagination. What is real are length, breath and weight. Those become primary qualities and primary qualities become tertiary, secondary, constructed.

We have been doing a lot of work on water. In fact, we had a public hearing on 22 March 2002, the World Water Day. We have been doing public hearings in different regions. Arthur Anderson, who got into trouble on the Enron issue, basically says that the current concerns with water relate to health, supply and demand, and environment and that as the primary concerns move in the future into tertiary concerns, they will become very remote issues. The primary ones will be competition, technology, new entrants and new economy. The new entrants, of course, will be the global corporations like Suez & Vivendi. In the new economy, water is a commodity, water is tradeable. So, we have seen Descartes and Bacon escape from the ecological embeddedness, saying our knowledge is gained through our senses. Our knowledge as ecological beings on the planet is un-reliable. But the tools that allow us to make an escape from that rootedness are primary. We are going deeper down the same trajectory of alienation.

Even though I have been trained as a physicist, thank goodness my Ph. D. was beyond Cartesian and Newtonian physics, it was on quantum theory which taught us actually that a lot of work done in the century before was very crude and crass. The crudeness lay in the fact that we treat things as separable when they are ecologically connected and not separated. Things are related to each other, they influence each other and they influence each other at a distance. The second crude assumption was that everything can be fixed, determined, made objective and immutable. Quantum theory teaches us that there is indeterminacy built right into the structures of the way this world is built and we have to live with that uncertainty, that complexity. Reductionism and the mechanistic world-view legitimise violence. Though quantum theory made mechanistic paradigms scientifically de-legitimate in thinking, it is still legitimate in terms of the dominant world view. These devices of chopping up work, in ways that allow you to constantly say that you are creating more reliable knowledge in the science and technology sphere, there is similar chopping up in the economic sphere, where every time something is taken through destruction, it is counted as growth and so much ecological literature is written on how the very assessment of the gross national product is based literally on two things: taking resources from nature and the life-replenishing processes and turning them into dead raw material, or taking activities and production from homes and villages and industrialising them.

Take the case of the 1 trillion dollar market in commodification of water. I did a calculation some time back I was carrying a water bottle and it started to get on my nerves. After a point, I said I have to go home and see how much this weighs. If we really imagine how much water each of us is going to drink every day, suppose 10-12 glasses of water, half of India will definitely start buying water, the other half will get polluted water. If that was to really happen, we are going to have a billion tonnes of plastic generated per annum. It is very efficient conversion of a renewable resource, water, into a non-renewable resource. We know in Jamnagar what the factories that are churning out petro-chemicals are doing to the water and the life support base of that region. There is a wonderful film made by the Foundation on Ecological Security on companies injecting toxins into the ground water to escape the pollution laws. In the middle of the night, tankers go out and inject pollutants into wells. But this one-shot use shows up a brilliant shoot-up in a curve of growth—plastics have grown and petrochemicals have grown because our ecological security and its undermining just does not get into the economic set-up and economic calculus.

The second aspect of the same construction of gross national product is how it takes women's strength, productivity and power and turns it into nothingness. A very dear friend of mine, who was the youngest member in the New Zealand Parliament, wrote a book called *If Women Counted*, largely as a result of her experience in trying to get money for what is needed for ecological security and not getting it, but there was always money for all the bombs and nuclear tests and missiles. So, she went back to study economics and why money is never available for schools, day-care centres, hospitals and everything that sustains life. And part of the problem she found was in the very definition of gross national product and the economics of it. The indicator, the measurement, was created to mobilise resources for war!

The definition in the UN system of accounts is basically that if you consume what you are producing then you are not producing. It is only when you buy someone else's production or sell your production to someone else, growth is happening. So all ecological maintenance becomes zero growth. Unless a river is tapped, and turned into a trans-basin movement, there is no water, the river is not water; the dam, the canal, the engineering works 'create' water. The forest does grow but once it is cut down, it creates growth. Genes in an organism have no value. It is only when our genes are moved and put into a sheep or a cow to make 'human milk' and then sell it back to us as 'human milk' or as mother's milk, then there is growth. It was actually said that Herman, the bull, was genetically engineered to produce a thousand cows which were supposed to produce mother's milk because they had genes from a human. It did not work. They changed their claims twice. First, mother's milk did not work because of the Nestle boycott. People got active and said 'No, don't fraud us again'. The next time they said this is an Aids cure. They got Aids cure in 6 months!

I am talking about fabrication and corruption of science in those cutting edge science areas.

I had to give a reply to the counter affidavit in our case in the Supreme Court on the genetic engineering trials. There was a line that said that there was no impact of Bt cotton on beneficial species. Bt is a toxin that is put in plants to make insecticide producing plants. The trials say 'no problem with non target species', when everything tells us there should be an impact. If there is a poison that kills one kind of insect because of a toxin, there is a very high chance of the toxin killing other kinds of insects. I found that there is no impact because there were no insects. The tables on insect population are zero in the control and zero in the test. There were no insects, so there is no impact, so it is fine, Bt cotton is safe and all of us working about the ecological impact are crazy. This is juggling with measurements.

Just like genetic mutations, we are witnessing cultural mutations and I think it is starting to now enter in a virulent form the very way we live our everyday lives.

We have been such a diverse society. We haven't just been diverse in the sense that each of us is diverse, but we have been diverse in that each of us is multiple. Our identities are not singular. We are multidimensional, we are not one dimensional beings and we are not, definitely not, a monoculture society. But the same monoculture of the mind that I have written about that has devastated agriculture, destroyed forests, destroyed fisheries, is starting to enter into our lives as we live daily. What is happening is two things: one, we are redefining our identities in the singular, excluding ways instead of multiple pluralistic inclusive ways. Second, we are re-moulding ourselves in the 'either/or' categories of the West which are mathematically called the 'Boolean' logic. I was in Trivandrum in early 2002 and there a Father Mathew talked to me about the Sabarimalai temple and how the pilgrims also pray at the mosque. Now that for us was Hinduism. A Hindu can go to a mosque and doesn't stop being a Hindu. In a Dhrupad festival in March 2002 Ustad Wasifuddin Dagar was singing the most beautiful music to Radha and Krishna and Shiv Mahadev. We have never had a problem with these interminglings. We have not been an 'either/or' civilisation. We have not had mutual exclusiveness in this civilisation, and that is why our mathematics is now being used for non-Boolean logic because we were experts in non-Boolean thinking and yet that Boolean logic is now being imposed in the most militaristic style and being dinned into us daily to make us accept it as the only way. I don't normally watch TV but I have been forced to watch TV because of the massacres in Gujarat. It was young men in triumph and joy coming to the streets after raping and killing. You never saw a woman as a violator, only as the violated. You saw the women crying, the children in hospital, the women talking about going back and mending and healing their society again. But you never saw triumphant women, thrilled at burning up someone else. So I do feel we are also talking about a gendered approach to things and at every step, the polarisation between the genders is increasing.

I have a deep feeling that three things are happening simultaneously. The first happened with the mal-development models that we adopted, the non-sustainable models, the Western models, in which the work of nature and the work of women got discarded. That led to the *first disembedding*. globalization is the *second disembedding* and this is more complex and confusing. If women were excluded by neglect in the first round of economic development, they are being excluded by appropriating their wealth and knowledge in the second round. Their output is recognised, their knowledge is recognised. That their neem (*Azadirachta*) is good for pest control, that the haldi (turmeric) heals wounds, that is recognised, but not the source, not the fact that it came from generations of women's innovation. The aroma of basmati rice is recognised and it is worthy of being pirated and patented; 200 kinds of saline rice varieties that are growing around our coasts and are very important with climate change problems, that is recognised, but that those seeds were bred with the intelligence of nature and women working together is again negated.

The gendering of our economics is related very intimately to the gendering of culture. And as more and more of our cultural sense of who we are is alienated from the earth, we lose our cultural roots. We are no more dwellers of *this* valley, this *region*, *this* forest. That is one reason I never leave Dehradun as my home, because the day I leave Dehradun as my home that is the day I will never really be able to be an ecological citizen. To know that this is the place where I was born, this is the valley whose future is my future, when you leave then the culture that you experience is the externally determined culture. And that externally determined culture then becomes more and more defined by others in terms of the negation of the 'other'. So you move from what I call positive identities, positive ecological identities to negative cultural nationalistic identities. From being ecological beings—biological beings who need clean water, air, food, economic livelihoods and ecological, economic and political security—to being consumers on the market place. All those securities are then replaced with a construct of growth based on undermining precisely those securities that give us identity and meaning.

As those identities and meanings go, it is a bit like what happened in the mad cow disease. In the mad cow disease, it was impossible to figure out what was really causing the infection to spread, because they couldn't find the bacteria, they couldn't find the virus, they couldn't find anything. The scientists who did the work got a Nobel prize some years ago. What was causing the infection was a deformed protein, it is the same protein, its chemical structure is absolutely the same, but it had got twisted and as a result of that change in structure, it was now becoming a self-infecting agent. Instead of upholding the organism—the cow, the sheep, the human being who got infected—it was now killing them.

Something very similar actually happens in factory farming. There are now huge movements to liberate animals from cages. It has been found that pigs, who love to snuff around and root in the soil, end up biting each other's tails when they are caged. The only way chicken can survive in the open is by getting worms and things in the field but when they are put in a cage, they use their beaks to kill each other. We still have the freedom to celebrate the horns of cows because our cows are still free and they haven't been dehorned, but when they are put into tight compartments or put into very concentrated habitat, they use their horns to attack each other. This phenomenon has been called the phenomenon of 'cannibalism' by the Agro-Business Industry. So there are two ways of looking at it. The non-violent approach would be to recognise that we have done horrible things to these animals, so they are attacking each other because violence is in their mode of living. The chicken's beak is meant to feed, the pig's tail is part of it and the horns of the cow are a significant aspect of its own anatomy. But that violent thought-frame says 'no'. So, what is done is that a day-old chick is taken and its beak is burnt at 800 degrees. The cows are de-horned as soon as they are born. And the teeth and the tails of the pigs are removed. I sometimes feel that the ecological space of human beings has been so shrunk and our ecological security so eroded that, like the pigs, the chicks and the cows who react when their ecological space is lost, the human beings are reacting and turning more and more violent and inflicting violence on each other because even though we are not living in iron cages, in terms of us being ecological beings, we are sensing our cage. We are experiencing our cage, we are experiencing the shrinking of the space in which we live. So, we are seeing cannabalism on the streets of Gujarat, we are seeing cannabalism everywhere in the world just growing in an epidemic way. And I think it is related very much to the way we decided to structure our economies and societies.

Another thing that is definitely related to this, especially in this period of globalization, is that the sectors that women were primarily responsible for—food, water, bio-diversity—were the areas which we called non-work till literally five years ago. These were called unproductive sectors; these were not considered sectors where knowledge was produced. Now suddenly, these are the fastest growth sectors. About $800 billion worth of profit is predicted in water privatisation and water trade and $800 billion profit in trade in seeds, and in monopoly on seeds and on food. Our budget says that agriculture is going to be the big growth area, but they are creating growth by destroying the very agricultural base in nature and the small farmers. Besides, such commodification also means a transfer of those areas from women's control, not to men in the community, not even to men in the country, but to fictitious individuals—the firm, the company as a corporate fiction, as a legal personality which has a personality only on paper but its ownership rights start to determine all arrangements, those arrangements that necessitate agreements like the WTO agreement. What does that necessitate? It means we cannot make a decision about how we handle our seed, what we do with our water, what we do without food. There is a TRIPS agreement that says this is how you are supposed to change your patent laws. This was discussed in Parliament and the last Patents Act was shaped after twenty years of public debate. On water, the World Bank has a structural adjustment programme that basically says you have got to privatise water. I have just come back from Orissa where small irrigation is being privatised. The prices have shot up ten-fold, while the price of rice has come down to one-third. So, the same farmer is spending ten times more for water and getting one third of what he got for rice, and within two years he will be in the situation of the Warangal farmers, who were pushed to commit suicide because of the price of seeds and the monopolies. When we worked out the pesticide use increase in the high suicide zone areas, it is about six thousand per cent. And all that financial burden is being put on the peasants with no money at all. It is all in the form of debts and when the debt becomes impossible to pay, the outcome is suicide.

Food, water and bio-diversity are the three key growth areas. They are also what used to be women's areas. But if our communities and our Parliament cannot decide who will own, how they will be used and distributed, then what do our politicians go to get votes for? I think that is where the constellation of non-sustainable anti-life structures becomes even further enforced. We have got economic thinking that works against life and now we are getting a political arrangement that basically says since I can't offer you water, I won't talk water, I will talk caste. Since I can't offer you a school, what I will do to get my votes is to make you afraid of the next community. It is this erosion of sovereignty, this erosion of democracy, on which the current global, economic model is built. We are feeding into a politics that must necessarily create fundamentalist, communalist responses. It is built into the very structures that the political system reinforces. The alienation that is already being experienced at one level, that is alienation from ecological grounding and second level of alienation because of economic insecurity, as more and more people are rendered redundant to economic activity. About two million weavers lost their livelihoods with one season of exports of cotton when the liberalisation policy started. The animal husbandry and dairy producers are at serious threat, if the policy for liberalising milk imports goes through. Now, when that redundancy happens, it is the mother and the young girl who work four times harder to make ends meet and usually the young man joins some kind of a militaristic 'club'. I think we should start using the word 'militia' because they join militias. The burning we have seen in Gujarat does not happen spontaneously; it is engineered. I feel that the new wave of communalised fundamentalist politics is really the highest employment sector for the unemployed men in society. Women have always found other ways to keep life going. But young men are now being pushed into this way of employment and in search for identity, as a way of getting into the niches of survival, which is no different from what happened earlier when over the diamond trade armies were formed and little kids of less than ten years joined those armies. It's no different from civil wars taking place in societies elsewhere—Sierra Leone, Rwanda, Yugoslavia, Sri Lanka. The dominant model of security, in response to these three levels of insecurity—one being cultural insecurity, the second being economic insecurity and the third being ecological insecurity in the sense of our life support systems—is responding by one method alone, and that is arms, more arms, more uniforms, more arms.

In March 2001 I went to Bastar where the tribals wanted to exercise their rights to decide whether or not they would allow a steel plant there. They wanted the Gram Sabha to decide according to the 73rd & 74th Amendments to the Constitution. Now, the Gram Sabha made a certain decision, but the records were forged and destroyed by the district administration. The Gram Sabha said no, you can't get away with this. They submitted a petition to the SC/ST Commissioner who verified and found that there was a fraud and the records were changed. Then, the Gram Sabha convened another meeting and just to be sure that this time there was no fudging, they invited some of us. Travelling down to Bastar, there were goons all along the way and the police took us into custody saying that our lives were in danger. We said, if our lives were threatened, why don't you handle the anti-social and anti-lawful elements? If there is threat and violence, why don't you deal with the people threatening to use violence, why are you taking into custody those who are committed to peace and non-violence. The fact is that in a context of brutalisation and cruelty, the institutions of society are basically affirming that violence is the norm. Anyone who does anything to create peace is a threat to public order. They don't say that of violence. If the order is to become an order of violence, then obviously any intervention that is based on peace is seen as a threat. In a system that is based on economic violence against nature, any ecological intervention is being defined as 'terrorism'. Hundreds of time I have been labelled as an 'ecological terrorist'. I have always returned the compliment to Mr. Bush, who is going to raise temperatures by 8.8 degrees in the next fifty years, because of his refusal to sign the Kyoto Protocol. Almost 67 per cent of our glaciers have disappeared. And if global warming continues, we will not have a Ganga or a Yamuna, we will not have those rivers, and the island states because of a 3-feet sea rise level within the next few decades. In fact, some islands were vacated last year. All this happens because of the wonderful constellation of convenient arrangements. There are the oil companies giving 64 million dollars a year for elections and the White House making laws according to it. We have the same phenomenon here; we have our Enrons and our Dabhols and others, and the machinery keeps working further and further away from building the real securities, the first of which is ecological security, because first and foremost we are biological beings. Second comes cultural security because before we vote for who will represent us in the Parliament, we are members of communities and societies. The third is our economic and political security in terms of how the larger structures work. Insecurity arises from the imperative towards negativity in all our structures. We are moving into negative economies, in the sense that the farmers are being forced into spending more than they are getting, the societies and countries are spending on collecting in terms of revenues on customs, etc. Everywhere at the economic level, there are economies of bankrupcy, they are bankrupt in respect of the economics of nature but they are also bankrupt in their own measure of what is an economy. We are running into negative politics. We are definitely running into negative culture, where we are not allowing our future generations to experience culture as a positive experience of who one is, but only as a negative experience of who one is not, and, therefore, who you are not must be annihilated to re-affirm who you are. Extinction is built right into that 'either you are me' or 'you are not me', 'either you are with us or you are not with us'. And, of course in society we are moving into the logic of live and live not.

I was interviewed recently by someone making a documentary on stemcells research. Stemcells are allowing us to grow out our own organs, so if I want to replace my kidney I can use stemcells to grow it out. The stemcells come from embryos which basically come from abortions. This research is a hotly debated political issue, commercialisation is even more hotly debated. A think tank in the U.S. says that as a result of these new breakthroughs, we are moving from the situation of have and have nots, to a situation of live and live nots. All the people on this planet cannot survive. Definitely not all of them can have the food systems that are being put into place because there are such huge ecological foot prints. Europe requires seven Europes outside Europe to grow the feed for the cattle. Therefore the dispensability of 80 per cent is built into the ecological model that has been evolved, which requires the resource base of the 80 per cent for the lifestyle of the 20 per cent. What about the remaining? You can either let them starve and die of thirst or shoot them. The other day I was sent information that there is a new contraceptive 'Corn' coming. Earlier, we had the 'terminator seed', which would be sterile in the next generation. Now we have got a contraceptive built into the corn, so that when supplied to regions where there should not be too many children, you would have sterility spread through the population just by the food you provide. In a way, the culture of violence has reached its limits, as war against life itself. I don't think it can go further really. I can't imagine that there is another step beyond this. I am saying I don't think there can be. The negative constellation of the forces of greed, of fear, of violence, of patriarchal control, which have this funny, funny response to everything living, I am not going into the details of what I read in the literature. For instance, the bees when pollinating crops are stealing pollen, because all pollen belongs to the patent holder of the plant, and bio-diversity in the fields is stealing sunshine, because only rows of ordered plants should grow as you tell them to grow. This much chemical, this much fertilizer only. Thus, our plants are stealing sunshine and the bees are stealing pollen. You can imagine the shrinkage of ecological space in our heads. We have already rendered ourselves ecologically insecure in the dominant model and of course we will act on that image. We will act it all out. I think we need to move from that 'fear of everything' syndrome to the 'love for everything' syndrome. I think that is a gendered issue. That's why the women will lead and women will teach. I am a mother and I have not seen too many mothers decide which of the children will survive and which will die. 'You are competitive and you are not. You are an efficient child, I will reward you, I will give you merit incentives and I will withdraw subsidies and support from you because you are not producing enough.' No mother can work on the logic of competition and dispensability. A mother gives more love to the child who is crippled, to the child who is disabled. The mother's love goes to the disadvantaged. It doesn't work in the logic of efficiency and market competition. So, we need to also move from the logic of greed to the logic of giving. I think there is a disease just now of wanting to own and control everything that lives. The patents on life are one of those diseases, but the attempt to own water is another. There are water wars across the world, and therefore my next book is called *Water Wars*.

When water is privatised and commodified, prices rise. People couldn't afford to buy food or water and the women were told they could not pull out water from their own wells because they belonged to the company who had the concession. This happened in Bolivia. Even groundwater has now become exclusive property. This attempt to own and control everything, I think, needs change to move again into that womanly sense of everything, especially the basis of life belonging to all and you belonging to everyone. Moving from owning and controlling to relating, connecting, belonging. I think the idea of exclusion, the idea of those singular mutually exclusive identities has generated too much violence.

We have just experienced the violence in Gujarat and it is not the end, it is going to continue. How many places, how many *dargah*s have we where Hindus and Muslims worship and yet these are being made to look as if they cannot be shared places of worship. I was with the Chipko women for whom every tree is a goddess, the forest is a goddess and every river is a goddess. Yet the forces of 'Hindutva' want to go for a little piece of land and say 'God, you get locked in here'. In this country where divinity is so pervasive, in every life form, in every ecosystem, in every cell of our body, in you and me, we have that privilege of experiencing life itself as sacred. The forces of Hindutva say 'no', that sense of what is divine and what is God must be given up for a jailed idol in one little stolen piece of land. I think that is violence to our basic culture. I think it is violence to the ecological culture because it is precisely the same forces that are killing in the name of religion, that are then saying we will also kill the tribals to get land for the steel plant, we will kill farmers to take over agro-business, we are going to be partners for that, because once your seeds are not sacred, your land is not sacred, your river is not sacred, your forests are not sacred, then only can you brutalise other human beings for your convenience. So, I think, reclaiming the sacred in nature, to rebuild ecological security, is both the healing for our ecological crisis and healing for the communal and fundamentalist crisis we are going through.

There is a need to move again from monocultures to the culture of diversity. That is the way we live, that is the way we thought and that is the only way we can have a future. The issue about diversity is that it let's you experience, know and recognise and produce abundance out of very little. Monocultures make you create poverty out of huge abundance. We need to move from monopolies to the culture of sharing and again it is from women that our society can learn what the culture of sharing is about. As Gandhi said, the planet has enough for everyone's need but not for some people's greed, that for some people's greed the planet is too small and there are too many people and too many interferences. I really feel that at least from my perspective as a woman, the market as well as religion have become such intense anti-life forces that need to be responded to by a deeper reclaiming of democracy—an Earth Democracy.

Ecological security needs to be built on the recognition that we can only have democracy as human beings if we have democracy as an earth species. If we learn to live with each other peacefully as one among diverse species, we will also live with others peacefully as humans. When Tagore started the Shanti Niketan, he said the reason I am starting a university in the forest is because our civilisation is a forest civilisation. It has learnt from the forest and it learnt democracy from the diversity. In a way, we need to learn democracy from nature. We need to learn co-existence from nature, we need to have a lesson in diversity from nature and then suddenly there is a whole new world, a positive world with positive constellation to be built, with hatred and violence being replaced by compassion and non-violence. While today, violence is growing and the institutions of our society are isolating the concerns of our people and ordinary citizens, at the same time, I feel in my bones and in my being that there is a whole new energy ready to burst forth. It might not be today, it might not be tomorrow, but there will be a burst of energy and there will be a return of sanity to our very brutal life and to our traumatised society.

7

Livelihoods and Ecological Security

N. C. Saxena

Natural resource management can succeed only with peoples' empowerment and social organization at the village level. In this context, I will examine the nexus between degradation and poverty in respect of key natural resources in India; land (croplands, grazing lands, forests), water (surface water and groundwater), and air. Then, I will present an analysis of the reasons for the degradation of these natural resources, and discuss the extent to which the poor are responsible for degradation, as also the impact on the poor due to environmental degradation. Further, we will look at the government programmes for the regeneration of natural resources, and then I will propose the most suitable means for strengthening the existing initiatives or designing new programmes for reversing the process of environmental degradation and impoverishment.

Conventional thinking on the environment blames the poor for over-exploitation of natural resources, as poverty and environment are considered linked in a 'downward spiral', in which the poor people, forced to overuse resources for their daily survival, are further impoverished by the degradation of these resources. The poor in this view are perceived as having a short time horizon, discounting the future benefits from conservation due to the urgency to eke out a livelihood and subsist. Such a time horizon leads to unsustainable use of natural resources. It is, therefore, believed that poverty needs to be eradicated first in the developing countries, before these countries can turn their attention to environmental protection. One may recall that in the UN Conference held at Stockholm in 1972, Mrs. Gandhi, the then prime minister of India, argued that the developing countries cannot undertake environmental conservation at the cost of economic development and that in the developing countries economic development must take priority.

The examples used to illustrate the vicious circle generally relate to common property resources (CPRs). As the poor cannot raise animal feed from their farms, which are meant for crops, their cattle depend heavily on common-lands for grazing, and hence this pressure on the grazing lands leads to their depletion and lower productivity. Encroachments on grazing lands and forests, done by the poor for crops, have the effect of depriving the other poor people of access to such resources, quite apart from the environmental effect of soil erosion. Cultivation on fragile mountain slopes leading to soil runoff and floods is another example. Shifting cultivation, with shortened fallow cycles, is often viewed as being ecologically destructive.

The important point here is that as the poor are dependent on nature for livelihood, they are very vulnerable to natural calamities, environmental degradation and ecological disasters. Some of these occurrences may be natural, like floods and droughts, and some may be man-made, such as the Bhopal Gas Tragedy or pollution caused in the river Yamuna by the industries and upstream rich farmers. Even natural disasters, like floods and droughts, may be aggravated by human action. For example, deforestation on the mountain slopes can increase the flood-proneness of the areas down below. Similarly, droughts may be aggravated by the neglect of water and soil management, resulting in soil erosion, increased vulnerability of crops to failure of rainfall and increased instability in crop output. Whatever may be the cause, the sufferers are the poor.

Once the ecosystems are degraded, they cannot sustain the human and livestock population, which results in migration (burden on distant natural resources) and reduced income of the already poor people, thus leading to widespread poverty.

In urban centres, the poor have to spend more on below-standard housing and thus face health hazards due to lack of safe drinking water, sanitation and exposure to industrial and air pollution. The pooled effect of these factors is a reduced life span, loss of income due to the job-days lost because of illness and increased expenses on health care. Again the poor remain in the poverty trap.

Probably the first victims of any environmental degradation are the women among the poor. A fuel-wood crisis as a result of deforestation, for example, forces village women to travel for miles in search of wood. This involves waste of energy and time, which the women could have devoted to more remunerative work. They have to bring water for cooking and washing from great distances. Fodder scarcity also affects the women first: the care of livestock is their responsibility.

This burden on women, in turn, has an impact on girl children. When the mothers' time is spent on fetching fuelwood and drinking water, the girl children are kept at home and discouraged from attending schools. They have to look after younger children, sweep the house and do other household chores.

Women are also the immediate victims of the smoke that fills the houses of those who cannot afford clean fuels like natural gas and electricity. Both rural and urban women, who have to wash clothes, are affected by the quality of the detergents they use, since washing is done mostly by hand.

Is Poverty the only Cause?

The 'vicious circle' hypothesis as characterising the environmental degradation caused by poverty in the developing countries, has been criticised on several grounds. First, the poor have hardly any autonomy of action, their behaviour is determined by the pressures put by the external socio-political forces, and hence blaming them does not lead to any corrective action. Second, the markets for environmental goods are highly distorted due to subsidies and wrong pricing policies leading to overexploitation, again generally benefitting the rich. Third, government policies have often converted community resources, such as forests, into open access resources, whereby the people withdraw from protecting them, while the government is unable to enforce the discipline necessary for its care. Fourth, technological advancement, though creating artificial capital, is often at the cost of natural capital. The deforestation that took place in India during the 19th century and the early 20th century was mainly on account of the pressure to meet the timber requirement of the expanding railway network and the wood requirement in urban areas (house construction, wooden poles for street lighting, etc). The Second World War put further pressure on the forests. The development of the iron and steel industry (in the initial stages) and the paper and rayon industries augmented this pressure on the forests. And last, economic change often bypasses the poor and reduces their access to the natural resources, thereby increasing their dependence on the fragile resources.

Thus, the blame for environmental degradation cannot be put solely at the door of the poor (in fact, the reverse is generally true, as environmental degradation hurts the poor and causes more poverty).

Faulty economic policies and subsidies for the rich are often greater explanatory factors behind deterioration in the quality of the environment. It is also argued that the poverty-environment nexus is formed through redistribution of economic resources from vulnerable sections of society to power holding elite due to monopolistic control exercised by these groups over productive and mainly non-reproducible natural resources, constituting the natural capital of a society. Monopolistic control enables the power-holding groups to: (i) transfer the cost of environmental pollution and degradation to weaker, disorganized, disenfranchised and marginalized groups, sexes and communities, and (ii) earn exorbitant profits by paying very low prices for accessing natural resources which do not reflect their natural scarcity and take undue share of natural capital in public domain due to non-availability of effective legal protection and poor governance.

We cannot also take it for granted that all economic development alleviates poverty. There are cases of destructive development which aggravate poverty and contribute to environmental degradation at the same time. An example of this is provided by shrimp farming in the coastal areas of Andhra Pradesh and Tamil Nadu.

The giant, global fish and seafood market worth $8,000 million has encouraged mushroom growth of intensive and semi-intensive prawn farms along the elongated coastline as well as intensive and mechanised fish fanning in the coastal waters. Boosted by the liberal Exim policy, shrimp farming developed feverishly and unpoliced. Of the 1.2 million ha. of brackish water areas, inclusive of ponds, lakes and lagoons spread along the coastline, about 80,000 ha. is under shrimp culture (80% under extensive methods and the rest under modified extensive and semi-intensive modes).

Semi-intensive aquaculture requires loads of organic and chemical inputs. At the end of each harvest, the waste is flushed out which pollutes the coastline and other receiving water bodies. These effluents affect the coastal fisheries and ultimately are, to an extent, responsible for depletion in the catch of traditional fishing in coastal waters.

Although no estimate is available, it has negatively affected the traditional occupations of local fishermen.

Moreover, leasing out of coastal lands for prawn farms has obstructed the flow of fresh water and thus people's livelihoods. The salt pans, which were a source for salt and thus supported the poor during the lean fishing period, have ceased to exist. The worst impact is on the ecological balance of the fresh water and sea water fauna that had dwindled due to lack of nutrients. On the other hand, it increases salinity of surface and groundwater. It affects the fertility of land in the adjacent areas and makes agriculture unsustainable, thereby causing occupational displacement of agricultural farmers. By displacing food crops, it dents the situation of food security. As aqua farming requires capital investment, the ownership of lands steadily gravitates to the cash-rich urban businessmen. Though there has been some investigation into the environmental impact of large shrimp farms, very little care has been taken of the above mentioned, done specially to deal with the loss of productive assets and the threats to livelihoods generated by aquaculture.

The enterprise may have created jobs for a few and raised their incomes. But for every person employed in shrimp farming, five agricultural workers have been rendered jobless. Moreover, it costs much more to create a job in shrimp farming than in agriculture, which it displaces. If shrimp farming had been confined to natural sites of brackish water, the tragedy would not have occurred. Another example is of cashew plantation in Orissa, which is discussed below.

In Orissa, cashew plantations have been raised by the Soil Conservation Department on about 120,000 ha. of 'Government Wastelands' in Schedule V areas. In many cases, such lands in the past were under the cultivation of tribals, but their rights were not recorded. In many regions of Central India the land records were generally in a bad shape, specially where land was of poor quality. As such lands did not have the potential of giving revenue income to the state. When settlement took place, the tribals were not in a position to get their possessions recorded, and thus the land under their possession got recorded as government land and some places were transferred to the Forest Department. Thus, the poor tribals got described as encroachers even on lands which were cultivated by their ancestors.

The cashew plantations, raised on land that was supporting the livelihood needs of the tribals, were handed over to the Orissa State Cashew Development Corporation for management. In such cases, no compensation was given to the poor farmers, because their land rights were not recorded. As the corporation could not run profitably, it started giving annual leases for harvesting of cashew crops to private parties through open auctions. Often such plantations are in a degraded condition because of lack of maintenance.

Two years back the Orissa government even contemplated giving long term leases to private parties for managing cashew plantations. One such advertisement appeared in the *Economic Times* dated 20/4/99. The leases would be given for a period of 35 years for a minimum area of 2,000 ha. Thus lands that were once with tribals would now be with private corporations, with the tribals getting no compensation, or rehabilitation. Many of them shifted to the hill slopes, and that resulted in more soil erosion, the prevention of which was the objective of the scheme. It is ironical that these plantations that deprived the tribals of their possession were funded by a scheme called, 'Economic Rehabilitation of the Rural Poor' (ERRP).

It is understood that in addition to cashew, there are similar plantations of coffee and other commercial crops in Orissa.

Thus the process of alienation of tribal land can be summed up as follows:

- State took over tribal ancestral lands presuming such lands to be government land for taking up cashew plantation for 'common good' i.e. soil and moisture conservation measures. The price paid by the tribals was discontinuation of the use of that land and its production. However, the improved conservation had a local benefit, at least theoretically.
- State handed over land to a government parastatal for commercial exploitation through cashew plantation in order to generate revenue for the state government. The local community has no share in the revenue.
- Failure of the parastatal to manage the plantation well led government to consider privatisation of cashew plantation and by implication pass on ownership of the land to the corporate sector. It would have meant closure of any access or any benefits to the local community from the plantation and land which is effectively privatised.
- Tribals shifted to the slopes that led to more soil erosion.

This is a typical example of lose-lose situation in which the poor lost heavily with no sustainable gains to environment.

Hypotheses

To sum up, a number of causal relations can be postulated that may explain the nexus between poverty and environmental degradation in India.

Hypothesis 1 : Poverty causes environmental degradation (HI).
Hypothesis 2 : Factors other than poverty, such as market failure, institutional failure and policy failure have greater explanatory power in describing environmental degradation (H2).
Hypothesis 3 : Environmental degradation harms the poor and often results in more poverty (H3).
Hypothesis 4 : Factors outside the realm of natural resources cause poverty (H4).

The findings on these hypotheses are summarised below.

H1 and H2

It is a fact that a majority of the poor have little option for income outside natural resources, such as land and water (60% of the entire workforce depends on agriculture, fisheries, and forests), and therefore use common resources, such as non-private land, tanks, ponds and rivers more intensively than the non-poor. Because of their poverty they cannot afford cleaner fuels, and burn bio-fuels to cook their food.

This not only degrades environment but also leads to deterioration in their health, especially of women, children and older people who suffer because of indoor pollution. This in turn reduces the number of working days available to the poor for earning their livelihoods and thus a vicious circle is established.

However it will be simplistic to come to the conclusion that poverty alone leads to resource degradation. If one looks at the totality of natural resources, much of environmental degradation, especially relating to water and air, is not caused by poor people, as their levels of consumption and production are much lower than those of the rich. Elite social groups with more resource-intensive lifestyles escape censure, but the poor get blamed for eking a fragile subsistence. Degradation is often due to excess consumption, and therefore the rich and their life-styles cannot be absolved from the responsibility of creating demand for goods being produced by the natural environment, be it timber, water for irrigation, or animal skins. After all urban pollution is caused by too many vehicles and industry, owned by the rich or catering to their demand. Similarly water pollution is mostly due to industrial activity or overexploitation of groundwater by rich farmers.

Groundwater is a common pool resource, but rich farmers consider this to be a private resource as they think that they have absolute rights to groundwater below their land. In over-drawing water they are able to deny poor farmers the right to use the resource. The high costs involved in accessing this resource makes the situation more complicated, and only the rich and well-to-do farmers are able to bear the high capital costs. Thus access to groundwater is mediated through technology and capital, rendering its exploitation inequitous (*see* box).

Water Famine—How Real?

During the summer months of April-May 2000, the Maharashtra Government was supplying drinking water through tankers in about 3,000 villages. Many of these had a standing and well-irrigated sugarcane crop. Thus groundwater that should have been a community resource was being monopolised by a few rich farmers, who also took advantage of easy availability of two other scarce resources—electric power and capital. The rich farmers thus transferred the responsibility of satisfying people's need for drinking water to the state, with community solidarity getting further punctured, and the state abetting in the overuse of water by supplying them cheap power.

Mid-term Review of the Ninth Plan

Similarly, river water pollution is either due to activities of the rich or inaction on the part of government to provide sewage systems in the towns. Thus water pollution is caused by industrial discharge, irrigation run-off and untreated sewage. About 75 per cent of the wastewater produced is from the domestic sector, but sewage treatment facilities are inadequate in most cities and almost absent in rural India. Only 25 per cent of Class-I cities have wastewater collection, treatment and disposal facilities. And less than 10 per cent of the 241 smaller towns have wastewater collection systems. Not more than 20 per cent of all the wastewater generated in Class-I cities and only 2 per cent of all wastewater generated in Class-II towns is treated. The water quality available in even Delhi is not of the desired standard.

Similarly major responsibility for causing outdoor air pollution has to be shared by the rich and the affluent. Industries, coal-based thermal power stations, vehicles and biomass burning are the main sources of air pollution in urban areas. The ambient air quality has deteriorated all over the country, especially in urban and semi-urban areas. Problem of air pollution is acute not only in the twenty-three cities of over one million population, but also in many middle sized towns. However, the brunt of polluted air is borne by everyone, and more by the urban poor, as they live in slums that have little municipal services to avail of.

Thus, not all environmental degradation is due to pressure from the poor, although their poverty does lead to land degradation, especially that of forests and common lands, which in return intensifies their own poverty.

Even when the poor over-exploit common lands it is often due to the 'tragedy of commons', that is, due to lack of clear tenurial rights. Forests and grazing lands become open access properties and the lack of clear property rights leads to their over use. It is significant that the poor farmers maintain their private lands and use them sustainably, but where property rights are not clear, such as on encroached or common lands, degradation is common.

The fact that environmental goods and services are not priced correctly also leads to their abuse. Industries getting subsidies on forest products; farmers getting cheap power, water, and fertilisers leading to excessive consumption, water logging or shortage for others; and polluting industries not paying for causing air and water pollution, as these costs have not been internalised, are good examples of market failure.

Distortions caused due to external costs not getting reflected in the price can be corrected through government policy and legislation. However such a step would need effective delivery and a regime that is not under the influence of the polluters. The experience has not been very positive. While deterioration in the quality of governance has affected all sectors, it has particularly been baneful on environmental issues, as here government has elaborate laws and regulations on almost every conceivable topic from hazardous waste to wildlife but monitoring and enforcement capabilities are weak, and often subject to extraneous considerations of corruption and nepotism.

The problem of market failure can also be addressed if communities are able to put pressure on the polluters, or on government. However, this requires effective group action.

Local collective action has been undermined in the last thirty years by a number of political and economic processes. Village societies have become heterogeneous, and market forces have commercialised the erstwhile subsistence economies integrating them with urban and national economies. Possibilities for migration and mobility tend to work against effective local management. As old authority structure crumbles appeals to government for conflict resolution and arbitration become more common, and dependence on government for local resource management increases. Thus neither are the village communities able to provide effective management for local resources, nor are they able to pressurise government to regulate the over-use of natural resources.

H 3

Environmental degradation affects the poor in a number of ways. First, it affects the economy's capacity to grow, because growth depends on the sustainable productivity of natural resources. Second, the poor bear a disproportionate burden of the costs imposed by environmental degradation, and this contributes to their further impoverishment. Third, it affects their health much more than it affects the health of the rich because of the poor peoples' inadequate nutrition, poor access to health care, and due to the places where they live. As the poor people are likely to live in the urban slums that have the worst air, water and solid waste problems, they get affected much more by pollution of various kinds. Fourth, the degradation of natural resources directly affects the poor because of greater reliance on them to meet basic needs. The State of the Environment Report published by the Government of India in 1999 estimated that the total costs arising from such environmental problems amounted to 9.7 billion dollars on an average, or 4.5 per cent of GDP.

H 4

There has been concern whether growth in the 1990s has been accompanied by a reduction in poverty. The official estimates show that the percentage of the poor in the total population has declined from a level of 36 per cent in 1993-94 to 26 per cent in 1999-00, but not at the targeted pace to reach 16.5 per cent in 2001-02, the level which was projected to be achieved by the end of the Ninth Plan period. This is due to sluggish agricultural growth which was also less well spread out; inadequate reach of TPDS to the poorest in the northern and eastern states; failure of watershed development and poverty alleviation schemes; fiscal crisis caused by the Fifth Pay Commission that led to reduced ability of the states to spend on social sector and maintenance of assets; and declining governance leading to inefficient utilisation of resources and even leakages. Thus there are several reasons for the continuing high poverty, not necessarily restricted to environmental factors.

The policy approach to agriculture, particularly in the 1990s, has been to secure increased production through subsidies in inputs such as power, water and fertilizer, and by increasing the minimum support price rather than through building new capital assets in irrigation, power and rural infrastructure. The equity, efficiency, and sustainability of the current approach is questionable. The subsidies do not improve income distribution and the demand for labour. The boost in output from subsidy stimulated use of fertilizer, pesticides and water deteriorates the aquifers and soil—an environmentally unsustainable approach that may partly explain the rising costs and slowing growth and productivity in agriculture, notably in the Punjab and Haryana. Moreover, the deteriorating state finances have meant that subsidies have, in effect, (i) 'crowded-out' public agricultural investment in roads and irrigation and expenditure on technological upgrading, (ii) limited maintenance on canals and roads, and (iii) contributed to the low quality of rural power. These problems are particularly severe in the poorer states. Although private investment in agriculture has grown, this has often involved macroeconomic inefficiencies (such as private investment in diesel generating sets). Instead of seeking low cost options that have a higher capital-output ratio, present policies have resulted in excessive use of capital on the farms, such as too many tube-wells in water scarce regions. A better strategy would be to concentrate on eastern and rainfed areas where returns to both capital and labour are high.

Similarly, poverty reduction would have been faster if poverty alleviation schemes, on which GOI spends roughly 10,000 crores a year, were better designed and implemented. Schemes such as ICDS, mid-day meal programme for school children, food for work, and old age pensions need to be given more resources, at the cost of schemes that have outlived their utility.

Suggestions for Environmental Improvement

Preventing further degradation of natural resources and improving their productivity would require better participation of the stakeholders at the local level. Second, it would need a powerful civil society movement that will educate opinion builders, watch the activities of the polluters, and offer equitable solutions. Sectoral suggestions are summarised below:

Forests and Common Lands

- A change in the silvicultural practices of managing forests, so that more gatherable biomass is produced in place of timber
- A change in the nature of species being planted on public lands from timber to usufruct based trees,
- Denationalisation of NTFPs, and greater control by forest dwellers over processing and markets
- Strengthening and sustaining Joint Forest Management (JFM)
- Better utilisation of degraded private lands through agro-forestry
- Imposition of tariff on import of pulp in order to encourage growing of trees on wastelands
- Integrated land use management by taking up all degraded lands for rehabilitation

Crop Lands in Rainfed Areas

Evaluation reports have shown that watershed projects cannot succeed without the full participation of project beneficiaries and careful attention to issues of social organization. Successful programmes that have adopted participatory approaches share the following characteristics:

- They devote significant resources to social organization
- A high proportion of staff members have experience and skills in social organization
- Project leaders are fully committed to participation and, in most cases, donors or senior officials place pressure to adhere to participatory approaches
- Project monitoring explicitly checks whether social organization is pursued
- Staff members have an incentive to undertake participation
- Communities being organized have some capacity to influence how the field staff work

Some other suggestions for government programmes are:

- High priority should be given to rejuvenation of village ponds and tanks, and recharge of groundwater.
- Government funds should be transferred to village local bodies, including user groups, who would handle funds and the job of government agencies should be to facilitate and train rather than to control funds.
- The ownership and control over revenue wastelands should be transferred to PRIs and village organizations to ensure certainty of tenure.
- Since a part of cultivable wastelands in many states has already been settled with the poor, special projects should be undertaken to make such lands productive (example, Sodic land project funded by World Bank in Uttar Pradesh).

Water

It is obvious that the past strategy of pumping money in the drinking water sector without looking at policy and institutional issues is not going to work. What we require is:

- People's control over management of water supply schemes
- Water to be managed as an economic asset rather than a free commodity
- Increased attention towards recharge of groundwater through afforestation and watershed development programmes
- Rainwater harvesting in water scarce regions

- Scientific utilisation of vast groundwater in eastern India through minor irrigation schemes
- Improving quality of potable water
- Better implementation of policy reforms introduced in 1999

The Rural Sanitation Programme has been restructured in 1999. However, most suggestions are still to be grounded. Some needing attention are as under:

- Shift from high subsidy to low-subsidy regime
- Greater household involvement
- Technology options as per choice of beneficiaries
- Stress on software programme (IEC)
- Emphasis on school sanitation
- Tie up with various rural development programmes
- Involvement of NGOs and local groups.
- Seek institutional finance (NABARD, etc.)

As regards river and surface water pollution, community sources need to be protected from industrial pollution through enactment and enforcement of appropriate legal provisions. Communities have a role in monitoring polluters and lobbying for effective control measures. Water bodies in the country are contaminated due to disposal of domestic sewage leading to organic and bacterial pollution. There is a need for close monitoring of the discharge of industrial effluents into waterbodies.

Progress of River Action Plans has been slack primarily because of slow preparation of DPRs by the state governments and withholding of Government of India's funds from executing agencies. Solution to the problem of Operation and Maintenance of assets under various NRCD programmes needs to be urgently found. Lack of motivation on the part of state governments in this national programme and the tendency of the programme degenerating into a routine municipal function needs to be seriously addressed.

Air

Large and medium polluting industrial units are not operating pollution control devices or meeting the prescribed pollution control norms. Many small-scale industries are not covered under common effluent treatment plans. The State Pollution Boards should ensure that the polluting industries install requisite pollution control systems within the specified time-frame. An important lacuna discovered in an evaluation of the State Pollution Control Boards completed recently by the Planning Commission suggests that the posts of chairmen of the Pollution Control Boards are occupied by politicians. The full-time technically competent and qualified Member Secretaries are absent and the posts supposed to be filled up by technical experts and representatives of local bodies are lying vacant. These issues need to be addressed.

Gender issues

As per the 1991 Census, more than 90 per cent of women workers continue to be struggle in the informal unorganized sector with no legislative safeguards. The prevailing social constraints of gender largely relegates women to the inside sphere. Added to this are the dual responsibilities of women tagged with heavy work responsibilities in agriculture, animal husbandry and other traditional sectors which create a syndrome of gender stereotypes, marginalisation, alienation and deprivation of women in the informal sector. Even when their hard work produces surplus (e.g. fisherwomen) they do not control its disposal, which has traditionally been and continues to be in the men's domain.

Almost 85 per cent of rural women in India still derive their livelihood from land and water based activities. The use and management of natural resources, such as forests and groundwater can easily be made more gender friendly through suitable policy changes. We have discussed these in the previous sections. Here in fact there may not be much of a contradiction in the interests of poor women with other classes of poor a people—poor men and children—who would like to use the common resource for maximising its livelihood value. There is not much difference between the needs of women and poor men, the underlying conflict is between the needs of the poor on the one hand, and those of commerce and industry on the other; or as in groundwater, between rich farmers and poor families.

Participation

As discussed before, people will benefit from natural resources only when there is genuine participation. Half-hearted measures towards peoples participation have only resulted in wastage of funds with no gains. It must be therefore understood as a process by which the people are able to organize themselves and, through their own organization, are able to identify their own needs, and share in the design, implementation and evaluation of the participatory action. Thus various elements of participation are: decision making at various stages; control and management of funds and resource; share in intermediate and final output; and, certainty of benefits. In other words, participation should not only stop at information sharing or consultation, but decision making and initiating action are important and essential components of participation.

One of the characteristics of participation is that it cannot be turned on and off like a tap, that is, 'now you participate, now you don't'. Participation is an evolutionary process that gathers momentum and defies breakdown into neat, self-contained categories, except for analytical purposes. Establishing participation is particularly important in the early stage, because expecting responsible behaviour in the later stages is not only misguided but may result in ineffective projects.

Participation should be viewed as a process that starts with planning of projects and ends with maintenance and sharing of profits/output, rather than as an element that can be injected in the later stages of a project whenever outsiders determine. For this we need to set up people's committees.

However, problems remain of providing adequate share to women in committees to manage natural resources. Even if adequate membership is provided, it is not synonymous with a share in rights or benefits. One needs to ensure both, and not one or the other. Forced inclusion of women through legislation has not led to genuine participation. Participation of women is cosmetic and symbolic. It is however better where NGOs or a gender-sensitive government official is active. Given the sex-segregated and hierarchical nature of Indian society, separate women's organizations and staff are needed to work among women, to instill confidence in them, so that they can fight for their rights. Therefore, whenever there is recruitment, more women need to be recruited in the relevant departments.

To sum up, ensuring the success of forestry or water supply schemes or rehabilitation of degraded lands would require strong people's groups (with women in the lead role) with enhanced management capacities which should then be harnessed by the concerned government department or NGO. This alone will fulfil the objective of the project for successful management of the assets created.

The two objectives that need to be kept in mind in relation to the role of women are: (1) reducing their drudgery and burden, and (2) giving them a voice in planning and management. As the availability of gatherable biomass and water gets augmented locally through the kind of reorientation that has been suggested, the burden of bringing these subsistence products from distant places will gradually diminish and perhaps disappear in due course. As for the 'voice', this is best ensured by mandating adequate representation for women in all the institutions (panchayats, consultative committees, 'river parliaments', etc.) that are set up for natural resource management at various levels.

Summing Up

There is enough empirical evidence to establish that environmental conservation must go hand in hand with economic development because any economic development which destroys the environment will create more poverty, unemployment and diseases and thus cannot even be called economic development. It may just be transfer of resources from the poor to the rich. This is because the poor depend on nature for their daily survival–for them the Gross *Natural* Product is more important than the Gross National Product. Environmentally destructive economic development will impoverish the poor even further and destroy their livelihood resource base. Therefore, the environment concern in the developing world must go beyond pretty trees and tigers and must link it with peoples' lives and well being. The environmental problems facing India are different from those facing the affluent countries and are more immediate and health and livelihood threatening in nature. Pollution in our air, soil degradation, deforestation, desertification, shrinking wetlands, inadequate public health and sanitation, indoor pollution in rural areas, growing water scarcity, falling groundwater tables, the lack of minimum flow in rivers, and over extraction of water for irrigation purposes are some of the environmental problems that need to be addressed first, along with poverty alleviation programmes. It does not mean that there are no strategies to address the issue of poverty outside environment.

In the ultimate analysis, environment management and economic development are mutually supportive aspects of the same agenda. A poor environment undermines development, while inadequate development results in a lack of resources for environment protection. The vicious cycle of the inter-relationship between poverty and environment can be broken through redistribution of economic opportunities and the empowerment of the communities. This is where participatory community-based development programmes appear as most effective entry points for reversing the existing trends. The two goals of environment protection and poverty alleviation reinforce each other. Ecological poverty may, in fact, be the starting point of dealing with economic poverty.

8

Lifestyles and Ecological Security

R. RAJAMANI

I will start with a dilemma which was brought to my attention by a schoolgirl a few years back. After retirement I settled in Hyderabad where I enjoy participating in environmental awareness programmes. In one such, where the schoolchildren had put up exhibits demonstrating the value of ecological preservation, a girl in her early teens showed me a model of a factory with air pollution control devices. When I asked her what we can do in daily life to avoid air pollution, she was hesitant and I prompted her by saying: 'Why use polluting two wheelers, why not just ride a bicycle?' She was quick in her response and asked: 'Uncle, do you ride a bicycle?' I was stumped, and found myself forwarding weak arguments about having used a bicycle in early age and having difficulties now, being a senior citizen. I have a similar problem in speaking on appropriate lifestyles, as I do not necessarily practice all that I may preach.

I have decided to take the plunge as I feel rather passionately on the subject and the emotional intensity could somewhat make up for intellectual deficiency. Also, I feel the subject is important enough for even a sinner to cast the first stone. Are not some of the ardent conservationists of wildlife in this world some of the best ex-*shikaris*? If there are still some who feel this is a hypocritical approach, I can only beg their indulgence and understanding.

Ecological security is well understood. I view it not merely as securing the biological diversity of which human beings are a part but the entire gamut of living and non-living natural resources, including the soil and the seas, minerals, air and water. The cultural diversity which has shaped humanity in different forms and is now in danger of being swamped by a monoculture dictated by globalization and similar phenomena is also part of the ecology, as far as I am concerned. I include among the living resources requiring extra security all the beings that do not have a voice, whether it be from the plant or animal kingdom and even among human beings. Our tribals, our grandmothers who practise traditional medicine, and others who have opted for a simple ungrudging life, where 'work is worship and words are superfluous', are part of the ecology as far as I am concerned. Their security has to be seriously protected and lifestyles that may threaten them have to be stood on their head.

Lifestyles defy definition. But then, they are like the elephant which you may find difficult to define but recognise when you see one! Living to meet our simple needs and ensuring our livelihood security are the first rungs of development of our lifestyles. These styles go beyond ordinary needs to keep us and our minds going. They mean more of the same things as well as new ways of gratifying desires that go beyond those that satisfy hunger and health, both physical and mental. The words 'needs' and 'greed' spring to mind as defining the difference between 'life' and 'lifestyles', but that may be simplistic, as there is no universally satisfying definition of 'need' and what looks like greed to someone looks like need to another! For our purpose, lifestyles represent a mindset that is based on continuing satisfaction of human wants beyond the basic level which assures us '*roti, kapda, makan*' as well as the means of satiating our knowledge and aesthetic senses with minimal effort. Therefore, it is linked to patterns of consumption which use up ecological resources to a point of no return or where the consumption of future generations is not assured.

The linkage is established when our collective lifestyles use the renewable resources beyond their capacity for renewal and the non-renewable resources beyond their capacity to be recycled or reused or be available for the generations to come. When these capacities are exceeded by the consumption patterns, ecological security is no longer assured.

How much then is enough if ecological security is to be ensured? The first requirement is perhaps the capacity and ability to say 'enough'. Doctors advise that in the interests of health and to avoid overeating, we should stop when we feel like reaching out for one more, last helping. But, often we do reach out for more, and we face the consequences. But if all of humanity reaches out for more and there is not enough to give, the damage to the whole world is irretrievable. Our lifestyles and consumption patterns affecting natural resources should ideally match the carrying capacity of our environment and ecology and should therefore be based on the 'enough' syndrome that is understood practically in individual as well as collective decision making or fulfilment of desires. This needs forethought and vision. Do we have it? Dr Albert Schweitzer was pessimistic when he said: 'Man has lost the capacity to foresee and to forestall. He will end by destroying the earth.' Was he right? The trends in consumption patterns seem to justify some amount of pessimism, especially when they are unbridled at one extreme and ignore the utter poverty of many in the world, especially among developing countries who are nowhere near getting even the basic necessities of life.

In a recent Lokamanya Tilak Award lecture, the distinguished scientist Dr M.S. Swaminathan drew attention to the linkages between lifestyles and ecological security. He said, 'The ecological footprint, which is the average amount of land and sea appropriated by each person for food, water, housing, energy, transportation, commerce and waste recycling is roughly one hectare in developing countries and ten hectares in the United States. If every citizen of this world aspires to reach the consumption level of an average U.S. citizen, we will need at least four more planet earths to fulfil such a desire. Gandhiji drew our attention to such an untenable situation in the following prophetic words: "*Nature provides for everybody's needs, but not for everybody's greed*".'

Unfortunately, the 'if' in the above statement about the citizen's aspirations is no longer 'if'. All citizens of the world are slowly being programmed in many ways to copy the consumption level of the United States. In an excellent study done in 1991 before the UNCED at Rio de Janeiro in 1992, Dr Jyoti Parikh, Dr Kirit Parikh and their associates had drawn attention to the average disparity ratio (ADR) and extreme disparity ratio (EDR) between the consumption levels of the developed and developing countries. The ratio of per capita consumption levels for food, forest, industrial, metals, chemicals and transportation showed on average that in almost all respects, the developed countries were far ahead. Within this, the ratio between the richest and the poorest tended to be even more. The authors concluded that despite having 76 per cent of the worlds population, the shares of consumption of almost all commodities of the developing countries are considerably less than 76 per cent. But it is clear that this will no longer be so if the developing countries slow down the rates of population growth, industrialise and achieve increases in per capita income by poverty amelioration and other measures. At that stage, they will also join the race to plunder the planet.

Is this a gloomy prophecy? Are there not signals already that unsustainable consumption patterns are increasing both in the developed and developing countries? If we were to compute in India the ADR and EDR between the higher income and lower income families, will we not already see the ratios going up in favour of the upper categories? What happens then to ecological security? Diagnosis and prescription can be found in the following passage from Chapter 4 of the Agenda 21 Document adopted at Rio in June 1992:

> Special attention should be paid to the demand for natural resources generated by unsustainable consumption and to the efficient use of those resources consistent with the goal of minimising depletion and reducing pollution. Although consumption patterns are very high in certain parts of the world, the basic consumer needs of a large section of humanity are not being met. This results in excessive demands and unsustainable lifestyles among the richer segments, which place immense stress on the environment.
>
> The poorer segments. meanwhile are unable to meet food, health care, shelter and educational needs. Changing consumption patterns will require a multi pronged strategy focussing on demand, meeting the basic needs of the poor and reducing wastage and the use of finite resources in the production process.

The widening gulf is not only between geographical entities of the North and South but also within the South where there is an emerging North. I had done an exercise to determine the driving forces or ideologies and sentiments that polarised the Environmental North and South in the following manner:

Environmental North	*Environmental South*
Might is Right and the weak shall be driven up the wall (AYN RAND)	The meek shall inherit the Earth (JESUS CHRIST)
Competition-survival of the fittest.	Compromise, consensus & co-operation.

Environmental North	*Environmental South*
Take	Give, like Forests, Emperors, SIBI & PAARI
Mammon worship—admiration.	You cannot eat money; it is but a veiled Midas touch.
How to make a million?	How much is enough? A World Bank Expert
Kaun Banega Crorepati?	How much land does a man require? Tolstoy
Materialism	Matters of the spirit not to be ignored.
Natural resources are forever; can be revived by technology and ingenuity.	Natural resources need careful husbanding.
After me the deluge.	Leave their due to the future generations.
Centralise; let MNCs flourish.	Decentralise. Let local and community action flourish.
Dole out small doses of aid & charity.	Lift up by own bootstraps.
Ostentation.	Simplicity.
Greed, grab and hog.	Need, give, care and share.
Keep up with the Joneses.	Be natural and what you are.

This may sound very subjective but does represent the polarisation which may require introspection and correction in the interests of ecological security. We must be clear that if the mindsets do not change, changes in policies alone may not work a miracle. We have the authority of the Global Environment Outlook of UNEP 1999, which states:

> Means must be found to tackle the root causes of environmental problems, many of which are unaffected by strictly environmental policies. Resource consumption, for example, is a key driver of environmental degradation. Policy measures to attack this issue must reduce population growth, reorient consumption patterns, increase resource use efficiency and make structural changes to the economy. Ideally, such measures must simultaneously maintain the living standards of the wealthy, upgrade the living standards of the disadvantaged, and increase sustainability. *This will require*

a shift in values away from material consumption. Without such a shift, environmental policies can effect only marginal improvement. (emphasis mine)

How do we effect a shift in values? History is replete with instances of attempts to instil values which have come a cropper. Yet there is no reason to share Dr Schweitzer's pessimism when we see some of the corrective actions on climate change, biological diversity, etc., already attempted, however fitfully and unequally. In countries like ours, we do have millions of people yet unswayed by consumerism. This gives us breathing space and time to start some initiatives. I draw upon the wisdom of my friend, Prof. Shekhar Singh, who has suggested some systemic changes. I must add his caution that behavioural changes of the type we may want to practise sustainable lifestyles, cannot be imposed in an enlightened society. Such a society, he says, can only create the sorts of conditions and circumstances whereby the members of the society make rational choices. Some of the measures he suggests are in the transport sector, where public transport should be preferred and the use of bicycles encouraged despite the dilemma I myself faced on this issue! Demand-side management in the Energy sector to promote energy efficient devices, housing, etc., has been proposed. He also suggests the regulation of advertising and marketing of luxury goods that are environmentally unsustainable. In the matter of finances and fiscal devices, he suggests that fiscal incentives must be designed to popularise environmentally more benign goods and services. In the same vein, measures for water conservation like rainwater harvesting, encouraging recycling, etc., have been suggested.

On the economic front, we need to introduce natural resource accounting and budgeting, which will induce rational thinking on the linkages between consumption and production of natural resources. But this alone may not be enough as found in the Colloquium on Science, Religion and Development in November 2000 at New Delhi: 'The disparities and inequities, now so widespread in the world, result in greater measure from the failure to place economic questions in the broader context of humanity's social and spiritual existence. Economic arrangements should serve people's needs; societies should not be expected to shape themselves to fit specific economic models, particularly those that embrace habits of unbridled acquisition and consumption.'

It is necessary to add that at the international level efforts to moderate consumption patterns must continue. This may not mean freezing lifestyles but other less painful measures, such as the transfer of resources to the developing countries, which should redress the balance somewhat. If the Commission on Sustainable Development and the UN agencies do not address these issues and perpetuate an unequal world, we should not hesitate to bring this out in the open. But this need not be done to invoke charity or aid but only for trying to have a more equitable world order.

There is no doubt that these devices and strategies, which promote rational choice, will bridge lifestyles and ecological security, if systematically pursued and wholeheartedly accepted by the people at home and abroad. But the best results can be obtained when this becomes part of even the individual's value system and avarice gives way to moderation. We can copy Nature herself in this as stated by Zarathustra: 'Nature abhors all extremes, and our salvation lies in nothing else than a state of equilibrium between the two opposing forces of the all pervading polarity of Nature.'

This approach requires a cultural change which can be promoted in many ways, but most importantly by the litterateurs and artistes (including the folk arts), drawing from the wellsprings of our ancient and modern thought which directs attention to the perils of unsustainable consumption. Equally importantly, all opinion builders, policy makers and leaders in society should be models of simple living and high thinking to be copied by others.

I can do no better at this stage than quote Swami Dayanand Saraswati who said: 'You consume and you contribute also. If you were purely a consumer, you wouldn't have hands and legs. There would be no such thing as parenthood. To be a father or mother means that you are a creator, and therefore naturally you are a contributor. You are a contributor and a consumer and you do not destroy the world, you do not destroy the environment.'

The spiritual dimension forever remains, cutting across all other considerations, even of disbelief and rampant selfishness. To demonstrate this, I quote a story narrated by a dear friend. This concerned a Sufi saint to see whom a traveller landed up at his hut one day. When he found only the Sufi saint there and no other material belongings, he asked the saint: 'Sir, where is your baggage?' The saint smiled and asked: 'Where is yours?' The traveller said: 'I do not have any; I am only passing through.' The Sufi saint said calmly, 'So am I.'

Not all of us can be like the Sufi saint though I believe that countries like India are not going under, along with their ecological security because the larger numbers of their people do not have the lifestyles that endanger ecological security. But, as I have also pointed out, this may not be for long, as the forces of excessive consumerism and its promotion in the so-called interests of economic growth are attracting may of us already. What is the solution?

The first principle is that we must be aware of the consequences of individual and collective action and let that knowledge influence our lifestyles. Before setting out to reform the world, we can begin by trying to reform ourselves. If in the process, many give up wrong lifestyles and others cling on to sustainable lifestyles, our ecological security may not be in danger. But human nature is fickle and homogenising attitudes and lifestyles in this manner may not always be practicable. The safeguard then may come from another natural principle hinted at by Zarathustra, viz., the polarisation in Nature which brings about equilibrium. Just as economic equilibrium is achievable between the body of savers as a whole and the body of investors, ecological equilibrium between unsustainable and sustainable lifestyles may be possible with a back up of the kind of systemic changes that we noted earlier. The world has continuously seen a balance between good and evil, optimism and pessimism, providence and improvidence and even the past and future. Not all sing with Omar Khayyam that we are 'dead yesterday and unborn tomorrow'. Will not some ecological equilibrium be achieved between these two extremes of lifestyles? Of course, we cannot take this to mean that we should encourage unsustainable patterns of consumption.

We may not totally lose hope of the whole world changing its lifestyles. But, I believe that with material and spiritual pursuits going in tandem, we may achieve at least a steady state. With apologies to eminent gastroenterologist friends of mine who have detected that I harbour plenty of 'wildlife' in my guts in the form of bacteria, I may add that I have taken courage from interpreting their advice on various occasions on the following lines. I harbour some bacteria which have lifestyles that do not affect my health and other bacteria which do cause me problems with their appetites. So long as these two categories maintain a balance in their relative populations by the sheer pressure of having to share from the same resources, I am in less danger of frequent infections affecting my health security. May we hope too that our ecological health may be maintained by the forces of differing lifestyles reaching a balance both due to internal and external causes? I should end on an optimistic note that the balance will be struck and the external pressures of not only our saints and seers, but also our own reasoning processes and policies, and also the efforts of organizations like the Foundation for Ecological Security, will maintain it.

9

The Earth Charter and Ecological Security

KAMLA CHOWDHRY

Earth: Ancient Cultures

Do you remember the picture of the Earth that the astronauts took from way up from the stars? It is beautiful and awe inspiring. For the first time, we saw the living Earth in its wholeness. Looking at that beautiful blue ball out there was an experience of great spirituality, of a connectedness with Truth and Beauty. For the first time in human history, we had a God's-eye view of our planet and saw the Earth in its wholeness and beauty.

Ancient cultures had a belief system and a spirituality which meant an intimate relationship with the Earth, a relationship of reverence, of worship, of spirituality and sacredness as also of protection. In Vedic times, man's attitude towards the Earth arose from mankind's primordial experience of being, on the one hand, a guest, and on the other hand, an off-spring of the Earth. The Vedic hymns speak of the Earth as an object of worship, of awe, of beauty, but not of exploitation. Exploitation of the Earth came with the 20th century, its technology and colonialism which helped in ravishing the Earth. These Vedic hymns speak about man's role on the Earth—that it is not one of despoiling the Earth of her possessions, but one of enjoying the blessings of the Earth because the Earth is his home, his own family, and his body.

The Vedic hymns have also emphasized man's role of protectiveness towards the Earth. Here is an example of a Vedic hymn:

'Whatever I dig of thee, O' Earth,
may you of that have quick replenishment,
O' purifying One,
may my thrust never reach right unto your vital parts,
your heart.'

There is a sense of compassion, of gratefulness, and of protectiveness in these hymns to the Earth. These hymns to the Earth depict her as a universal mother, dispenser of every sort of good, and therefore the need to protect her and to seek her blessings.

In other native indigenous cultures too, cultures which were brutally dealt with by colonial nations, there was a deep reverence for the Earth and for nature. The Western nations, however, on their way to industrialisation, denigrated and used nature for accumulating power and wealth. Listen to the anguished cry of Chief Seattle, when in 1854 Washington pressurized and pushed him to sell the tribe's land:

'How can I sell this land,' he cried with great anguish.

'How can you buy or sell the sky, the warmth of the land? The idea is strange to us. How do you own the freshness of the air and the sparkle of the water, how can you buy them?

'Every part of this Earth is sacred to my people. Every shining needle, every sandy shore, every mist in the dark woods, every clearing and humming insect is holy in the memory and experience of my people.

'Whatever befalls the earth befalls the sons of the Earth. Man did not weave the web of life, he is merely a strand in it. Whatever he does to the web, he does it to himself.'

Today, scientists and ecologists agree with Chief Seattle that whatever we do to the Earth, we do it to ourselves as well.

The Earth: Science and Technology

The 20th century has been a century of great scientific and technological achievements, a century of increased physical comforts and living standards, especially in the North, a century in which we landed man on the moon, a century of computers and communication technologies, which have changed the concept of time and space. But, it has also been a century of wars and conflicts, of nuclear bombs, of land mines, of missiles and other technologies of mass destruction and violence to the Earth and its eco-systems.

The so-called great achievements of science and technology have raised serious questions about the future survival of the Earth and of humankind. We now have daily news of collapsing fisheries, shrinking forests, eroding soils, deteriorating rangelands, expanding deserts, rising CO^2 levels, falling water tables, rising temperatures, more destructive storms, melting glaciers, rising sea levels, dying coral reefs, and disappearing species. The challenge for us is to reverse these trends before it is too late.

Oppenheimer once said that his hands were soiled by the atom bomb. He was a scientist with a conscience (and a great Vedanta scholar) and was deeply troubled about the destruction and devastation of the atom bomb. Are we troubled with the destructive technologies involving the death and destruction of other species and of eco-systems for gaining wealth? We have seen what pesticides have done to our soils and water and to the health of the farmers and their children. We have built dams uprooting thousands of people, destroying homes and cultures, and ways of life because of our vision of progress and development. Have we not soiled our souls with the kind of development we have pursued?

Gandhiji had said his greatest ambition was to wipe every tear from every eye. Have we so completely forgotten Gandhiji and his vision of development? To give an example of progress, Japan, the leader in industrial growth and modern technology, has developed a driftnet to catch squid in the deep sea. A single net stretches out underwater 50 km wide and 10 km deep. The technology is an indiscriminate killer of every form of life that gets entangled in it. Other countries too are following suit, killing millions of sea birds, dolphins, sea turtles and varieties of deep sea fish entangled in the net.

Acid rain is a by-product of industry, a man-made gift of death from the USA to Canada, from Great Britain to Norway, from Germany's heartland to neighbouring countries. Wherever the acid rain falls, it destroys forests, lakes and agriculture. Acid rain is a kiss of death, wherever it goes.

More recently, Dr Rosalie Bertell, a distinguished US scientist, who is an expert on radiation and winner of major international science awards, mentions in her latest book, *Planet Earth: The Latest Weapon of War*, that in the name of security the US has developed weapons of choice against terrorists which threaten the future of life on Earth and consequently of Earth itself. She points to the creation of new electromagnetic belts in the atmosphere, causing damage to the vital Van Allen belts circling the Earth, which she points out will take hundreds of years to recover. The damage has upset the Earth's magnetic field, leading to massive earthquakes. She further points out that globally the number of earthquakes a year has more than doubled since the inception of some of these weapons, as also unpredictable weather and freak storms. According to her, the greatest danger of all lies in the fact that the ELF waves can disrupt the tectonic plates of the earth's crust, causing major disasters. From the military standpoint, these weapons, in their effects, can look as if they were acts of God!

The so-called great achievements of science and technology have raised serious questions about the future of humankind and the future survival of the Earth.

Economists and Ecologists

The economists as also our politicians look at the unprecedented growth of the global economy and of international trade and investment as signs of progress and see a promising future with more of the same. The ecologists, on the other hand, look at this same growth and see climate change and the destruction of the Earth's resources. The ecologists view the market with less reverence because they see a market that will not and does not tell the whole truth.

Lester Brown points out that 'as we begin the 21st century our economy is slowly destroying its support systems, consuming its endowment of natural capital. Demands of an expanding globalised economy as now structured are surpassing the sustainable yield of eco-systems'. A third of the world's cropland is losing top soil, endangering food security; 50 per cent of grazing lands have become deserts; the world's forests have shrunk by 50 per cent and are further shrinking fast. Two-thirds of the ocean's fisheries are over-fished; and overpumping of underground water is leading to serious water shortages.

Modern business has played a major role in the Earth's destruction. Listen to what Paul Hawken has to say:

> Quite simply, our business practices are destroying life on Earth. Given corporate practices, not one wildlife reserve, wilderness,

or indigenous culture will survive the global market economy. We know that every living natural system on the planet is disintegrating before our eyes. The land, water, air and sea have been transformed from life-giving systems into repositories of waste. There is no polite way of saying that business has ravaged the earth.

The adoption of the Western economic model means a certain death of the eco-systems and of the Earth itself. It is essential that we transform our destructive economy and transform our way of life, so that simplicity and sustainability can be achieved, so that the Earth is saved from man's greed and his murderous ways.

The Rio meeting, about ten years ago, was an attempt in this direction. One hundred and forty Heads of State came and agreed to Agenda 21, but nobody followed it. President Bush, the senior Bush, said, 'We will not jeopardize our way of life'—but, they seem more than willing to jeopardize the life of the Earth itself!

So, because of our greed and our use of violence we have raped the soils and denigrated the eco-systems and caused irreparable damage to the Earth—and its soul. In the process, we have lost touch with our inner self, with the sacredness of the Earth, and the pilgrimages to the Ganges and the sacred mountains that nourished our spirituality and sustained us. It is time we brought our Vedic sayings and our spirituality to center stage—and remember that everything we do to the Earth, we do to ourselves as well! If we tear her apart, we do so to ourselves as well; with violence to the Earth, we have become violent to each other as well.

In the pursuit of science and technology we require *supreme wisdom* and supreme ethics and spirituality. The lengthened reach of our actions in space and time has put man's responsibility and ethics on to center-stage.

Gandhi and Other Voices

There are many voices that are challenging the direction in which the world is moving—the direction of economic growth, of the development paradigm, and of Western civilisation itself. The Earth Charter has listened to these many diverse voices from all over the world and is urging for a new direction to heal the Earth and to heal the spirit of man.

Gandhi was a man far ahead of his times. Voices all over the world are now echoing what he had said as early as 1908. In *Hind Swaraj* Gandhi had warned that Western civilisation was heading towards violence and destruction. His arguments were based on his concern for the poor, his emphasis on moral and ethical considerations, and his concept of what constitutes a good life and a good society. The production and consumption of more and more goods, considered as a sign of growth and development, was evil, according to Gandhi. Real development, he said, was that mode of conduct which points out to man the path of duty. And that a good life was based on truth and non-violence, which ultimately led to the liberation of the soul.

Wolfgang Sachs and other development writers echo Gandhi's concerns. 'The time is ripe to write its (development's) obituary—delusion, disappointment, failures and crimes have been the steady companions of development, and they tell a common story: it did not work.'

The World Bank President, Mr. Wolfensohn, too, seems to be saying the same thing,' '...the World Bank's central mission is to weld economic assistance with spiritual, ethical and moral development'.

Veer Bhadra Misra, a priest in one of the principal temples in Benares, but also a professor of hydraulic engineering in Benares Hindu University, and deeply dedicated to the cleaning of the Ganges, says: 'The Western approach will not work here. You need to use a different language, a different relationship with the Ganges.' And he adds, 'Life is like a stream. One bank is the Vedas and the other bank is the contemporary world, which includes science and technology. If both banks are not firm, the water will scatter. If both banks are firm, the river will run its course'.

Like Misra, the Earth Charter too is trying to firm both the banks, so that science and spirituality can mesh, and life can flow like a pure mountain stream.

Agreeing with the critics of Western civilisation, Mathew Fox says: 'The addiction to avarice and greed is deep within our civilisation. It is built in the very structure of capitalism; this quest for more. Avarice is not a problem of materialism, it is a soul issue, it is our quest for the infinite but it has been misplaced. Consumerism cannot satisfy us and this is why we are always looking for the new model next year, it is an infinite progression in the consumer addiction.' Further, like Gandhi, he emphasizes the spirit within: 'If we want to remake our civilisation we must remake it around what is the spirit in us. It is because we are violent inside that our environment is dying all around us. The nest in which we live we are fouling.'

At the heart of the matter is the need to consider and strengthen the inner aspect of man, to make moral and ethical choices, to move towards a technology with a human face, and a non-violent economics that would cooperate with nature rather than exploit it.

The Earth Charter

The Earth Charter is a document which attempts to deal with man's responsibility towards the Earth and towards each other and brings man's ethics to the center-stage—as the Vedas did for us many centuries ago.

The Earth Charter is a declaration of fundamental principles for building a just, sustainable and peaceful global society in the 21st century. It seeks to inspire in all peoples a new sense of global interdependence and shared responsibility, for the well-being of the human family and the larger living world. The Earth Charter is an expression of hope and a call to help create a global partnership at a critical juncture of our history.

As mentioned earlier, the dominant patterns of production and consumption have caused serious environmental destruction, and devastation and depletion of the Earth's resources. The 'benefits' of development have been hijacked by the rich nations and the rich people, widening injustice, poverty, ignorance and increasing violent conflicts. September 11 is an expression of this divide. We must reverse these trends, if the Earth and humanity are to survive.

The Earth Charter is a document which hopes to halt these destructive trends of industrialisation and of consumerist societies, and thereby hopes to advance the building of a just, sustainable, peaceful and compassionate society. It recognises the value of cultural diversity and the importance of local concerns and local commitment.

The Earth Charter also seeks to build a sense of shared responsibility for the well-being of the Earth. Caring for people and caring for the Earth are inseparable. In a world of increasing poverty, injustice, inequity, and violence, caring and compassion are important. If we do not learn to care for the Earth, we also do not learn to care for its people.

Compassion and non-violence are central themes in the Earth Charter. The Dalai Lama, reciting an ancient verse, conveys the caring and compassion needed, 'May I be a guard for those who are protectorless, a guide for those who journey on the road. For those who wish to go across the water, may I be a raft, a bridge.'

One important aspect of the Earth Charter lies in understanding that the extent of happiness and well-being, as individuals or as nations, is determined by the extent of our compassion for others. The obstacles to compassion are greed, hatred and ignorance.

The world is at the crossroads. If the Earth is to survive, and if humanity is to survive, we will have to take serious cognizance of the Earth Charter—and of the respect and compassion it stresses for the Earth and its beings.

The Earth Charter is a document that has emerged after much discussion with concerned people and communities all over the world. Different cultures, different countries, different religions, different age groups have discussed and contributed to it, and after many drafts and redrafts a final document has emerged. Like the Universal Declaration of Human Rights, it is our hope that the Earth Charter will also be endorsed by the members of the UN, so that the Charter becomes a guide for human action towards sustainable societies.

The core principles of the Earth Charter are four, which are embodied in Part I of the Charter. These are:

1. Respect Earth and Life in all its diversity.
2. Care for the community of life with understanding, compassion and love.
3. Build democratic societies that are just, participatory, sustainable and peaceful.
4. Secure Earth's bounty and beauty for the present and future generations.

The rest of the Earth Charter spells out more fully, both in scientific and spiritual terms, the interconnections and the meaning of the above four core principles. It is hoped that the UN adoption of the Earth Charter will become the road map to peace and compassion, to sustainable development, and towards non-violence. The Charter's final section is 'The Way Forward', and it ends with the hope, 'Let ours be a time remembered for the awakening of a new reverence for life, the firm resolve to achieve sustainability, the quickening of the struggle for justice and peace and the joyful celebration of life.'

If we really wish to move forward and if we are serious about sustainable development, and about justice and peace, it will mean a change in the business and the corporate sector, where profit will not be the only measure of success; it will mean a change in government economic policies where an increase in GNP will not be the only measure of progress in a country; and it will mean simpler lifestyles and living in smaller communities.

Moving towards a simpler lifestyle, towards sustainability will be very difficult. It is neither more scientific studies nor more conferences that will lead us to change our lifestyle. We need the Earth Charter's guidance, but even more so, we need an inner change, an inner conversion, an acceptance that you have to be the change you want others to be.

Where Shall We Begin?

If the Earth Charter is to become a reality, we must learn from Gandhi and other spiritual leaders how to change oneself before changing others. Gandhi had emphasized throughout his life that we must change ourselves before we can change others; that our real enemies are within, our greed and our fears. If we want the Earth Charter to become a reality, a mass movement, we must be able to say as Gandhi did: 'My Life is my Message.'

The Earth Charter will mean that we must modify our social, economic and political institutions. For too long we have been at the mercy of those selling dreams of progress without a whisper of where it is taking us. It is *dharma* that we need to bring center-stage, if we wish real change and real transformation to take place.

The *Mahabharata* has laid down the foundations of *dharma*, of sane living, individual and social. The Earth Charter too is about sane living. Let us see what *dharma* has to say about sane living.

'All the sayings of *dharma* are with a view to nurturing, cherishing, providing more amply, endowing more richly, preparing, increasing, enhancing all living beings. Therefore whatever has the characteristic of bringing that about is *dharma*.

'All the sayings of *dharma* are with a view to supporting, sustaining, bringing together, upholding all living beings. Therefore whatever has the characteristic of that is *dharma*.

'All the sayings of *dharma* are with a view to securing for all living beings freedom from violence. Therefore, whatever has the characteristics of not doing violence is *dharma.*'

The Earth Charter is promoting the *dharma* of man in the twenty-first century. *Dharma* in the 21st century means the healing of humankind, and the healing of the Earth. *Dharma* has been interpreted and reinterpreted in terms of *desa* and *kala*, that is, place and time, the two coordinates of history. In the 21st century, we need the *dharma* of healing the Earth, and healing humanity—and the Earth Charter is that *dharma*.

The Earth Charter heralds the world the United Nations wishes to create. It represents the future of development, and it represents the oneness of the world and the survival of the Earth. And it represents the return of spirituality and the sacredness in our lives.

10

Human Rights and Ecological Security

J.S. VERMA

Let me begin by pointing out how ominous are the times in which we are living. One of the questions posed—and I think that is once again the most relevant question to pose for all problems—is, 'What to do?' Gandhi was quoted to say, 'You have to purchase everything that is needed with suffering.' In other words, you have to stand up to injustice and you have to stand up to any erosion of values or sense of justice, even though there may be suffering for those who stand up. But that is the only way, and therefore the word 'purchase', I think, is very indicative because you purchase the good things by paying for them. Therefore, those of us who are facing this situation have to pay for it.

I think that is also the answer in respect of the theme of human rights and ecological security. Sustainable development based on inter-generational equity is really the proper balance which has to be struck, and the inter-generational equity requires us to remember that the present generation can make only a judicious use of the natural resources, keeping in mind the fact that we are trustees of what we have, and not owners thereof, and we must ensure by judicious use that the future generations—who would be none other than our children, grandchildren and great grandchildren—have enough left for them. As a matter of fact, our culture has taught that we leave more for our children and grandchildren than what *we* had. We are doing just the reverse. I think that is the answer to this problem, and that alone will ensure a proper balance and inter-phase between human rights and ecological security.

In recent times, beginning with the Stockholm Conference in 1972, fortunately the awareness was growing in this direction. But once again, after thirty years there is a serious doubt whether we have translated the rhetoric we began decades earlier into some action. As a matter of fact, I read in the *Asian Age* an interview of the Indian Minister who had gone to participate in a recent conference—there was also a comment about the absence of the Heads of the Government of India and the United States, two very important nations in this context. When the Minister was asked what was hoped to be achieved, or what could be the gain of this world summit, the Minister said the gain was that 'the developing countries could ensure that the developed countries would not be able to dilute the Rio principles'. Now, that is hardly a gain worth being happy about. If we are trying to save that which was decided ten years back, that only goes to show that there is no progress, at the most there is a status quo, and an effort to take a backward step alone has been stopped and nothing more. And, therefore, the need really is to ensure the proper balance.

The rat-race which has been accentuated by the greater advancement in science and technology should not lead to more arrogance. This is really the need of the hour. What is needed is application of the knowledge which is acquired in a manner which is profitable and useful and meant for social good. India's former President K. R. Narayanan, in one of his speeches, referred to the role of the United States as that of a headman in the global village—some people may not have liked it but the reality is something like that. It is this which has got to be arrested. The absence of the United States, and particularly Heads of the Government, in the world summit was, to my mind, the most ominous thing. Therefore, care must be taken to ensure, as early as possible, that the commitment which has been seemingly made is kept up.

The UN Secretary General Mr. Kofi Annan in his message for the United Nations Day of 2002, referred to the Millennium Summit declaration of the world leaders as follows: 'They pledged themselves to free their peoples from the scourge of war, from abject and de-humanizing poverty and from the threat of living on a polluted planet with few natural resources left. They undertook to promote democracy and the rule of law, to protect children and other vulnerable people, and to meet the special needs of Africa, and they promised to make the United Nations itself more effective as an instrument for pursuing all those aims.' And then he uttered the important words. He said, 'These pledges give us cause for hope but they will change nothing if they are not followed by action.'

The Stockholm Conference did initiate a worldwide programme of awareness and it proclaimed that natural and man-made environment are essential to the well-being of man and to the enjoyment of basic human rights, the most significant right to life itself. India responded in theory immediately and the 1976 Constitution Amendment Act, which was brought into force from 3 January 1977, inserted Article 48A in the Directive Principles, indicating that one of the principles that is fundamental to governance, and has to be kept in view by the state in the formulation of its policies, is that which requires the state to protect and improve the environment and safeguard the forests and wildlife of the country. Simultaneously, Article 51A enumerating ten fundamental duties of every citizen was also inserted in Part 4A of the Constitution, wherein in clause (g) the fundamental duty of every citizen to act likewise was also emphasized.

This had the effect of enabling the interpretation of Article 21, guaranteeing the Right to Life, which was construed as 'life with dignity', to take the aid of these Articles 48A and 51A(g) to expand the meaning and scope of Article 21, but that was through the process of judicial creativity or intervention in several judgements of the Supreme Court, to which I refer later.

The United Nations General Assembly has recognized clearly the linkage between the quality of environment and the enjoyment of basic human rights. The Rio Earth Summit of 1992 carried forward this programme, laying emphasis on sustainable development to ensure health and harmony with nature.

Later in 1993, at Chicago and Vienna, another important development which took place was to indicate that the faith traditions and human rights are related to the issue of environment. So far as we in India are concerned, it should come to us naturally, but then it was the recognition elsewhere in 1993—why I say so because our faith traditions indicate much before the Constitution or any of these international conventions the rich heritage of our composite culture had (as one of its part the faith tradition which showed, for example, the worship of wild life, trees, etc). In a place near Jodhpur a sect called Bishnois, 365 of them, laid down their lives a couple of centuries back in order to protect trees. Those are the faith traditions of our country, which came to be recognized and linked with the issue of environment and human rights much later in 1993. The concept therefore of the global village in which there was the need for a joint venture by everyone to participate in that direction in order to ensure sustainable development was the progress made.

The recent world summit was imminent. It is interesting that the preparation for the world summit at Johannesburg was considerable and there was a meeting of experts on human rights and environment in January 2002, preparatory to the seminar held at Geneva, to assess the progress made since 1992. The conference concluded that the developments indicate the close linkage between the protection of human rights and environmental protection in the context of sustainable development and the growing inter-relationship between the approaches to each of them as well as the synergies that have developed between these previously distinct fields. So this development—what was considered to be distinct fields earlier—that gap had vanished and the admission that they were closely related and inter-dependent was something that was a distinct improvement.

The reference was made also to the ILO Convention 169 concerning the tribal people and the value of environment and the system of protection. It was emphasized that human rights and environment are inter-dependent and inter-related, and therefore what was emphasized further was that poverty was at the centre of all deprivations just as it is at the centre of deprivation of human rights. We have 55 per cent of the poor living in Africa and Asia. One of the targets for 2015 is to halve the number of people living or surviving on less than one dollar a day. That is the extent of poverty. Obviously then, when that is the situation, unless there is a rights-based approach adopted, there is no possibility of any progress being made.

The Agenda 21, which was formulated to implement the Rio Declaration, how far we have taken it, that is what was discussed. Let me now refer to the mixed reaction which I saw from some papers and newsletters. The United Nations Secretary-General Dr Kofi Annan no doubt had described it as 'the major leap forward' which will 'put us on a path that reduces poverty while protecting the environment, a path that works for all peoples, rich and poor, today and tomorrow.' Of course, he mentions one concrete and positive outcome, which our Minister also said later in the interview which was published in the newspaper yesterday. He pointed out that the participating governments had agreed on an impressive range of concrete commitments particularly in the five priority areas of water, energy, health, agriculture and bio-diversity. The only thing I can tell you is that we are busy trying to carry forward what we said there. So, we are in the process of doing as best as we can to implement it. So here, in the World Summit, it was in substance a repetition of what had been said time and again earlier also.

Then he further said—this is a point which has to be remembered, because this really is part of the solution, if not the whole of it—that the governments alone cannot meet environmental challenges and civil society groups have a critical role as partners, advocates and watchdogs, which is certainly very true. So partnerships have to be forged between different sections of the society and the corporations also have to remember that they are not being asked to do something different from their normal business. They are merely being asked to do their normal business differently, so that they ensure security of the ecology and thereby also respect human rights.

Of course, the Secretary-General obviously did not refer to the absence of the United States but that is one comment very strongly made, and I think rightly, because the direct commitment at such a conference of the United States was certainly very important, not merely for the purpose of ensuring implementation of the programme that was adopted but also for ensuring the prevention of damage to environment and ecology, to which their contribution is considerable. As a matter of fact, when we were in the Court, one matter which we were hearing related to dumping of toxic waste. If it is toxic waste you cannot have in your house, then why should you throw it into the neighbour's yard? That is the whole point. We thought that it was only our trait that we clean the room and throw the dirt at the doorstep of the neighbour, but there are others also! We might only be throwing some dirt which may not be so harmful, but they are dumping toxic waste, which is directly linked with ecology.

In this connection, you will also recall the Supreme Court's intervention with regard to shrimp cultivation and the commercial activity in the coastal region. Why all that here? For being exported to developed countries? What is needed therefore is a control on such activities, and for that reason some kind of an arrangement—just as we have duties corresponding to the rights—similarly here also to ensure that those who are more powerful and in a better position don't take advantage of their superior economic strength and other strength to put us to greater disadvantage. The risk for the developing countries must always be kept in mind.

Even in the area of armed conflict there are provisions which require ensuring that there is respect for the principle of military necessity and proportionality. The damage which ultimately affects ecology also must be not more than what is absolutely necessary and it should be proportional, so that it does not leave any permanent damage so far as ecology is concerned. But all the same we have the recent instances and so many threats of all kinds—the Gulf War, so many other things. All these things are regulated by laws. Once again this is an area that the law, if properly implemented, will take care of, but then the difficulty is that these laws are followed more in breach than being followed.

Not merely armed conflicts, we have situations like September 11. It was on September 11, 1893 that Swami Vivekananda gave the message in the Parliament of Religions in Chicago. And incidentally, near Chicago, we had the incident in 2001. So, we have no reason to think of September 11 only for the purpose of everything which you need to do. For example, the global frenzy of war against terrorism has itself become a serious threat. We have also to take into account so many other factors which are related to it.

Take the example of narco-terrorism. That is something which is also instrumental in the degeneration of all these things—for which we use the expression eco-terrorism. Probably it is easier to comprehend and appreciate that in the present context, because all of us know what terrorism is. Anything which causes or can lead to an ecological disaster is eco-terrorism. If you use those very methods, in terrorism very often you can kill people you do not know. Eco-terrorism is much worse. Probably a terrorist very often knows whom he is killing, but eco disasters result in killing several unknown people. All this merely for some personal gain and for commercial benefit.

Natural disasters and calamities, like the Orissa cyclone and the Gujarat earthquake, cannot be prevented, but they also are relevant in this context because they result in damage to ecology. But what do we say about man-made disasters? Take Bhopal in 1984. It is now eighteen years, but the lessons of Bhopal have not yet been learnt. If we compare the Alaska oil spill with Bhopal, there is discrimination. Why? Even today, whatever compensation may have been ultimately decided to be taken or given for the victims, they still continue to languish in those very conditions without even medicare. If you see the average of 500 dollars per person—those who have got it—people continue to come to us even today. Nothing has been done for them, as against the result of the Alaska oil spill, where those responsible for the spill were made to pay compensation through their nose and the people were not merely awarded but given much more compensation. These are all related matters. Unless you punish people responsible for these disasters, you cannot stop these things. And the victims are more numerous in the developing countries—Bhopal is a typical example to show that the more powerful can get away with things.

Some material facts are also very revealing. The Asia Pacific region has lost 88 per cent of its original forest cover and only 5 per cent of the remaining area is protected at present. It is apprehended that within the next 25 years only 10 per cent of the Asia Pacific original forest will remain. Tropical forests are being destroyed at the rate of 17 million ha per year. The rich bio-diversity of Arunachal Pradesh and the mangrove forests of Sundarbans and other coastal regions are being fast depleted. Some facts are really disturbing. Arunachal has one of the richest bio-diversities in the world. When we tried through the Court to stop the de-forestation in that area and degeneration of ecology, we were told that the main source of revenue for the State is only from that. We asked the Attorney General the amount. He told us after an enquiry that the amount was Rs. 50 crore. I responded that Rs. 50 crore was a mere pittance; it was not even a fraction of each scam which we read so often about! I said that a similar amount could be given as a grant to the government of Arunachal Pradesh and this would help save the rich bio-diversity which cannot be replaced at any cost.

What is needed, therefore, is more action in that direction, particularly here where the pressure of the population has grown so much. During the last 30 years, from 1971, the population of India has doubled. The population at the time of Partition in 1947 was 35 crore. It is now 100 crore. When the pressure of population is present to that extent and we continue to be so cruel to our natural resources, which are directly affecting the ecology, it is a matter of serious concern.

Recently we in India witnessed the vagaries of the monsoon. Now, one of the theories is—and that is what one of the UNEP studies suggest—that the Asian blanket haze, i.e. a vast blanket of pollution across South Asia, is damaging agriculture, modifying the rainfall patterns and risking the lives of thousands of people. Why is it only here? Our wild life is being severely depleted. As far as tigers are concerned, we are reduced only to about 3000, from 40,000, according to the figures I have. So this is the extent of damage to wild life. Air pollution, water pollution, we all know to what extent it is on the increase.

So far as the Indian scene is concerned, as I said, we have several laws, including those enacted after 1972, such as the Environment Protection Act, etc. I can say from whatever I know that the Pollution Control Boards have been activated considerably during the last few years. It must be said that during the last few years the awareness has increased considerably. In 1976 as a Judge in Madhya Pradesh High Court, when I was hearing a matter relating to discharge of industrial effluence in the Tapti river near Burhanpur from the Nepa Mills, no one knew that there needs to be a State Pollution Control Board. There were then also some concerned citizens who brought a suit for injunction. That was the usual remedy which we knew at that time. There was some sensitive subordinate judge, who, without bothering about the law, thinking that the Tapti River, which was the only source of water supply to the town, was getting polluted, granted an injunction.

The judiciary has a very important role to play. A Judges' Colloquium was held from 18 to 20 August at the time of the World Summit. Several senior judges from all over had collected there. They adopted an action plan which emphasized something which fortunately in India has been happening for quite some time. They said, we agree that the judiciary has a key role to play in integrating human values set out in the UN Millennium Declaration—freedom, equality, solidarity, tolerance, respect for nature, and shared responsibility into contemporary global civilisation by translating the shared values into action through strengthening respect for the rule of law, both internationally and nationally.

Fortunately, the Indian Supreme Court has been involved in this process for a long time and that is something which is very welcome. They have been doing it for so many years, relying on the standard meaning of Article 21—Right to Life with Dignity, in which the right to healthy environment has been expressly read into Article 21 and the Supreme Court, acting in exercise of its original jurisdiction under Article 32 for the protection and enforcement of fundamental rights and using wherever necessary a power authorized under Article 142 to make such orders as are necessary for the justice of the cause, has been issuing directions from time to time and that to a great extent has been able to translate the rhetoric into action.

Another very significant development in a positive direction is that the society has become quite aware and conscious. In Delhi itself during the last few years we certainly find a visible change. I remember some years back when I was in the Court I had gone to the Escorts Hospital to see a friend of mine who had undergone a by-pass surgery, and the doctor took me to his chamber to have a chat. He was wearing a steel-grey bush-shirt. Touching the bush-shirt, he said that whenever he opened the chest for surgery of even a young man living in Delhi around forty or so, the colour of the lungs was like that of the bush-shirt. Well, I said, a man coming from the village, 70 years or so, the colour of the lungs is pink, as it ought to be. That was the state, and I think all of you will agree that this kind of judicial intervention by the Indian Supreme Court has certainly made considerable gain, and what is most important is that the people have become conscious and aware of it. You see children today, if you commit a mistake, they will point it out to you. That really is the biggest hope. So the right to clean and healthy environment being included in the Right to Life under Article 21 is reason for us to be happy.

The Supreme Court has also developed and applied 'the polluter pays principle' on the principle of strict liability in torts. The precautionary principle is that if anyone wants to disturb the status quo, the burden is on him to show that it is not going to adversely affect environment and ecology. This is an important development for the purpose of ensuring the protection of bio-diversity, ecology, etc.

In this context, it was very heartening to hear in a very significant order made by the Supreme Court on 23 September 2002. Sometime back a news item had appeared about defacing of rocks on Kulu-Manali-Rohtang road. The Supreme Court made an order applying the 'polluter pays principle' and in one respect I think carrying it forward, as it ought to have, because of the emerging principle of human rights jurisprudence. In addition to imposing a fine of Rs. 4 crore on the polluters, on the polluter-pays-principle, they also imposed a fine of Rs. one crore on the Government of Himachal Pradesh for its neglect in protecting environment and preventing this damage. Now, this is in line with the emerging principle of human rights jurisprudence, which says that for any violation of human rights within the jurisdiction of a state, the state is responsible whether the violation is committed by the state agents or even by the non-state players.

This is the principle which we had, in as many words, indicated in the Gujarat communal disturbances case. We had included in our order made on 1 April and later on reiterated on 31 May these emerging principles of human rights jurisprudence. Why? Because the state is responsible for the protection of human rights, so that it is not made liable only after a violation is attributable to a public servant or a state agent. It has the duty within its jurisdiction to protect the human rights of all. If that is the responsibility, any neglect or failure in the protection of human rights committed by anyone, whether you have facilitated it or not, you are responsible. In substance, it is the very same principle which has been applied in the sphere of environment protection, and therefore I think that is a very welcome development.

To conclude, I have only this much to say that the right to life with dignity is a recognized fundamental right under Article 21 and it is a basic human right inherent in human existence. Being inherent, it is not the gift of a new law; it is merely recognition under the law. Therefore, the law may at best also, in addition to recognizing, provide a remedy for its enforcement, but it is not the source of that right. A healthy environment conducive to the health and well being of human beings must therefore be an essential component of the right to life.

Now, there are two categories of environment problems. Under the first category are, those which have negative effects on development projects. One of the recent on-going debates is about the utility of these mega projects. It is not necessary for me to go into that debate, except to say this. It has been recognized, on the lines international conventions also, that a rights-based approach is really what is needed to be applied in decision making, when you decide about whether a particular mega project should be undertaken or not, and not as earlier the cost-and-benefit question. The question of large-scale displacement is also a factor which has got to be taken into account, because tribals are indigenous people who are mainly displaced as a result of the development projects coming up. They have had for long a direct linkage with the protection of environment and ecology and therefore that aspect has also to be borne in mind. Let us keep in mind also what the Stockholm Declaration had stated. It had stated, 'to defend and improve the human environment for present and future generations has become an imperative goal for mankind, a goal to be pursued together with and in harmony with the established and fundamental goals of peace and a worldwide economic and social development'.

So, what is needed is really a holistic approach and that alone will ensure sustainable development, keeping in mind the inter-generational equity. Sustainable development in that sense needs to be more clearly defined in order to set down parameters which must be borne in mind. I am conscious of our failings, but the fact remains that whatever progress in this direction has been made has been possible to quite an extent because of judicial interventions. When I say judicial interventions, please do not think that I am trying to give credit to the judges, the category to which I belong. It is because of the awareness of the people who brought the issues before the Court in the form of Public Interest Litigation.

Another message to be remembered is that this was the result of a joint venture between the civil society and the institution of the judiciary, which means not merely the judges, but also the lawyers, because without then it would not have been possible for us to do what we were able to do. While criticizing the lawyers for being fat-cats and charging fabulous fees, I have never hesitated to praise them for one thing: any lawyer, the costliest among them, would leave any brief and work without charging any fee in any of the public interest matters and also spend money from his/her pocket for the expenses. It has been possible because of the partnerships forged and developed between the several sections of civil society and the institution of the judiciary and some other institutions, for example, several NGOs. It is these kinds of partnerships which need to be forged more and more and that is what will make the other institutions of governance also alive to their duty. The judiciary has done nothing else except to make others work! Now, what we need to do is to ensure that everyone works. If everyone works, the question which was posed at the beginning, 'What to do?' would be answered. All of us need to do our job instead of expecting someone else to do his job.

11

Globalization and Ecological Security

JAIRAM RAMESH

I am not from the mainstream environmental, sustainable development movement. And when I was asked what I would like to speak on, I suggested this somewhat controversial topic, which is globalization and Ecological Security, because economic system is seen to be eroding ecological security.

The common conventional wisdom on globalization and ecological security is that these are fundamentally conflicting goals and that globalization actually is eroding the infrastructure for the ecological security. This is perhaps the most succinct and most eloquent description that I have ever read. It is also the most profoundly mistaken and wrong statement on the subject that I have read.

Let me begin by saying that there are two themes today, and it is only appropriate that we are discussing this in the background of the Climate Change conference that is going on. Because what has happened in the last few years is not just a question of globalization *and* ecological security, but what we are seeing is the globalization *of* ecological security. That is really the issue that has sort of fixed in the public agenda of both the developing countries and the developed countries. We understand less the link between globalization and ecological security and we are preoccupied more with the issue of globalization *of* ecological security. And I would like to make a distinction between these two, because each has its own economic and political consequences.

Let me begin by saying that many of the problems that we associate with ecological insecurity—the over-exploitation of natural resources, the damage to the water system, the enormous increase in the pollution load in terms of air pollution, water pollution, land pollution, the deforestation that is taking place in the upper catchment areas, the degradation of forest lands—these all pre-date globalization. These are all processes that have been going on over the last few years. Perhaps they have come into public focus in the last decade or so. But it is important to realize that the so-called romantic period of planned development that we had was actually a period in which great damage to the entire foundation of ecological security was done.

I make this point not to criticize the past, but to draw attention to the fact that very often we tend to make the assumption that market economies are environment-unfriendly and somehow planned economies are environment-friendly. The greatest environmental disasters that the twentieth century has seen were in Central Asia under Communist regimes. In fact, Communist regimes in Europe and Central Asia have been the most environment-unfriendly governments the world has ever seen. The type of ecological disaster that has been visited upon the Aral Sea, for example, is something that could never have been possible in a market-friendly environment. So this conventional assumption that people make that somehow if you make the transition from a planned economy to a market economy, the casualty is the environment or ecological security is not borne out by facts. There have been market economies in the world where environment has been at a discount, there have been planned economies in the world where environment has been at a discount. So I do not think the issue really is the choice between a planned economy or a market economy. I think the issue is between countries which follow environmental policies that are integrated with the overall mainstream of development concerns and countries that do not really pay serious attention to the whole environmental dimension of what they are doing. In fact, the paradox is that—we do not realize this—very often even in market economies many of the great environmental movements have been actually the result not of market forces but either of judicial pronouncements or of regulatory instruments that have been adopted in response to popular pressure from civil society. So even in market economies it is the inter-play of regulation and technology and public pressure that has forced a certain pattern of environmental behaviour.

So, the first point I want to make is that we need to get out of this mindset of looking at the market economy as a villain and to romanticize the planned economy environment and as a friend of ecological security. I think it has less to do with the choice of the economic model and more to do with the type of instruments that you adopt for managing the environment, if you decide that indeed environment is a worthwhile objective to pursue.

Let me then move on to the second theme that I want to talk about: to give some content to what is globalization, because everything now comes under the rubric of globalization. It is a catch-all phrase, sort of a hold-all phrase under which anything can come, and anything that you want to criticize can come under the word 'globalization'. I would tend to argue that if you want to look at globalization and want to make some sense out of it, and look at its link with ecological security, you have to look at it in four different dimensions. There is trade globalization; there is globalization in finance—financial globalization; there is the globalization in people, i.e. the movement of labour both within countries and across countries—and then, of course, there is the broader issue of cultural globalization. So first, trade globalization, trade both in goods and services; second, financial globalization, basically movements in capital; third, labour globalization, which is the movement of people, both within and across countries; and fourth, the cultural globalization.

It is important to look at each component separately, because I believe to confuse the issue of the impact of trade globalization with the movement of capital, with the movement of people, and this broader issue of cultural globalization, does not do justice to the whole concept. The paragraph that I read from Dr Amrita Patel's lecture really refers to globalization of trade, i.e. the opening of markets, the movement of goods and services, the linking of producers in one country with the consumers in another country. When we use the word globalization, the tendency is to think of globalization of trade, which is the movement of products from one country to another, the linkage of market—the producers in one country to the consumers in another country. This need not be across countries; this could be within the geographical boundary of one country itself. So, by and large, when we say globalization we are talking of the movement of goods and services both within geographical borders and across geographical borders.

I want to ask the question, what is the evidence in fact that this movement of goods and services is in the economic and ecological interest? I think one has to separate these issues. Clearly, if it is not in the economic interest of countries or communities, there is no worthwhile objective in pursuing this process. The question of ecological security then becomes secondary. But, if there is an economic benefit being obtained, then there is a trade off between an economic benefit that may be obtained and an ecological cost that may be incurred. So, I think it is important to spend a few minutes trying to understand this whole question—a very controversial question—about the impact of globalization of trade in goods and services on the local economies.

If we take livelihoods as the base, then there could always be evidence to suggest that globalization has had both a positive as well as a negative impact. But here, I am going to use the country basically as the unit of finances. I am not looking at local communities as a unit of analyses. If we take the country as a unit, there is enough evidence to suggest that actually globalization of trade makes the country's economy much more resilient and, in fact, leads to security of the most fundamental kind, which is employment security. There is no empirical evidence to suggest, except in the case of some African countries, which are a separate category and have to be dealt with separately, for the rest of non-Africa's world that the globalization of trade has actually led to a weakening of a country's economic position. The reason why Africa is different is because Africa's agriculture is very fragile, most African economies are mono-crop or mono-product economies, and basically the starting point of Africa's diversification of economic structure never really took place, unlike other countries in Latin America and Asia.

So, when we look at the empirical evidence of the last twenty years and ask the question, which most people are beginning to ask, has globalization made the countries poorer or richer, I think the evidence is very clear—that globalization of trade, in terms of trade, in terms of opening up of new markets, in terms of integration with the international product markets, has in fact made countries richer by creating more jobs at home. In the process, some livelihoods may have got lost. In the process, the employment structure may have got diversified—less people involved in agriculture, more people involved in industry, less people involved in industry, more people involved in services. We are not now talking of individual cases, we are now talking of the broad macro economy, and when we talk of the broad macro economy, I want to reiterate that there is absolutely no empirical evidence to suggest, barring the unique case of Africa, that globalization in trade has actually led to a weakening of a country's economic security or employment security.

The two outstanding examples of this are basically India and China, China much more dramatically than India. In the case of India's own experience during the last ten to fifteen years, all the evidence certainly suggests that the opening up of the Indian economy to trade has, in fact, made the Indian economy stronger and much more resilient and much less vulnerable to international shocks.

Now, I am not going to talk about globalization of finance, globalization of labour, globalization of culture, because I think that takes us into a completely different dimension and the links with ecological security are far less explicit and far less clear. Therefore, the focus of my talk is exclusively on the globalization of trade, on which really much of the debate is taking place in forums both within the country and outside.

Therefore, to summarize the second point, over the past decade economies, large economies particularly, have become more resilient. Economic security has actually increased, particularly to external collapse. And again, taking the example of India, comparing 1990 with 2000, there is no doubt that the opening up of the economy, going by the lose term of globalization in trade, has in fact made the economy stronger.

The question is, has ecology become stronger or not. That is really the question, whether in the process of globalization, in the process of integration, in the process of international re-location of labour and capital, the local ecological structures have in fact weakened. Here, it is necessary to note that we are not writing on a clean slate, that over the last thirty or forty years we have accumulated a set of problems, on account of development strategies that have been adopted. However, people ascribe water-logging in the Punjab to the opening up of the WTO, but clearly there is no link between WTO and water-logging in Punjab. Likewise there is no link really between deforestation that has gone on over the last thirty-five years and integration of world trade, because if we look at the pattern of international trade for India, very little of our export trade is in forest-based products or natural-resource products, as we have diversified away from that structure. It could be true of Africa, but certainly it is not true in India.

The question whether globalization of trade has in fact had a deleterious effect on ecological security is very difficult to answer because of the accumulated set of problems that we have inherited on account of a certain pattern of development. And, this is where I think one needs to distinguish between the stock and the flow. At a given point of time there is a certain stock of problems that have accumulated. For example, the stock of accumulated greenhouse gases. The real question is how is the flow?

Is the increment to the stock accelerating, decelerating, or is it constant? What is the globalization process doing to the accumulated stock of problems? That is really the issue that we have to come to grips with.

On the issue of economic integration, which Dr Amrita Patel had talked about, that the process of economic integration is leading, as she says, to adverse ecological and environmental consequences in areas where these resources are exploited, I would argue that the fundamental impact of globalization of trade, going by the evidence, has been less on environment and more on employment. And, a strategy of globalization that actually increases employment, in my view, strengthens the foundation of ecological security, because it could be argued, and it has been argued in the Indian context, that most of our ecological problems arise out of poverty. Most of our ecological problems arise out of lack of access to economic resources and in empowering the communities economically, the transition to a safer ecological regime is made automatically. Therefore, I would argue that globalization, by increasing opportunities for employment, by increasing opportunities of specialisation of trade in the resource in which a country is surplus, namely, labour, leads to increased employment, and certainly it is a strategy that has led to greater ecological security.

The fact of the matter is that India has not done very well in this regard compared to China. That has more to do with the fact that we have not been able to exploit the opportunities of globalization because of our own policies and less to do with the fact that globalization does not open up these opportunities. If we again compare India and China, and look at India and China ten years ago and India and China today, most of the successes that China has had in terms of globalization of trade are in precisely those areas where India also had a comparative advantage—whether in textiles or labour-intensive manufacturing of consumer goods. These are all industries in which basically local jobs have been created. And the fact that China has been able to do this and India has not has to do more with the nature of domestic policy and less to do with the nature of the external constraint. But we tend to blame the external world much more for our own failure, whereas the clear evidence is that there are other countries which have been able to exploit these markets to good advantage.

So on globalization of trade, I would say that the verdict today is that globalization of trade certainly creates far greater economic opportunities for countries that participate in this process of globalization. There is enough evidenced to suggest that closed economies grow at lower economic growth rates and that economies that have opened themselves to trade as opposed to capital—now I am making a distinction between financial globalization and trade globalization—that economies that participate in the process of integration of international trade, namely, goods and services, are countries basically which have increased economic wealth and therefore they have increased their ability to deal with their ecological security.

Now, from this it does not follow that a country that has become economically more resilient out of globalization automatically increases the strength of its ecological structure. I think nobody in his right mind—and if anybody has in fact argued this he or she is wrong—nobody in his or her right mind would argue that there is this automatic link between economic development and ecological security. The question really is, what are the safeguards and what are the instruments that one should adopt in order to ensure that the goals of environmental and ecological protection and conservation are fulfilled while at the same time the objective of economic growth is also maximized?

I think there is a great belief in this country, particularly, that a low-growth economy is more protective of the environment than a high-growth economy. Somehow if you are growing at 7 per cent or 8 per cent and industrializing faster, you are imposing a great cost on the environment, whereas if you had a low rate of economic growth you would have a low level of equilibrium with the environment. But I think we have enough evidence to show that this is really not the case. So the real challenge, in my view, in the years ahead—to shift this debate away from globalization *vs.* ecological security to globalization *and* ecological security—I think is to recognize that globalization of trade has a positive effect on a country's economic position and it provides an opportunity for the country, then, to follow policies and instruments in order to meet the requirements of environmental protection.

The second issue is of globalization of ecological security. It is only appropriate that we are meeting today in the background of the negotiations and the discussions on climate change, because this is one of the issues really that has come up in the public arena in the last ten or fifteen years, which epitomizes what I am trying to talk about—which is that ecological security has become more globalised. Rather than the link between globalization and ecological security, the concerns of ecological security themselves now have become a globalised.

What are the issues we have to be worried about in this area? I think the most important issue here is that there would certainly be attempts made to link trade with environmental concerns. There is a large community of people, particularly among civil society organizations, among the NGO community, certainly in the Western countries, which believe that this link should exist, that in fact the only way to ensure ecological security is to impose trade sanctions, that the most effective instrument that the international community has for enforcing desirable patterns of environmental behaviour is to use trade sanctions. In fact, the entire debate on trade and environment in the context of the WTO is about this. Now we have a large body of material, jurisprudence, law, that we have accumulated to show the conflict that exists between the promotion of globalization of free trade and use of globalization of free trade to meet the objectives of environment.

The famous case is the shrimp-turtle case. I do not know how many of you are familiar. There is a famous shrimp-turtle case in the international community today which is redefining the whole link between trade and environment. The United States banned the import of shrimp from countries like India on the grounds that the way shrimp is caught in these countries kills turtles. This is a very famous case. The first ruling went in favour of India, Malaysia and Thailand but subsequently when the United States went back to the appellate body, the World Trade Organization, the appellate body seemed to give a ruling which seemed to justify the application of domestic environmental standards in what is essentially a matter of international trade. Now there is a big question mark, whether in fact the WTO has sanctioned the use of environmental safeguards and the use of trade sanctions basically to meet domestic environment goals.

So I think the big issue here is to what extent trade sanctions would be used to enforce desirable patterns of environmental behaviour. We are seeing this not only in the area of environment, but also in social areas. We have legislation pending in many countries, which says that we should not import carpets from India because these carpets use child labour. This is an example of a link between trade sanctions and social issues. There are important issues pending, for example, in Europe, where there is a movement to ban imports of leather from India on the ground that tanning uses carcinogenic chemicals. The shrimp-turtle case I have already mentioned. There are a large number of instances where I think today there is a progressive move towards the use of trade sanctions in order to meet the objectives of ecological security.

Some people actually welcome it. Many people actually welcome this and say that the only way we are going to get environment integrated with the development process is if you start using trade sanctions. I think this is going to be a very contentious political issue—the use of trade sanctions to control market access. And all I can say at this stage is that the next three to four years is going to be absolutely critical in the international negotiating process.

The second issue of course is the whole issue which is being discussed today in Delhi, which is on the climate change. This again is a good example of the globalization of ecological security and some of the principles that I have been talking about. The whole Kyoto Protoçol, which has been a subject of great controversy, is based on a fundamental distinction between stock and flow. There are countries which have contributed to the stock of Green House gases and there are countries which are contributing to the flow of Green House gases.

The first problem you have to really address is the responsibility of those countries which have contributed to the stock and then address the problem of what is the responsibility of other countries who are contributing to the flow. I think it is this inability to have an equitable distribution in the eyes of many countries between those who contribute to the stock and those who are contributing to the flow that has led to the political controversies over the Kyoto Protocol, but I am sure this is something that is going to get resolved.

The key issue here, whether it is the WTO or the Kyoto Protocol, is that environment/ecological security is becoming an instrument of protectionism. I think that is the real issue here. The real danger here is that if ecological security is going to be raised to the level of godhood, as it should perhaps be and it certainly has, then the countries are going to use the environmental arguments, the ecological arguments, basically as an instrument of neo-protectionism. I think that is the danger, that having seen the positive effects of globalization of trade, if ecological security is going to be used as a criteria for restricting market access and for actually making free trade un-free, then I think we are going to be denying many countries the benefits of the globalization process.

Therefore, to summarize, what I want to say is that ecological security really is a matter ultimately of domestic policy. Ecological security is a matter of economic policy of agricultural policy, of how you deal with water, air and land. It has really nothing to do with the globalization process. I think the globalization process really, as I have explained to you, largely in terms of globalization of trade, is basically an opportunity for specialisation in capital, in labour, in factors of production, and basically an opportunity for a country to ex›and its presence in international markets, to create jobs at home, to increase its prosperity, which creates the conditions for addressing these questions of ecological security.

As I said and I want to reiterate, it is not that when countries have in fact become much more global, then, automatically, ecological concerns become addressed. Ecological concerns need to be addressed as matters in their own right. And the real challenge for countries like India is to ensure that the globalization process moves in a manner that not only increases its economic wealth but also actually enhances ecological well being. Therefore I would say that, contrary to what most people think, the objectives of globalization and ecological security are not in fact mutually exclusive and in fact can be reconciled in a proper economic framework, and I hope that this is done sooner rather than later.

12

Ecological Security: Backbone of National Food Security

M.S. SWAMINATHAN

Sustained food security will be possible only if farm productivity can be increased in perpetuity without associated ecological or social harm. This will call for the conservation and enhancement of our land, water (inland and marine), forest and biodiversity resources, in addition to the protection of the atmosphere including the ozone layer. There is thus a feed-back relationship between ecological and food security.

Right to Food

The Right to Food has been recognized as a fundamental right. Many industrialized countries including the United Kingdom are now shifting their approach from food aid to enabling countries to build sustainable food security systems. This is because of the growing realisation that agriculture is not just a food producing machine, but is the very backbone of the livelihood and ecological security system in most developing countries. Hunger is the extreme manifestation of poverty, since the poor spend over 70 per cent of their daily earnings on food.

In addition to chronic protein-energy malnutrition caused by poverty, two billion people in the developing countries, many of them being women and children, suffer from hidden hunger caused by one or more micronutrient deficiency, like lack of iron, iodine or Vitamin A.

Ecologically sustainable agriculture, including crop and animal husbandry, fisheries, forestry and agro-processing can help to strengthen the livelihood security system in rural areas. Household food security in such countries is best defined in terms of person years of jobs or livelihoods, rather than in terms of tons of foodgrains. A famine of jobs or of purchasing power leads to a famine of food at the level of consumption. Agricultural progress serves as the best safety net against poverty, hunger and unemployment. Therefore, sustainable agriculture is the foundation for sustainable human security. I coined the term 'ever-green revolution' to indicate sustainable advances in farm productivity.

E.O. Wilson has stressed the importance of an ever-green revolution in the following terms:

> The problem before us is how to feed billions of new mouths over the next several decades and save the rest of life at the same time, without being trapped in a Faustian bargain that threatens freedom and security. No one knows the exact solution to this dilemma. The benefit must come from an evergreen revolution. The aim of this new thrust is to lift food production well above the level obtained by the green revolution of the 1960s, using technology and regulatory policy more advanced and even safer than those now in existence.

Food Security has three major dimensions:

- *Availability of food*—a function of production
- *Access to food*—a function of purchasing power/access to sustainable livelihoods
- *Absorption of food in the body*—determined by access to safe drinking water and non-food factors like environmental hygiene, primary health care and primary education.

The capacity to support even the existing human and animal populations has been exceeded in many parts of the developing world. Hence, the future of food security depends upon population stabilisation, the conservation and care of arable land, through attention to soil health and replenishment of fertility, and the conservation and careful management of all water sources, so that more crop can be produced per every drop of water.

Much of the degraded and desertified land belongs either to resource poor families, or constitutes over used and over-grazed common property. Ownership pattern of land and water determines the feasibility of introducing integrated and sustainable land and water management systems. Even where land is individually owned, locally acceptable systems of social management may have to be introduced through legislation, education and social mobilisation. Women's access to land is also important. Water, particularly ground water, should be a social resource and not private property. Creating an economic stake in conservation is vital for ensuring the sustainable use of natural resources.

Degradation and diversion of arable land and the depletion and pollution of water resources results in the loss of rural livelihoods. This triggers the unplanned migration of the rural poor to towns and cities, resulting in the proliferation of urban slums. The rise in the numbers of such environmental refugees threatens peace and security. Norman Myers has chronicled the seriousness of the situation. Hence, there should be a monitoring mechanism for avoiding the loss of rural livelihoods. Development programmes should strengthen the linkages between ecological and livelihood security.

Grain Mountains and Hungry Millions: The Growing Paradox

There are now unique opportunities for launching a Food for Sustainable Development initiative, in the form of a 'grain for green' movement. Such a programme could accord priority to the:

- Restoration of hydrological and biodiversity 'hot spots', particularly in mountain ecosystems
- Coastal agro-aqua farms (planting of salicornia, mangroves, casuarinas, palms, etc., along with coastal agriculture and aquaculture)
- Water harvesting, watershed development, wasteland reclamation, and anti-desertification measures
- Recycling of solid and liquid wastes and composting
- Agro-forestry and other sustainable land use systems in the fields of resource poor farmers.

The Government of India is now in a position to launch a Food for Sustainable Development and Hunger Elimination programme. About 20 million tonnes of grains would provide nearly 100 million person years of work designed to eliminate poverty, induced endemic hunger and at the same time restore and enhance environmental capital stocks.

The Food for Sustainable Development Initiative could be managed at the local level by Community Food Banks (CFB) operated by women's self-help groups. Such CFB's can be designed in a manner that they can address concurrently issues relating to chronic, hidden and transient hunger. The merit of CFB's will be low transaction cost and transparency. They can also help to widen the food security basket, thereby saving what could become 'lost crops'. Wherever animal husbandry including poultry farming is important to provide additional income and nutrition to families living in poverty, CFBs can also operate Feed and Fodder Banks.

Conferring the right to food and thereby an opportunity for a productive and healthy life on those who go to bed undernourished is now the fundamental duty of the state as well as of the well-to-do sections of the population. Thanks to both the spread of democratic systems of governance at the grassroots level and technological advances, there is now a unique opportunity to foster a Community Centered and Controlled Nutrition Security System. Such decentralized community management will help to improve delivery of entitlements, reduce transaction and transport costs, eliminate corruption and cater to the twin needs of introducing a life-cycle approach to nutrition security and to meeting the challenge of seasonal fluctuations in nutritional status. If such CFBs are operated by women, this will help to bridge the gender divide in the area of nutrition.

Short and Long Term Strategies for Sustainable Livelihoods

1. Both in terms of incidence and absolute numbers, India has the largest number of children, women and men going to bed undernourished in the world. Although the Food Corporation of India has currently over 60 million tonnes of food grain stocks, and there are numerous safety net measures of the Government of India for the economically and socially underprivileged sections of society, the FAO has listed India as one of the countries which has not been able to achieve the targets of the World Food Summit of 1996 in terms of reducing the number of undernourished. This calls for serious introspection of both our strategies for fighting hunger as well as of our ethical commitment to the cause of a hunger-free India.

2. The prevalence of endemic hunger should no longer be accepted as unavoidable. The social security systems for the able-bodied poor should include a food component in the form of a National Food Guarantee Scheme on the model of Maharashtra's employment

guarantee scheme. The public distribution system should be strengthened and should be designed to reach the unreached. On the basis of ICMR norms, about 158 million persons, belonging to about 32 million households, fall under the category of ultra-poor and need immediate assistance to help them to lead a healthy and productive life. They are best identified by Gram Sabhas and local bodies. They can be issued with Food Entitlement Coupons, which should entitle them to work under the Food Guarantee Scheme. The total requirement for such an open-ended employment-cum-food security project may need at the maximum about 10 million tonnes of food grains per year. Meeting this need is well within our national capacity.

3. Consumption inequality decreases as income increases. Diversification of diets also happens with increased purchasing power. Unfortunately inequality of income distribution is growing. A job-led economic growth strategy will help to reduce protein-energy malnutrition, and at the same time stimulate farming systems' diversification.

4. A whole life cycle approach should be introduced by providing a horizontal dimension to the numerous on-going vertically structured programmes supported by the central and state governments as well as by bilateral and multilateral agencies. At the local level, the management of a life-cycle based nutrition security system, beginning with pregnant women and extending up to old and infirm persons, is best left to the one million elected women members of the Panchayats.

5. Decentralized procurement and decentralized storage will help to minimize transport and transaction costs. Uttar Pradesh, Madhya Pradesh, West Bengal and Tamil Nadu have accepted the principle of a decentralized procurement system. The storage can be done through a national grid of Community Food Banks (CFBs) managed by self-help groups. The construction of CFBs can be done at the local level under the food for work programme. CFB's can help to implement these social safety net programmes in an effective and transparent manner. We must end the prevailing mismatch between production and consumption as soon as possible.

6. Short-term problems should not blind us to long-term realities. The population is growing and per capita land and water availability is decreasing. We have to produce more but produce it differently in a manner that high yields can be obtained in perpetuity without associated ecological or social harm. Farming systems' intensification, diversification and value addition are extremely important to generate

the needed on-farm and non-farm employment. There is also an urgent need for greater attention to the nearly 100 million ha. of rainfed land. Better dry farm techniques are available. They offer great opportunities for increasing the production of pulses and oilseeds. Productivity improvement in both irrigated and rainfed areas will help to increase marketable surplus at the household level and thereby the cash income. The gap between potential and actual yields even with the technologies currently available is high in most farming systems. Livestock husbandry and livelihood security tend to be closely correlated in the case of poorer households. There is greater equity in livestock ownership as compared to land. Hence, support services should be organized for small-scale livestock farming families in the form of Fodder and Feed Banks and health care and insurance facilities. With increasing urbanisation the demand for animal products will grow.

7. There is an urgent need for spreading quality literacy throughout the country, which will help to sensitise both producers and consumers on issues relating to food safety, Codex alimentarius standards and sanitary and phytosanitary measures. In addition, there is need for greater research in the field of breeding crop varieties having the quality characteristics needed for food processing and exports. If productivity and quality are improved, farm income will go up substantially.

8. Sustainability of food security measures should be ensured. PDS at the local level should provide reasonable income to those operating the ration shops. Community Food Banks may receive their initial food supply from government but subsequent replenishment should come from local communities. A wide range of grains and wild foods can be stored in CFBs. This will help to widen the food security basket. Also, the silos can be locally manufactured, thus providing another source of rural employment in the non-farm sector. Further, the silos will help to reduce post-harvest losses considerably. Both private and public sector institutions and companies have the necessary technical capability to launch the CFB movement.

9. Organization of a National Consortium for Sustainable Food Security. Indian farmers have shown that they will produce more if there are given opportunities for assured and remunerative marketing. Agriculture is the backbone of India's food, livelihood and ecological security systems. Therefore India's agricultural image within and outside the country needs to be refurbished. At the same time, chronic, hidden and transient hunger should be eliminated as soon as possible. It will be appropriate if NAAS promotes the organization of a National

Consortium for Sustainable Food Security consisting of representatives of FCI, CII, FICCI, ASSOCHAM, NHDB, NDDB, APEDA, TISCO, Hindustan Lever and appropriate Agricultural Universities and ICAR Institutes for fostering sustainable food security both in the hunger hot spots of India as well as in other countries in Asia and Africa.

10. There is no time to relax, both, on the production and consumption fronts. The stock of 60 million tonnes should not lull one into complacency. Concurrent attention to production and consumption is important. Enhancing production through an ever-green revolution is a priority task. However, eliminating widespread endemic hunger is a priority responsibility and ethical obligation. A universal and user-sensitive public distribution system, food guarantee scheme, community food banks and various other food entitlement projects need to be implemented in an integrated manner, so that the goal of hunger-free India can be achieved. Nutrition status will, however, continue to fall, unless the purchasing power of the poor is increased. Hence, livelihoods for all should be the bottom line of all national development and import and export policies.

Jal Swaraj

Since water will be the most limiting factor in the coming years in relation to domestic and agricultural needs as well as for ecosystem maintenance, it would be useful to develop a strategy for a sustainable water security system.

The Water Emergency prevailing in the country both due to drought and the unsustainable and inefficient use of most water resources, particularly of ground water, has brought home the urgent need for launching a Jal Swaraj movement based on the conservation of every drop of water and its sustainable and equitable use for domestic agricultural and industrial purposes. This was the vision of the late Anil Agarwal, Founder of the Centre for Science and Environment, New Delhi, while coining the term 'Jal Swaraj'. In 1980, when this author was in charge of Agriculture, Rural Development, Irrigation and Science and Technology in the Union Planning Commissions, a 5-point strategy was included in the Sixth Plan (1980-85) for developing a sustainable water security system for the country:

1. Rainwater harvesting and storage in a manner that evapo-transpiration losses are minimized.

2. Participatory watershed development and management and desilting and renovation of ponds, tanks, lakes and reservoirs.
3. River water sharing and efficient use.
4. Waste water (including sewage water and industrial effluents) treatment and recycling.
5. Sea water use along the coast for raising mangrove and salicornia plantations together with aquaculture.

All the above water sources need to be used in a conjunctive manner. Also, in the case of dry farming areas, community conservation of rainwater will happen only if there is equity in water sharing. For this purpose, all farm families should agree to grow only low water requiring but high value crops like pulses and oilseeds. Such a method of water conservation-cum-improved livelihood security can be achieved through the organization of Pulses and Oilseeds Villages.

In addition to the above immediate measures, steps were proposed in the Sixth Plan for developing a long-term plan for linking the major rivers of peninsular India, like Krishna, Godavari, Mahanadi and Cauvery, as well as for the desalination of sea water. Peninsular rivers are under our political control, unlike the Ganges, Indus and Brahmaputra which have international dimensions.

The suggestion for linking our major rivers is not new. Dr K.L. Rao is famous for his advocacy of the Ganga-Cauvery tie-up. Various experts have also been writing books and papers from time to time urging steps for linking India's major rivers. During the tenure of Morarji Desai as Prime Minister (1977-79) a proposal for constructing 'garland canals' in the Himalayas, central and peninsular India attracted his serious attention. He however abandoned the idea when it was pointed out that constructing a canal at a high altitude in the Himalayas was beset with serious ecological, political and national security issues.

The revised National Water Policy (April 2002) of the government of India contains the following statement:

> Non-conventional methods for utilisation of water such as through inter-basin transfers, artificial recharge of ground water and desalination of brackish or sea water, as well as traditional water conservation practices like rainwater harvesting, including roof-top rainwater harvesting, need to be practiced to further increase the utilizable water resources. Water should be made available to water short areas by transfer from other areas including transfers

from one river basin to another, based on a national perspective, after taking into account the requirements of the areas/basins.

Thus, inter-basin sharing of waters is an idea whose time has come. The present time is particularly a propitious one, since there is scope now for launching a massive Food and Cloth for Jal Swaraj programme, organized on the model of the Employment Guarantee Scheme of Maharashtra.

Based on the financial provision made in the Sixth Plan for initiating steps for linking the rivers of peninsular India, the Central Water Commission had undertaken detailed studies. Given the necessary political will and consensus, the linking of the rivers of Peninsular India and the equitable and efficient use of this gigantic water grid will help to create a 'win-win' situation for all the states involved. If there are winners and losers, there will be only conflict and confrontation, as is happening now.

It is high time India moves in the direction of rainwater harvesting, watershed development and conjunctive use of rain, river, ground, treated sewage and sea water on the one hand, and river water linking on the other. China, which has taken a long-term view in the area of building a national water security system, has already made much progress in building the gigantic Three Gorges Dam, for taking the waters of the Yangtze River to the parched lands of the northern parts of that country. The Three Gorges Dam will confer multiple benefits in the areas of flood control, irrigation, drinking water supply and power generation.

India unfortunately is a country where there is often paralysis by analysis, particularly in vital areas like inter-basin sharing of water. For example, a National Water Policy was adopted in September 1987. It remained largely on paper. This policy was reviewed and updated in April 2002. However, implementation structures for converting the policy into reality do not exist. There has been no effort to mobilize the Panchayati Raj Institutions for harvesting and sharing water at the local level. The Centre for Science and Environment and the Akash Ganga Trust have established in Chennai a Rain Centre which is a single-stop information centre on all aspects of rainwater harvesting, storage and use. Such rain centres are needed in every village and town in the country. In each Panchayat and Nagarpalika, at least 2 women and 2 elected members should be trained as Water Security Managers, capable of looking at water security issues in their totality, namely, the consumption of water to meet the needs of human settlements, agriculture, industry and ecosystem maintenance.

While there is discussion and debate relating to the quantitative aspects of water needs, the same interest is not evident with reference to the qualitative aspects of water, with particular reference to domestic consumption. For example, the CPR Environment Education Centre in Chennai has observed the following position in relation to ground water quality in the Chennai area. Water samples from 25 different locations in Chennai, collected from wells and bore wells were analysed for their potability in the Center's laboratory. The pH of the samples ranged from 6.50 to 8.81. The Total Dissolved Solids (TDS) exceeded 500 mg/l (the desired limit of TDS in drinking water) in 88 per cent of the samples, and 64 per cent of the samples contained more than 1,000 mg/l of TDS. 28 per cent of the samples contained more than 2,000 mg/l of TDS, the maximum permissible limit as per IS 10500;1991. twenty-four per cent of the samples contained high level of iron content. This clearly indicated the sad state of ground water quality in Chennai.

The Ganga Action Plan, after huge investment and many years of work, could not succeed in making the water of this 'holy' river potable. This is attributed to non-point pollution, caused by human beings, many of them being pilgrims. The same fate is true of most of the rivers and tanks revered for their spiritual significance. It is clear that unless water becomes everybody's business, as Anil Agarwal put it, it will remain a source of conflict and contamination.

India has enough water resources to fulfil everybody's need. We live in a democracy. Let us designate 2003 as a Water Emergency Year and initiate during the year a Water Literacy Movement which will stimulate State and Central Governments to launch an integrated water security strategy with the following short and medium term action plan. In the short term, emphasis may be given to the following:

- *Collect* every drop of water and use it for raising more crop per drop.
- *Treat* all wasted water and use it conjunctively with ground and surface water resources.
- *Ensure* that drinking water is not polluted.
- *Create* consciousness of the need to regard holy rivers,

reservoirs, lakes and tanks as gifts of God on earth by not polluting them

- *Manage* ground and surface water resources in a sustainable and equitable manner through regulation, education and social mobilisation.

All the above steps are politically doable and economically affordable. The short-term steps mostly need non-monetary inputs, since they depend upon people's awareness and participation on account of enlightened self-interest.

In the medium term, we should initiate action to use conjunctively sea and ground water along the nearly 8,000 km shore line of India for rising plantations of mangroves, salicornia, casuarinas, cashew nut and coconut. Also, agro-aqua farms can be established all along the coast for promoting integrated systems of aquaculture and agro-forestry.

Above all not a day more should be lost in fostering political consensus to link all peninsular Indian rivers in the form of a Dakshin Water Grid. When coupled with the prime minister's National Highways Project, the Dakshin Water Grid will usher in uncommon opportunities for strengthening both food and livelihood security, leading to a hunger and poverty free Dakshin.

Jal Swaraj will become a reality only if such a movement is built on the foundation of the twin pillars of equity and ethics. For this purpose, all political parties must agree to abide by the rule of law and respect the findings of institutional structures set up to settle disputes relating to sharing of water, particularly under conditions of scarcity. When Lal Bahadur Shastri coined the slogan '*Jai Jawan, Jai Kisan*', he wanted to respect the contributions of every Indian '*Jawan* and *Kisan*', to national security. Since about 75 per cent of India's water resources go to agriculture, sharing the joys and sorrows of all Indian farmers in an equitable manner is vital for both agrarian prosperity and sustainable food security.

Peace, Food and Ecological Security

The world is facing today a trilemma, or a triple dilemma. Over 3 billion struggling to survive with an income of less than US $2 per capita per day, are crying for peace and equitable economic development. Countries in Southern Africa, Ethiopia and Afghanistan are in the midst of serious famines. There have been reports of children being sold for bags of wheat. The Roman Philosopher Seneca said 2,000 years ago, 'A hunger person listens neither to reason nor religion, nor is bent by any prayer'.

Thus, one aspect of the trilemma is the craving for peace, and development which is equitable in social and gender terms. On the other, there is a growing violence in the human heart. Terms like ethnic cleansing and biological and biochemical terrorism are being widely used in the media. The revival of small pox is becoming a possibility; the nuclear peril has again raised its head. There are over 30,000 nuclear weapons in the arsenals of major and minor nuclear powers. The availability of large quantities of highly enriched uranium increases opportunities for nuclear adventurism.

The third side of the trilemma is the spectacular progress of science and technology, resulting in increasing technological divide between industrialized and developing countries. If access to technology has been a major cause of economic inequity in the past, the challenge now lies in enlisting technology as an ally in the movement for social and gender equity.

In 1994, the report of the International Commission on Peace and Food which I chaired was released in UNESCO by its then Director-General, Prof. Federico Mayor. Unfortunately, the Peace Dividend we had then anticipated, as a result of the end of the Cold War and the break up of the Berlin Wall, is yet to materialize. In fact, the expenditure on military hardware and internal security is increasing day-by-day, particularly after the tragic events of September 11, 2001.

Contemporary developmental challenges, particularly those relating to poverty, gender injustice and environmental degradation are indeed formidable. However, the remarkable advances now taking place in information and communication technology, space technology, biotechnology, agricultural and medical sciences, and renewable energy and clean energy technologies provide hope for a better common present and future. Genomics, proteomics, internet, space and solar technologies and nanotechnology are opening up uncommon opportunities for converting the goals of food, health, literacy and work for all into reality. It is however clear that such uncommon opportunities can be realized only if the technology push is matched by an ethical pull. This is essential for working towards a world where both unsustainable life styles and unacceptable poverty become features of the past.

Also, there is a growing mismatch between the rate of progress in science, particularly in the area of molecular biology and genetic engineering and the public understanding of its short and long-term implications. There is an urgent need for institutional structures which can inspire public confidence that the risks and benefits are being measured in an objective and transparent manner. Scientists and technologists have a particularly vital role to play in launching an Ethical Revolution. The Pugwash movement, which I now have the privilege to lead, is an expression of the social and moral duty of scientists to promote the beneficial applications of their work and prevent their misuse, to anticipate and evaluate the possible unintended consequences of scientific and technological development, and to promote debate and reflect the *ethical obligations of scientists in taking responsibility for their work.*

It will be appropriate to quote in this context, what Bertrand Russell and Albert Einstein said in their famous manifesto of 1955 issued on the occasion of the 10th anniversary of the use of atom bombs on Hiroshima and Nagasaki: 'We appeal as human beings to human beings. Remember your humanity and forget the rest. If you can do so, the way lies open to a new paradise; if you cannot, there lies before you the risk of universal death.'

Shall we renounce war and violence as a method of settling disputes, or shall we put an end to the human civilisation? This is the question facing us today. We are witnessing a growing intolerance of diversity and pluralism in human societies, as for example in terms of religion, ethnicity, political belief, colour, culture, gender and language. In contrast, the goal of sustainable development, accepted in various UN Conferences including the recently held World Summit on Sustainable Development at Johannesburg, as the only pathway to a happy human future, can be realized only if there is harmony between human kind and nature. It is obvious that we cannot be non-violent to nature, if we are going to be violent to each other.

We now have a Global Convention on Biological Diversity to help in the conservation and sustainable and equitable use of biodiversity. We need urgently a similar convention on Human Diversity. While a convention alone will not be able to halt the growing intolerance of diversity, particularly with reference to religion and political belief, it will help to foster a mind set which regards diversity as a blessing and not a curse. Both biodiversity and human diversity are essential for a sustainable future.

It is also necessary to reflect on methods of giving meaning and content to the ethical obligations of scientists in relation to society. The World Conference on Science held at Budapest n 1999 called for a new social contract between scientists and society. With a rapidly expanding Intellectual Property Rights (IPR) atmosphere in scientific laboratories, the products of scientific inventions may become increasingly exclusive in relation to their availability, with access being limited only to those who can afford to pay. The rich-poor divide will then increase, since orphans will remain orphans with reference to scientific attention. How can we develop a knowledge management system which will ensure that inventions and innovations of importance to human health, food, livelihood and ecological security benefit every child, woman and man, and not just the rich? I propose that the UN may explore the possibility of establishing an International Bank for Patents for Peace and Happiness. Scientists and technologists from all parts of the world should be encouraged to assign their patents to such a Bank, so that the fruits of scientific discoveries are available for public good. Such a Patents for Peace and Happiness Bank would stimulate scientists to consider themselves as trustees of their intellectual property, sharing their inventions with the poor in whose lives they may make a significant difference for the better. The French mathematician, Marquis de Condorcet, who was a contemporary of Thomas Malthus, said over two centuries ago that the human population will stabilize itself if children are born for happiness and not just existence. The Government of Bhutan has taken the lead in developing a Gross National Happiness Index, based on the economics of human dignity, love of art and culture and commitment to spiritual values. Making all well-to-do members of the human family regard themselves as trustees of their financial and intellectual property will be essential for fostering a human happiness movement. We already have many philanthropic orgnizations for harnessing financial resources. The organization, under UN auspices, of an International Bank for Patents for Peace and Happiness will help scientists and technologists to practice what the great Indian spiritual and intellectual leader, Swami Vivekananda, advocated as the true pathway to human fulfilment.

'In this life, give everything you can—give money, give food, give love or anything else you can—but do not seek barter.'

Not seeking barter with nature is the basic pre-requisite for ecological security. Harmony with nature and with each other is the recipe for achieving food security in perpetuity.

13

Political Process and Ecological Security

NAJMA HEPTULLA

In the recent past, there have been the debates in and outside Parliament on drought conditions prevailing in the country. Specific instances of the plight of our farmers have been given by several Members of Parliament. The Judiciary had to direct the government to formulate ambitious plans to harness the water resources lest conflicts are created among the states and the people. The new Vice-President and the Chairman of the Rajya Sabha, who is very pro-active and understands grassroots realities, called a meeting—this was the first time the Chairman of the Rajya Sabha called such a meeting—on the issue of drought in Rajasthan and other parts of the country, which I appreciated very much. There have been instances when desperate farmers have taken recourse to the superstitious also and people are forced to seek supernatural remedies for nature's rage. The most feeble and vulnerable of us are in the frontline for behaving in this way.

Year after year, Parliament has discussed the issue of drought and floods. Predictably, the government is at the focus of accountability. Indeed, the government is obliged to provide immediate relief. Yet, in fact, we are providing quick-fix solutions to a long-term phenomenon of climatic change due to sustained environmental degradation during the previous century.

We have to recognize that ecological security has a significant bearing on sustainable human development and social security. Nature's temper has a significant bearing over our well-being. I can say from my own experience as Chairman of the MP LADF Committee—the Member of Parliament's area development fund which the government gives—about the magnitude of the human tragedy caused by natural calamities. It is a massive task to rehabilitate those whose lives have been devastated by the cyclone in Orissa or the earthquake in Gujarat. The Committee has mobilized the MP's annual funds to undertake rehabilitation and community work in the affected areas. We often miss a simple point that we have betrayed nature for our own greed and lust. Surplus and easy availability of natural resources has been taken for granted by us. Human beings have callously disregarded nature. We rejoice in our technological marvels by trampling upon nature. We forget that nature has been a trusted partner in man's evolution. We as the supreme creation of God arrogate to ourselves the attitude of masters of nature. Unfortunately, technology has become an instrument of human greed for reckless consumption.

However, it is encouraging to see that environment has come back on the social agenda. There is a growing awakening and awareness in society. The issue has a potential to provide alternative agenda of development with closer interaction with the local community—a development that is compatible with local environment and the demands of the local community. Environmental issues have attracted spontaneous and voluntary popular participation from the local community. This is a clear indication that the local communities have a greater stake in their ecological surroundings than the prevailing market-driven development model.

In a democracy, we should be receptive and responsive to change. We must respond to the social aspirations. There is a persuasive discourse on environmental issues. It is interesting to note that non-state actors have been very prominent on the environment issue. There is greater activism and advocacy campaigned by the NGO network. Often NGO reports have contradicted government claims. They have been able to assert moral and democratic pressure over the government on environmental and related humanitarian issues.

To make environment issues a part of the development discourse, our educational institutions have made environment part of their curriculum. They have taken up ambitious research and development programmes to explore new eco-friendly technologies. There has been a lively debate in the media on environment, environmental development and international ramifications of environmental politics.

All these are the non-state, actors who are an integral part of the wider political process. The civil society world over is geared up to provide the alternative developmental model that is de-centralized, sustainable, and environment-compatible. The new model will redefine new concepts in governance. It can inspire a new democracy, a democracy that has a massive capacity to broaden its agenda to be more responsive and comprehensive.

In India too, we have recognized the growing environmental consciousness in society. The Constitution envisages concerted efforts by the state and its citizens to protect the environment and the natural heritage. Article 48A of the Directive Principles of State Policy and Article 51A of the Fundamental Duties obliges the state and citizens squarely to protect the environment and wildlife. Indeed the state, as the planner of the nation's socio-economic development, has the larger responsibility. Here, I would like to say that we have passed a lot of legislation in recent times for the protection of wildlife. Very recently, only last week, we had the Bio-diversity Bill in the Rajya Sabha. I wanted to participate in the debate, buy I could not do so, as I was chairing the House. However, I gave a few points for the consideration of the government.

While devising our strategies, we have come to realize that nature has to be our partner in development. The new development planning has to be eco-friendly. With my long experience as a parliamentarian and also as the President of the Inter-Parliamentary Union, I can say that parliamentarians the world over' as the interlocutors between people and their governments' are abreast with the issue of ecological security and sustainable and equitable development. As the law-makers, parliamentarians have to guide the government about the imperative to recognize environment as the key factor in sustainable human development. In our Parliament, I have taken initiative to sensitize fellow MPs on the issue. We had convened and intervened with Parliament and other resource agencies. The proceedings have been compiled in the form of a book. We also joined with the WWF-India in convening an international conference on the issue. Such sustained interactions are essential not only to renew the agenda for environment protection but also to create an environment constituency in society. As Chairman of the IPU Committee on Sustainable Development, 'I' had convened a special meeting of parliamentarians and other resource agencies at Brazilia in 1992. As an appraisal of the outcome of the Rio Conference, we adopted the Brazilia Plan of Action for Parliamentarians in support of the Agenda 21.

Parliaments can be the focal institution in providing eco-sensitive governance. They can devise mechanisms to scrutinize and sensitize governments and also seek statutory environmental audit. In Indian

Parliament, we have a parliamentary committee on environment to scrutinize the government's working. There is now greater appreciation of the wider social and gender issues enjoined to ecological security. Eco-sensitive development offers greater opportunities to empower women and other vulnerable groups. We are also concerned about the unsustainable patterns of production and consumption that have put a heavy burden on environment. Recent consumption patterns have put unsustainable burden on ecology. In fact, the consumptive population of countries like Canada is much higher than that of India. During the 107th conference of the Inter-Parliamentary Union at Maracas, the parliamentarians reviewed the state of global environment and implementation of various international instruments. The global parliamentary community, expressed its support to these instruments to contain further degradation. We have been concerned about continued degradation of the environment and have reaffirmed our commitment to protect the global commons and biological diversity.

Again, at the recent World Summit on Sustainable Development at Johannesburg, which I attended, the parliamentary community supported the new partnership between government, civil society and business on environment and development issues. In this era of globalization, business too shall have to share the obligation towards humanity. Increasing commercialisation has put pressure on nature. Business has a greater role in sustainable development and must not only employ eco-friendly technologies but also help in stopping the destruction of nature.

The obligation of restoring and protecting environment lies predominantly with the developed countries. Twenty per cent of the world's population consumes eighty per cent of the resources, while 8 per cent of the population is sustained on meager 20 per cent resources. Hazardous and nuclear waste is dumped by these countries in various parts of the globe. This can cause massive catastrophe. Our marine life has been polluted due to this waste and oil spills. The CFC emissions in the United States is higher than that of the entire world. The green house gases have begun to warm up earth's atmosphere. There are reports of the gradual melting of the Antarctic. These changes are massive. A friend from Canada, who was a Member of Parliament and then a Minster, once told he that the grass is growing in that part of Canada where they never saw anything but snow. The magnitude of the consequence is beyond comprehension. Still countries like the

United States, who are the major polluters, continue to shirk their obligations, and continue to defy the Kyoto protocol. The natural resources belong to humanity and the progenies of a few rich cannot lay a predominant claim over these global commons. However, the current trend of globalization may expose these resources to unscrupulous exploitation by the richer countries. This is what happened with the rain forests of Latin America. globalization cannot be allowed to become an excuse for unrestricted exploitation. Polluter must pay. Developing countries cannot continue to pay the cost for the sins of the affluent.

Financial and technical resources are indispensable to the implementation of Agenda 21 and other Conventions. The Inter-Parliamentary Union has sought the developed countries to fulfil their obligations under Agenda 21, which have not been fulfilled in spite of the fact that we took the five-year or ten-year appraisal of what was decided at the Rio Conference and the commitments made over there. Parliamentarians are mindful that natural resources like water, land and soil, forest and global commons cannot be divided among countries. These have already been exploited beyond sustainable limits and global health is under serious threat from waste products and harmful emissions. There is a growing concern among Parliamentarians that global emissions of greenhouse gases continue to rise. This has resulted in climate change which, in turn, has enhanced the frequency and severity of natural disasters. Most of these human tragedies due to natural disasters occur in developing countries that lack resources and technologies to face them. Therefore, it is vital to address the human tragedies caused by climate change.

We need to recognize the close links between poverty and more effective management of environmental resources. There is a need to incorporate environment issues into national poverty reduction strategies. Parliamentarians are concerned about the spread of droughts and desertification. We have called to implement measures to combat droughts and desertification. We seek suitable forest eco-system and land management. It is essential to conserve and protect biological diversity and genetic resources. There is also a need for greater investment in alternative energy technologies and to promote environmentally sustainable practices. Much of the environment is destroyed due to our growing energy needs. Mankind shall have to look for newer and safer sources of energy.

Beyond temporal sustenance, nature remains a part of our cultural heritage. In its sublimity we find a sense of belongingness. It renders a sense of collectivity, a sense we have lost in the competition of markets. Are we entitled to deprive people of their cultural heritage? Can such development be sustainable that erodes nature and deprives people? Ecological security is high on the agenda of the political process. Parliamentarians have been debating on the strategies to harmonize developmental imperatives with environmental ethics. It is a question of altering development thinking and strategies. Parliament looks for the inputs from civil society and expert groups. We recognize the voluntary movement by local environment groups and consider them as a significant trend in evolving a political culture based on decentralized democracy.

I have myself, through my Parliamentarians Forum for Human Development, been closely associated with the issue of sustainable human development. Several complex issues are enjoined with environment security. It entails a paradigm shift in our economic planning and industrial technology. Both these require gradual but sustained change. Also associated with it are the international obligations and cooperation. The issue has the potential to cause revolutionary changes at global level. Every revolution is preceded by revolutionary ideas that provide the foundation. To me a political process in democracy has a much wider concept. It includes creating awareness through debate among political parties, media and educational institutions. This can build an environment constituency. It is also about factoring environment into the development paradigm. Parliament as the highest forum to build an awareness of natural issues can become the focal point in integrating environmental issues in national development strategy. Here, I can say that the political process has gained momentum in India and there is a consensus in society and it is reflected in the polity too. Parliament will give eloquence to the silent millions in remote regions who have stakes in their surrounding ecology. Let me assure you, I shall always be available for such noble cause.

If all of us join hands we can really create awareness in society. For instance, take the issue of plastic bags being thrown around. These are all non-bio-degradable and the use of non-bio-degradable packaging material is becoming more and more popular. Some years ago, we decided to bring in the New Year with our children in the bird sanctuary in Bharatpur. We decided to spend our New Year with the birds and animals there. To my horror, when we went for a walk in the park, I found 'pan parag' pouches and plastic bags lying all over. The animals and birds can swallow these, which can be very harmful. Then, though no vehicles are permitted inside the sanctuary, we saw a jeep full of children and noisy people. We decided to tell the park-keeper about it. To our horror, when I was complaining to him about this, the jeep entered his house and we discovered that it was his children who were breaking the law! I made much hue and cry about it and on return to Delhi, I made a statement in Parliament and also told former Prime Minister Rajiv Gandhi about it. Since then, I have not gone back to Bharatpur. I do not know whether things have changed since.

There are other people also. My daughter went on a hiking trip to Madhya Pradesh, specially to Pachmarhi, along with a group of young boys and girls. They found a very eco-friendly guide, who was a forest officer. He was so concerned about the trees and the ecology of that place that he took them around and showed them what was going on there. So, it depends on individuals. I also feel that it is important to get trained and to be committed to one's work and to protecting the environment. While it may not take much to protect the environment, it takes a lot of effort to destroy it.

Essentially, it is at the grassroots level that we have to create awareness. Last summer I met to some young children who had taken a summer school programme at the Alliance Francaise. I asked them if they had ever seen any butterfly or birds. They looked at me as if I was talking something funny. I said when we were young we used to see butterflies, dragonflies, etc. Now I do not see any butterflies in my garden. I do not see even birds. Occasionally, crows used to come; lately I have not seen crows either. This is how degradation is taking place. Human beings are encroaching upon the animals. That is what I said in the Parliament once. When a Member of Parliament said 'they are fighting like dogs', I told him, look, I am a zoologist, not only do I protect the right of the humans, I protect the right of animals also! Let us not denigrate animal life, they are also like us. They also have a right to live.

14

Education and Ecological Security

ERACH BHARUCHA

Ecological security can be seen from very diverse perspectives depending on one's own life experience of diversity and ecology. Besides, there are many different perspectives in all walks of society, including tribal culture, urban culture, rural culture, and each will look at ecological security from its own perspective.

Environment pollution relates to all the sectors, e.g. agriculture and pesticides, urban areas and traffic, and a whole set of things that threaten ecological security. Take the example of land degradation. Land degradation comes about in various ways. Even urbanisation is a sort of land degradation to a certain extent. Take a city like Pune, where I was born and brought up. Today, it is a very different place, the city has spread into the most ecologically sensitive surroundings and undergoing very rapid urbanisation. It is incredible.

I think the extinction of species is a very key aspect in understanding threats to the eco-system, threats to eco-security. Each extinction can trigger hundreds of other extinctions—this perhaps again is a very important thing to understand. The disruption of all our natural resource bases, water being the key one, seems to threaten ecological security.

I believe the prime cause of all this to be lack of awareness. Awareness of these issues is very central, very patchy. I am going to demonstrate to you through studies which we have undertaken, that inadequate educational strategies both from the non-formal and the formal sector of education seem to be the most enormous threat to eco-security. The largest threat seems to me to be the inadequate educational strategy.

What people do know about ecological security comes from very different sources. When a child grows up you don't have to teach him the difference between clean and dirty water. You do not have to teach him the difference between bad air and the good air that he has to breathe. You do not have to teach him what is dangerous in his own environment. These are things that the child learns through his own life experiences. I can give very many examples of what children, especially rural children, learn from different types of environments on their own.

It is the learning process which is so exciting. I am very fascinated by the way people look after sacred groves. One day, while studying some sacred groves in the western *ghats* in Maharashtra, I came across a little configuration on the ground. I was walking with the local *pujari* (temple priest) and asked him about it. He said, 'Oh, this is nothing for you, not important.' On my persisting, he called a little shepherd boy and asked him to explain. This little boy said, 'These are things that I collect from the forest. These are my buffaloes, the leaves that I have collected, and the pebbles that I put around the walls of my house'. I realized that the children in this area know where to collect these natural resources, in which season they will get which natural resource, and they change according to the season. What an incredible way to learn something from their own living experience.

With this as an example, I started looking at it in various ways. I found the children of the Ratnagiri coast making small bounds when the sea is receding and then with little nets which they had made, catching crabs, just like their parents did. So this is learning from nature. This is something that we ourselves have not done in our schools. Our teachers never came out of classrooms. This we realized very early in the Bharatiya Vidyapeeth at Pune and over the last six or seven years we have started focussing on things like this.

We did a small exercise with a group of school kids. We took them to a hill next to their village, and told them to mark the places from where they obtained their resources. For instance, where does your mother get water from? Where do you get your fuelwood from? Where do you graze your cattle? They created a little map which was linked to these resources.

In this area much of what was community land is now being sold for developmental purposes. Therefore, the children get an awareness that many of these things are disappearing very rapidly. We have used this kind of an exercise to see that community processes continue through an educational process. So we are running an environmental educational programme in about sixty village schools there and we are using these kinds of methodologies.

There are so many traditional knowledge systems, viz., water harvesting, conservation practices, rotational grazing, farming techniques and this whole concept of sacred groves which I have mentioned. When we think of ecological security, it splits into various components—water, soil, fuel, forest resources, and so on. For each of these, there is some sort of traditional methodology by which people guarded them. There is a sacred grove in the western *ghats*, with a temple inside, a tiny little structure. There is a tribal fisherman who looks after the deity. He has a very interesting ceremony called a 'call ceremony'. If he needs to cut a branch of a tree from this grove, then he has to take the permission from the deity. The way he does it is very interesting. He takes two glasses of water. He puts two drops of water before the two little figures in the temple. Then he takes a little grain which he places on these two little figures. If the grain placed on the right falls down first, he can cut a branch from the tree. If the grain placed on the left side falls, he cannot cut the branch. This is one way in which there is 50:50 per cent chance of saving that resource. So this is ecological security, it leads to ecological security.

Our history also indicates interesting examples of ecological security. Take the Ashoka edicts. If we look at the list of species Ashoka wanted protected, they are incredibly fascinating. Many of these are species which only very recently have come to our present schedule of protection. Likewise, there is Shivaji's edict. First of all, he laid down that one should not cut any tree. The edict also slabs that people have to especially look after the mango and jackfruit trees like their own children. This edict was effective in the Peshwa period as well. It was obviously very effective. Most of the trees were being cut then for making ships. Later on, the British actually turned this edict around to be able to make ships of their own.

This traditional knowledge of ecological security went into the formal educational processes. This happened in the British era, and it happened in a very odd way. The British wanted to take spices from our country. Therefore, they needed to understand more and more about botany. They realized that besides the spices, there were many other forest resources in the country. There were not too many botanists from England who wanted to come to India. Those who actually did botany in the early part of British East India Company's time happened to be, like myself, surgeons!

Those selected were told that they were to not just look after the well being of the British people here but they would also be collecting plants. So, these surgeons or medical doctors were used for collecting plants, documenting something, making herbalia sheets, making drawing bases, and sending the herbalia sheets back to the East India Company. There are many fascinating stories about this.

Many of these doctor botanists lost their specimens when a bullock cart, for instance, turned over in the water or a ship sank somewhere. So a lot of botanists' specimens were lost. However, that was the early start to Botany in India. There were also some Zoologists and, *Shikaris* or Hunkers. Most of them were Army or British government officers or people from the States in India, the Maharajas, who really studied intensively the zoology of this country. Of course, before that the Mughals had already documented a lot of species in zoology.

How did this interest change to ecology? From there to the behaviour of species and to ecology took a long time. Probably the earliest eco-system studies were established through the Bombay Natural History Society (BNHS), long before the Bhartiya Vidyapeeth Institute of Environment & Education & Research (BVIEER). When I joined the BNHS as an Executive Member about 18 or 20 years ago, I had debates with major scientists there. Their response was that once their research work was documented, it was regarded as completed. It was placed on record and that was the end. My response to that was, no, it is not finished until you do something about it. The same scientists, who at that time said, 'No, no, that is not our job, our job is to do science' are today running *padyatras!* But that change took 20 years to happen. The scientists today are now gradually becoming activists for conservation, but that has taken many, many years.

What do we know about the current environment education and awareness strategies? At the formal environment education at the school and college level, there are two aspects to understand: (a) the curricular aspects and how teaching/learning methods are used, and (b) how to create a non-formal environment education strategy?

First, the non-formal environment education. The late Dr. Salim Ali used to put me on his motor cycle as a school boy (he did not know that I actually wanted to have a ride on his fantastic motorcycle)—and then he started showing me birds. That is how I became a bird watcher. Incidentally, Salim Ali's first job in the Bombay Natural History Society was as an Education Officer. So BNHS's tradition of doing nature study with school kids and adults is something pretty old—starting in the thirties. Then came the World Wildlife Fund. I joined that as well. It has the largest 'Nature Clubs of India' movement in the world. This is the non-formal strategy which we use. But, the strategists from these two big organizations were then primarily urban. It is only very recently that they have realized that they have to do this in the rural sector, in tribal groups also. This is the non-formal aspect. We have a lot of these kinds of activities through my own institute. It is the nature trail we have developed, with the kids doing an environment programme.

In the mid-1990s, there was a big experiment in the home of the Bio-diversity Conservation Prioritisation Project. We were asked to do the education awareness and training aspect of this big project. We did 22 focal studies on the knowledge of biological diversities among different groups of people—tribals, urban people, urban school kids, rural school kids, and so on. We began to understand where the gaps in knowledge lay. We all think of the tribal people having enormous knowledge of plants and animals. That turned out to be very, very true. Certainly most tribal people I accessed in the Western Ghats, parts of Gujarat, the north-east, knew many plant and animal species, much more than an M.Sc. student in Zoology or Botany would know. There is no doubt about this. They had enormous local knowledge of their own plants and animals.

When you look at the plants and animals they know, very interesting facts emerged. They know plants which they use, they know plants which are dangerous—and have names for those—and they know plants which are sacred. But other plants that do not fall into these categories are just called wild plants. Similar facts emerged for animals as well. They may have gaps in taxonomical knowledge, but for their traditional use the knowledge seems adequate and appropriate.

Among school students, with and without environment programme, we have found a lot of differences. We have also looked at the role of bio-diversity in school curricula, in college curricula, and so on.

We are able to raise levels of bio-diversity knowledge by doing non-formal education in the schools as extra curricular activity. Having done that, our strategy has now changed. We have started using the same non-formal environment education technology in the formal curricula, which then brings about an enormous change.

We have also tried to understand something about college students. Where do the college students get their knowledge of bio-diversity? We gave a large number of students from different colleges a sort of a proforma to fill in. Twenty-five per cent said their knowledge base was their school curricula, 14 per cent said it was their college curricula. When we looked at what sort of knowledge there was, it was extremely basic. They did not even know many common species. They did not know, for instance, the difference between Cheetah and Sambar. But they had some basic knowledge about bio-diversity which they said they got from school and college. Then, we dealt with groups of people who are knowledgeable about bio-diversity and asked them how they got their knowledge. We found that they said they got their knowledge from early childhood experiences with nature. This was the major difference and the whole pattern began to change with this perspective.

Let us now look a little at the formal environment education aspects. There is a Supreme Court directive which tells the government that it should put environment education into formal school and college curricula. This has led to certain changes in the working in the NCERT. We have conducted a study on this through a content analysis of the textbooks on science, geography, social science, language, civics from every state in India. It is a tool that assesses educational aspects in a school textbook. We also wrote a computer programme to be able to do this.

What were we looking for? We wanted to see what concepts of environment exist in formal textbooks today across the country, in every state. If you look at the content, that can be divided into natural resources, bio-diversity, pollution, energy, people and environment. When we did this study we found that there is a smattering of knowledge within textbooks. But it does not go into the process of learning. It gives a concept, it does not say why that concept is fitted there, because it is probably pushed in there by the Supreme Court judgment. And, therefore, the process of learning which occurs from knowledge, to a greater degree of awareness about environment, and from there to a concern for environment and from that to action, just does not occur. While the statement is there, the process of learning is not there. This is what we found by and large—the absence of what we can call 'action-links'.

This is to tell you how this programme runs. I know you can't see this from the back. This is the text, this is about activity, visuals, and questions and answers, and so on. And there you have got parameters. Ninety-eight concepts we identified which go into various aspects of the contents. Is it accurate? Is it relevant and applicable? Is it comprehensive, and what biases does it have?

Finally, does it have any action linkage? This kind of structure has been created for every lesson of every textbook of every state in all the subjects from standard 1 to 12. This data is enormous. Each state's output varies between 1500 to 1800 pages—an enormous amount of material per state.

Once all this is into the computer, it gives a textbook analysis which looks very complicated, but it is not. This way one gets to know a particular text book has 67 per cent positive information and 32 per cent negative. Practically every textbook in the country had no action links, no processes of learning about the environment. This is a common pattern. This is something which we have realized now. How do we take this knowledge base and shifting into some sort of an active learning which the child can understand and do in his own life?

All state textbooks are supposed to be based on the NCERT framework. But when it gets translated at the state level, many changes take place, especially when language translations have to be done. It differs very considerably from one state to another.

You may have a concept in a science book in standard 5 which is fairly complex. The same concept in standard 7 may be on eco-systems and it comes back in Geography at a lower level. So, the science and geography text-book writers have not coordinated their effort to bring about a gradual progression in the learning process on the environment. The years between standard 10 and 12 are the two years when students really make enormous efforts to learn—for obvious reasons, there are Board examinations. When we went back to textbook boards in many states and asked them why they had not introduced learning about the environment, they said they did not want to put in too many 'outside' things. That was the word used by two or three official representatives. We are very concerned about this. If the subject does not get strongly into the state board exams, then it will never be taken seriously.

We had thought that there would be a lot of material on pollution in the textbooks. No, it is not there. It is very scattered, it is very inadequately dealt with, it talks about pollution without saying what is the cause, who makes that pollution, how does that pollution happen, and how does it affect human beings.

We then went into what we could do. We had identified most of these gaps in textbooks at the school level. We found we could not fill these gaps, but only somebody who had done a very exhaustive content analysis of these kinds of textbooks can actually do this. Unfortunately, the Ministry in its knowledge and wisdom asked somebody else to do the phase II study, which meant a lot of this material today has not been used. But we have got an attempt to change textbooks in the phase II study, where we have tried in eight states to change textbooks for standards 5, 6 and 7 in 100 schools each. This is the model. I think this is a good model. In Maharashtra probably it has been done best, because the SCERT there had a deep interaction with us while doing this. We have now got a tentative method of filling these gaps on understanding what ecology and environment mean to school kids.

We have also looked at the college curricula. Botany students at the B. Sc. and M. Sc. levels are still given more marks when they go out into the field for collecting botany specimens and additional marks if they collect rare plants. This has just not changed. They go on collecting the same rare plants. It took many years, for instance, for the medical colleges to stop using frogs for absolutely useless experiments. I happened to be part of the students did an agitation against this, when I was a medical student, and later was given up this practice through the help of BNHS.

There are many of these learning processes which we need to look at to sensitize people. I think this is also part of ecological security. The University Grants Commission (UGC) now has a committee—I happen to be on that committee—which is trying to look at ways to add environment subjects to all the graduate degree courses. The committee is expected to form one common paper for every graduate subject. It is a very difficult task. Now, having done this content analysis up to 12th standard, we know what has happened up to standard 12. Using that as a base, we are trying to decide what sort of things can go into that single paper. It will be a compulsory paper which everybody will have to appear for. This is what the UGC says at the moment. It is a long way from getting implemented, but we are trying to see how this can be done. This will change a huge amount of concepts in terms of environmental learning.

I think we need to use all sorts of methods to bring about this awareness of ecological security. I believe it is very locale-specific. I believe it has to be done for different target groups in different ways. The very tools that you use to do this are very divergent. We are a long way from a success story, but if you do not really move into this—and I am not a pessimist, I am an optimist about this—I believe it can happen, we have seen this happen. In Bharatiya Vidyapeeth, in the 160 schools where we run this programme, we have found it trickling into the community, especially in the rural sector. That is very interesting. In the urban sector one does not get feedback from families, one does not get feedback from teachers. In the rural sector, where we run a slightly different programme, of course, we get enormous feedback.

One starts by running teacher training workshops. Over the last 7 to 8 years we found that even without invitation, if we run a school teacher-training programme in the village community, the Sarpanch and the Panchayat members come on their own. We had posters made for schools which we found hanging in the village square, in market places, on temple walls, which we had not been the ones to put up.

If one goes to Almora and sees Uttara Khand Sewa Nidhi's (UKSN's) programme, which has been environmentalising textbooks, you will find that the knowledge has reached the community, they understand land resources. It makes me feel very optimistic.

When I started saying this earlier, about five years ago, many people said that I should wait till the children become adults and become community leaders. I did not have an answer to this at that time, I thought maybe they were right, maybe it is going to take a long time. But today we realize that it happens very fast, it trickles into homes and community lifestyles. Those of you who have children who come to environment programmes will probably respond by getting conscious of the dos and don'ts, about not wasting water, and so on. Come to one of our schools where we run this programme, and you will find there are no leaky taps, there are no plastic bottles and plastic waste, the school is obviously different from other neighbourhood school. But it has taken seven years of very hard effort. It takes time and effort. It is important to link it to formal curricular processes. If the teacher does not believe in it, it will not happen. If the school principal does not believe in it, it won't happen. The most important thing that we do is that we talk to the district education officer before we start a programme like this. And it works.

Having done this experiment for so many years, we innovative another programme. After listening to teachers' responses we decided to start a diploma in environment education for in-service school teachers. We conduct four batches for 30 to 50 teachers each. The response has been incredible. Many of those teachers are now able to run many environment programmes in their schools on their own.

There are many other interesting things like this. We run fairs. We take a bunch or a cluster of schools in the same area—usually village schools and now also urban schools. We run an environment fair where the kids run dramas, drawing competitions, put up displays, the teachers create environment games and put these things up in a fair. It is a fun thing. Children enjoy this and they learn about the environment. We have also been able to make interpretation centres to do this.

We need a mass environment education movement. It takes a critical mass of people before one can have a political party that will become green, or a politician who will become green. That is where we need to grow. Therefore, my belief is that we need to move away from the NGO models, use those NGO models in formal curricular-based content. There are an enormous number of young people whom we can energize. That is what will bring about ecological security.

15

Institutional Framework for Ecological Security

DILIP K. BISWAS

An institutional framework as needed for ensuring ecological security is closely intertwined with the governance structure. As such, the subject relating to institutional requirements for ecological security should be necessarily discussed as an integral constituent of the governance system.

The Legislature, Executive and the Judiciary are the three important wings of governance. Over the years, elaborate institutional mechanisms at the central and state levels have been set up for framing policies and laws, and for their execution through the administrative machinery and resolution of conflicts through the judiciary at various levels. With the increasing concern for ecological security, a newer set of organizations/agencies to deal with the ecological issues have been added to the governance structure.

However, barring a few exceptions, the existing institutions have not been able to meet the expectations. This is primarily attributable to the infirmities in the institutional framework which include the following:

(i) Most government structures are highly differentiated along sector-wise lines with their tasks compartmentalized within narrow jurisdictions;

(ii) Rules and regulations designed for exercising controls and prohibitions have led to excessive bureaucratisation;

(iii) The governance system is highly centralized. Local bodies are vested with little or no control over development planning and resource generation;

(iv) Despite proliferation of rules and laws covering a gamut of activities, enforcement and monitoring have been lax;

(v) Apathy for regulations, rent-seeking and corruption are among the major impediments in enforcement;

(vi) Command and control measures are predominant rather than incentives for better environmental management practices;

(vii) Ecological issues do not necessarily coincide with the administrative and legal boundaries. The spatial dimensions of the ecological impacts are often ignored in the existing system; and,

(viii) At the policy level, professionals and trained human resources are conspicuously lacking in most of the institutions.

The water management situation in the country is a typical example of the compartmentalized approach and associated deficiencies in the institutional structure. As a result, the quantity of available water has been on the decline and the quality of water has been deteriorating despite a multitude of agencies which are meant to serve as custodians for water management.

For integration of diverse ecological concerns in the development plans, it is necessary to restructure the policy-making and decision-making processes from their vertical-horizontal segmentation to a holistic system. Envisioning the development plans should be based on understanding the interdependence of technical, economic, social and environmental concerns. Alongside, it is necessary to define the responsibilities of various constituents of government and to define a framework within which all policies and programmes of the government and the private sector should be undertaken.

To this end, a national-level body higher than a Ministry should provide direction and guidance to all Ministries. At the national level, the Ministry of Environment under the guidance of a National Environmental Protection Agency (NEPA) needs to translate the policy vision in terms of action points and programmes for implementation through the concerned agencies. The Ministry of Environment has to function as a watchdog to monitor and ensure that the activities of different line Ministries/Departments are in unison with the ecological requirements.

In designing a nodal agency and outlining its functional domain, the policy makers have to bear in mind the 'Allocation of Work' as assigned to various Ministries. For instance, the Ministry of Finance is allocated the work on macro-economic policies relating to taxation and subsidies that impact the environment, but these cannot be taken away from that Ministry and given to the Ministry of Environment. As such, working arrangements need to be devised for incorporating inputs from the Environment Ministry into the economic Ministries.

At the state level a body along the lines of the national body needs to be created for determining critical regional resource use, assessment of resource use, implementation of the national goals, coordinating the functions of agencies involved in different sectors of the local economy and vested local authorities with environmental jurisdiction.

Local authorities, such as the municipal bodies and village councils, and the project authorities would constitute the lowest rung of the institutional ladder. They would play the most important role in micro-planning and in the execution of measures relating to management of commons including land, water and such other natural resources.

The holistic administrative structure will be difficult to achieve in the short run considering the legacies of existing structures and the organization of government. In fact, existing structures have a tendency to resist change and reinforce their positions. However, a holistic paradigm needs to be viewed as an end towards which the design and shape of government structures can be directed. Furthermore, each layer of administration needs to serve as an integral component of one another. In such a system, flow of information and ideas are facilitated allowing better coordination and flexibility. The problem of an escalation in bureaucracy is also controlled as no new channels have to be created and with some modifications and training it ensures better utilisation of the existing staff component.

The administrative mechanisms also require a set of tools and methodologies to work on the pathway to sustainable development. Rules and regulations that incorporate environmental concern with development and growth have to devised, measures to promote sustainable use of resources have to be put in place for implementation and ambiguities and conflicts in policies have to be removed and reconciled. The so-called externalities, which include environmental costs and social costs, have to be incorporated into decision making. Externalities lead to inefficient allocation of resources and their misuse. If the cost of pollution, and its attendant health and environmental hazards, is excluded from the cost considerations of a thermal power plant there will always be the possibility of the plant increasing pollution to enhance its private profits. Therefore, for sustainable development, mechanisms are required to internalize the external costs and benefits. These tools would have the twin objectives of ensuring that environmental and social costs are integrated into cost-benefit analysis and by implication restrict or prevent indiscriminate depletion of natural resources, and simultaneously, they would ensure that the development achieved is optimal in its consumption and production mix.

Effective integration of environmental concerns in the development process will depend on strategies to tackle the problems with the available techniques based on intervention through the national government, provincial authorities, sector-wise agencies or local bodies. To evolve an effective institutional mechanism, the strategies may include the following components:

- *Identification of issues*: This involves recognizing the main environmental and economic issues. The major areas of concern such as soil erosion and degradation, deforestation and bio-diversity loss, urban pollution, water pollution, energy shortage, loss in agricultural productivity or sluggishness of exports, need to be spelt out.
- *Enlistment of bio-physical, social and economic indicators*: The problems are reflected in a variety of ways and their specifications need to be classified in terms of socio-economic parameters, phase of economic development, level of environmental degradation (pollution, emission etc), natural resource base and regeneration and depletion rates of resources.
- *Defining the jurisdictional domain of different agencies*: This entails linking the different aspects of the problems to appropriate levels of intervention. The horizontal and the vertical spread of government departments and agencies need to be listed and their functional responsibilities connected to each indicator recognized. There could be overlaps between agencies and these too have to be identified. The purpose of such an exercise is to ensure that the appropriate level is made responsible for implementing a specific policy and to remove bottlenecks of inter-agency coordination. An understanding of this will also be useful in assessing the enforceability of various policy options.

- *Identification and selection of policy options*: Policy options have to be identified and linked to the administrative mechanisms that exist. The objective of the exercise would be to ensure that policy measures do not remain mere statements of intent but translate into actions.
- *Assessment of likely impact of the policies*: The actual impact of policies may take time to discern given the time lag in implementation and gathering of data. However, the probable impact can be assessed on the basis of past trends and data. Some policies may have positive results in terms of growth but can lead to negative environmental consequences in the short run. On the other hand, positive environmental impact of policy may lead to short run retardation in growth rates. The trade-offs involved and the time dimension of the impact can become an effective tool for weighing the options and devising corrective actions.

The Brundtland Commission stressed in its report that, 'Governments must begin now to make the key national, economic and sectorial agencies directly responsible and accountable for ensuring that their policies, programmes, and budget supports development that is economically and ecologically sustainable' (*Our Common Future*, 1987). Development planning has hitherto been based on aggregation of sectorial plans linked to broad economic objectives set by the planners and coordinated through a central planning body, while macro-economic policies are dictated by the Finance Ministry. If environmental concerns are to be integrated in the economic policy making matrix, we need to understand the various dimensions and connotations of sustainable development as distinct from the conventional development model as also the operational requirements for both the policy making and implementing agencies.

16

Natural Resource Management and Ecological Security

P. S. Ramakrishnan

Natural Resources and Ecological Security is a very difficult subject, of which food security is an important component. Much of the natural resources in the flat lands of the country having been decimated, it is simpler to speak about natural resources. There are some still left in the uplands, in the mountain regions, which pose a variety of special and unique problems in terms of our ability to understand those systems and in order to be able to make sense out of what we are trying to do in the mountain areas.

Looking at the country as a whole from an ecological perspective, I would classify Indian society into three categories: (1) the urban people, (2) the people living in the rural areas, who are still traditional in the sense that they live fairly close to nature and natural resources, although there is very little in terms of natural resources still left in the plains, and (3) the mountain people, who are very closely linked with nature and natural resources and can still largely be considered to be part of a cultural landscape—cultural landscape as distinct from the bio-physical landscape and the human landscape. It is very difficult to make a clear distinction between where one ends and the other starts. It is a very integrated unit in which people are still living, despite the fact that we have already caused a lot of deforestation. When I say 'we', I mean those of us who are living in the plains. We have caused a lot of deforestation over a period of time, right from the British times, and even more so during the first few decades after independence by over-exploiting the resources, for which, for very strange reasons, the blame is put on the poor hill people. This is what I heard when I was working in the north-eastern region during the 1970s. If you ask a bureaucrat the reason for the deforestation, he will insist that the 'shifting agricultural farmers are damaging the forests and destroying everything'.

What is unique about the mountain systems? Before detailing the mountain systems, let me add that food security has got two components. The first component concerns all of us. Ten years ago if one talked to an agricultural scientist, he would say that we do not have a problem, we are self-sufficient in food and the country is proud of the fact that we have achieved self-sufficiency, that at one point of time we were getting food as aid from different countries, and now the green revolution has done wonders for us and we are doing very well. No doubt about that. Much of the green revolution is in two major states, Punjab and Haryana as well as in a part of western Uttar Pradesh, and it has done well. There is no denying the fact that India has been doing very well.

Around the 1990s, if one talked to an agricultural scientist he would look askance and insist that whatever India had been doing was the greatest thing it had ever done and there was no looking back. Five years ago, towards the end of the last century, the realisation suddenly dawned that the yield that the green revolution had started had reached a plateau and there was great concern that the yield may in fact be going down. There is a whole variety of reasons for it. India was involved in an inter-academy project involving three countries—India, China and the United States—and one of the conclusions arising from that project was that the yield was not only going down but that there was no alternate technology in place in order to push up the yield. This was largely related to land degradation.

One of our studies happened to be in Haryana and so we had an opportunity to look very closely at the farmers' perception of the green revolution agriculture as it is currently operating. One conclusion that emerges is that the yield is going down. On the other hand, a whole variety of tinkering was done by a number of non-governmental organizations to develop what they termed 'organic agriculture', but it has not made much of an impact. If at all there has been some impact, it has been very patchy. Therefore, one concern that we have, particularly when talking about 60 per cent of the population living in the flatlands of the country, is, how do we make this green revolution agriculture more sustainable than what it is at this point of time?

What is so special about the mountain systems? In India, we are very uniquely placed in the sense that we have got this great mountain range called the Himalaya in the northern part, which determines almost everything that happens in the northern plains, apart from determining what happens to the region itself. On the other side, there is the southern part of the country, the Ghat region, the Western Ghat and the Eastern Ghat. The Western Ghat, in particular, determines to a very large extent what happens in the flatlands of peninsular India. Therefore, what we do or what we do not do with respect to our mountains is also going to have considerable impact in terms of the food security or the ecological security of the rest of the country.

We know that mountains are much more fragile than the flatlands. Compared to the flatlands, bio-diversity is concentrated in the mountains and the people are dependent upon this bio-diversity for their livelihood needs. Therefore, if there is going to be any tinkering with the bio-diversity, it is likely to cause social disruption, something that is already happening in some parts of the mountainous region. If the social disruptions are slow, taking a longer period of time, society adjusts itself and is able to make adaptations in order to cope up with these uncertainties. If these uncertainties are very abrupt or happen all of a sudden and on a larger scale, the system breaks down.

One major activity is deforestation, which is being caused mainly by us, the people living in the plains, and not by the mountain people. The mountain people get involved for a whole variety of reasons, but the key drivers are operating from the plains of the country. There are a whole series of problems—land use changes happening at a very rapid rate, soil infertility, rapid soil desertification, and declining water sources. Water resources and the quality of water available to the mountain people also has have their impact on what comes down to the plains, to the river systems, and so on.

One finds a large amount of abandoned terraces all over the mountain region. Since the natural mechanism of traditional knowledge around which agricultural systems have been built over a period of time, over many hundreds of years, is no more possible, and since the forests have started degrading, the people dependent upon these forests for their agricultural activities are leaning more and more towards energy subsidies being promoted by the people living in the plains. Energy subsidy creates its own problems. It has a cyclical effect. There is population migration. Many of us are aware of the fact that the central Himalayan region has got a money order economy because able bodied men are migrating out from the region, causing eco-system instability and a whole variety of problems. The people living in the mountains are getting disheartened with what is happening.

What is it that we can do in order to be able to set the system right? It is a very difficult task and this has been one of my concerns. I would like to share some of my experiences as a scientist and what I feel can be done to find a way out of this dark tunnel.

Here, it is necessary to clarity that there are two types of knowledge systems. One that we study in our schools and colleges and in the universities, which we all do, and that is formal knowledge based on the hypothetical-deductive method that is de-linked from the human element. We make all kinds of generalisations and these generalisations are applied across the board, irrespective of the social systems that one is talking about.

The other knowledge system which is well understood is the traditional knowledge system, based on societal perceptions, and these societal perceptions take a very long period to accumulate and it is an experiential process. As an experiential process accumulated over a period of time, it has got a very strong human element attached to it.

When one discusses formal or traditional ecological knowledge, very often people tend to relate to it, linking it in their minds with the Ayurveda system or medicinal plants, and so on. But there is much more to it than traditional knowledge centred on medicinal plants. There are a whole variety of ways in which societies manipulate ecological systems. This manipulation of the ecological systems determines what they can get out of that system in a sustainable manner. In other words, they manipulate the system by altering the ecological processes—the social process and the ecological process inter-link with one another—and the system is able to make adaptations to the uncertainties that are arising in the environment or the changes that are happening over a period of time. The people are able to maintain a reasonable level of productivity till we intervene and try to screw up things for them. That is what has been happening in recent times.

Formal knowledge does not need any detailed explanation. Therefore, when you talk to a traditional ecologist, he understands it as having to create and sustain the bio-mass, that there has to be a forest cover, using the thumb rule that there must be 33 per cent forest cover. This is very important to sustain the nutrient state of our system and to enable the water balance and the bio-diversity to be maintained.

But if you talk to mountain farmers or hill persons, they will not understand what an eco-system is; they are so much a part of the eco-system, part of a socio-ecological system. There is nothing called a social system there and there is nothing called an ecological system. In spite of all the problems we have created for them, they still perceive themselves as part of a socio-ecological system. What is the uniqueness of this socio-ecological system? This socio-ecological system has all along had the capacity to adapt to changes that were happening in the environment. These changes have been rather slow and, therefore, they have been able to adapt to those changes. This socio-ecological system is not a static system, it is a dynamic system, both in space and time, which attaches itself to a whole variety of situations and that is what is called the sustainability of the system, and that is what contributes to the sustainability of the system.

In order to contribute to the sustainability of the system, they use a whole variety of knowledge systems that they have accumulated over a period of time. Those knowledge systems cut across anthropology, sociology, socio-economics and cultural dimensions. They operate at a descriptive level. To give one example, if you ask a tribal farmer what he would do if he had a stomach problem, the answer would be that he uses the juice of a certain plant.

If you ask a farmer why he practices agriculture in a particular manner, he cannot articulate a response. That is what I mean by the process level operation of traditional ecological knowledge. In the north-eastern region, a farmer may grow something like 30 or 40 species in a two-hectare land area. Looking at it in a casual manner, one would presume that some seeds are thrown here and there and whatever comes up is harvested and used. But on looking closely and taking time to study the system, it will be found that on top of the hill they use certain species and on the bottom of the hill they will use certain other species. This is a process of social selection operating within that society, whereby the crops that are emphasized on top of the slope: are very efficient in terms of nutrient use, and those crops used at the bottom of the slope are mainly suckers. This is done because there is a nutrient gradient on a hill slope at the top of the hill slope there is very little nutrient and if they put a sucker there, that crop will not do well in economic terms. Therefore, they try to move that crop down to the base of the slope. This is one example to illustrate how the process operates.

This is the traditional ecological knowledge operating at the process level. And understanding this traditional ecological knowledge is extremely important for managing the resources for the people living in the mountains and for the welfare of society. It is important for them because their livelihood is dependent upon it. It is important for us from the angle of agricultural bio-diversity, which is a feeder to modern agriculture, being practised in Haryana and Punjab or the Green Revolution agriculture whether it is by the traditional breeding procedures followed by the scientists or bio-technology. If you look at the life span of an agricultural variety used in Haryana and Punjab, it does not have a life span of more than four or five years. After four or five years, problems start surfacing with that cultivar and it has to be replaced by something else. That something else is available only in the traditional agricultural systems that the mountain societies are operating at this point of time. Therefore, even from a purely selfish angle, it is extremely important that we do our best to conserve the bio-diversity. But conserving bio-diversity is not possible unless we are able to give a sustainable livelihood, a better quality of life, to the mountain people themselves.

It is also necessary to reckon with uncertainties in the environment, a phenomenon with which the traditional societies living in the mountain regions have to deal with. We did a study in the North-Eastern region concerning largely shifting agricultural farmers. They do other forms of agriculture as well, like valley rice farming, home gardens, and so on, but mostly they practice shifting cultivation. We found that they try to modify their shifting agriculture in a variety of ways. This is not something that happened in one day; it takes several years to make it happen. They move into a rotational bush fallow system, which is again shifting agriculture, and then eventually they come to a sedentary system because they want to make money by being close to the market centre. Therefore, they make an adaptation in the cropping pattern to cope with the uncertainties which they face. Uncertainties arise on account of distance from the market centre, as also from the availability of forest resources. So, adaptations are made in terms of the natural resources that are available.

Traditional ecological knowledge has undergone a whole variety of changes, which can be observed at any given point of time. Looking at a particular system, you find the traditional shifting agriculture being practiced. In another direction, one finds that a lesser known crop, a leguminous species, has been introduced into the cropping system. It is of food value to the local communities. That is a species which, as analyses have shown, fixes something like 250 kilogram of nitrogen per hectare per year. They try to increase the component of this leguminous species, which is also a food crop, into their system for improving the soil fertility in the absence of forest cover. At the same time, they are able to make adaptations both in space and time with respect to their traditional ecological knowledge.

This is happening all the time. What we have done is to break this evolutionary process. This breaking down process is going to get even more aggravated in the context of global change. What is global change? Very often people confuse global change with climate change—there is much more to global change than climate change. Land use change and land degradation is a very important component. Biological invasion is another component. Arising from all this is the bio-diversity depletion that is happening. Climate change is reversible. It can be reversed over the next 30 or 40 years by taking quick technological decisions. It is also possible to reverse biological invasion, but it is much more difficult and will cost a lot of money. Land use, land degradation and the associated bio-diversity depletion, are happening all the time. And bio-diversity, once lost, is not replaceable.

Climate change as a phenomenon is not easy to sell to a developing country. But, in the context of landuse degradation, biological invasion, the exotic weeds coming into this area, and looking at it as an integrated whole, then probably many people will be able to appreciate it.

What will be the impact of global change? The impact of global change is as follows: it is creating a crisis and this crisis is a much bigger crisis than the kind of crises habitual to traditional societies. This results in the absence of an effective response from traditional societies, particularly the weaker sections of society. When I refer to traditional societies, I include the people in the rural areas and the plains. Therefore, the system starts breaking down with no alternative in place. They are used to this part of the curve, where the change is very slow, and adaptive changes have to be made to manage the resources. They get enough time to experiment. There are institutional adjustments that take place all the time in order to be able to cope with the crisis that arises. As long as the crisis is a slow process and it is not very abrupt, the people are able to make changes. Once it becomes more abrupt, it will get aggravated in the context of global change and globalization to a certain extent.

I was involved in a study of globalization *vis-à-vis* agriculture and one of the conclusions was that the developing countries are going to be more affected than the developed world, and within the developing countries, the poorer sections of society are going to be much greater victims than the developed sections of society.

And what does all this mean? It means that we need to have a different kind of approach towards natural resources management. So far, have been using traditional ecological approaches in order to manage the natural resources. A forester will say that this is what he has studied and this is how he has to manage the resources. However, this does not work. We need to have social dimensions integrated into the bio-physical dimension, we need to keep the economic perspective in view and we even need to incorporate the socio-cultural dimensions. We are a multi-cultural society and making generalisations on the basis of a standard approach and a standard way of development is not likely to prove successful. The key factors that connect all these things are the kind of institutions that we create.

An example is the very interesting experiment going on in Nagaland under a project which arose out of some research that we did in the north-eastern region over the past thirty years. The Canadians came and put it under the India-Canada Environment Facility, with a fund of a few million dollars. The aim is to involve the local communities living in about 1,200 villages and find a solution to the problem of shifting agriculture. The first five years of this interesting and innovative project have been completed and the results are unfolding.

Now, what is the key for the success of that project? One thousand and two hundred villages were given the option by the government, in their wisdom, to form village development boards in agreement with the value system of each one of the thirty-five or thirty-six tribes which form the state of Nagaland. In other words, the village development boards were formed not through a fiat from above and not through the so-called democratic process but by means of a value system with which the local communities are able to relate. There are thirty five different ways of forming village development boards in that kind of situation, but all of them have got one function, that is, to use the rural development money. That is one of the keys as far as the success of that programme is concerned.

It was possible not only because the right kind of institutions were created, but also because the ecological processes and the sociological processes were recognized to be an integrated whole. Considering all this as an integrated whole is very important for managing the local resources and thereby providing sustainable livelihood to the local community. There are more than 300 or 400 test plots established right across Nagaland where this experiment has been going on. I am not suggesting that this is a great success. There are problems in that kind of activity. But, even if there is 25 per cent, or even 10 per cent, success, that is a great move forward, compared to what we have not been able to achieve during the last hundred years.

In understanding sustainability issues it is wrong to use formal knowledge for arriving at conclusions. Formal knowledge is either bio-physical or social without any connectivity between the two. In the bio-physical, it is physics, chemistry or biology, and in the social it is anthropology, economics or geography. It is only in recent decades that people have started to look at the interface between the natural and social sciences and people have started realizing that at some point of time integration is extremely important.

What does that show? It shows that many myths are propagated in scientific literature—such as, population and poverty is responsible for land degradation and natural resource depletion; shifting agricultural farmers are responsible for land degradation; the carrying capacity of grasslands is determined by the number of cattle or sheep per unit of land. All this comes from hearsay, which gets repeated time and again without scientific verification. Recently some of us were involved in an international programme under IHDP (International Human Dimension Programme) to survey about 200 research papers published during the last hundred years, some of which were top quality. Nowhere was there concrete evidence to suggest that population and poverty are responsible for land degradation.

The point I am trying to make is that for getting to the root of the problem to address the sustainability issues in a meaningful manner, it is necessary to get the record straight right from the very beginning, even in terms of what it is that causes land degradation. There are evidences to suggest now that land degradation is caused by faulty decisions, incentives, market mechanisms, whether it is national or international market mechanisms. In a recent study in the western Ghat region, Kodagu district, where coffee is extensively grown, incentives were provided to the farmers by the government to increase the coffee plantations, when the coffee crop in Brazil failed a few years ago. First of all, the tree cover was removed to plant more coffee bushes. Then, coffee started extending into the drier zones in the Western Ghats. It resulted in large-scale land degradation and deforestation in that area.

So, for an objective analysis of a problem, it is more necessary now than ever before to realize that we need to get into the interface area of research. Moving into the drier zones would be unsustainable; everybody knows that coffee cannot be grown there. But people moved in that direction out of greed and within a few years the coffee plantations collapsed in the drier zone.

What are the kinds of possibilities that exist in terms of sustainable development? Here is a broad typology of an agricultural system about which many of us do not know anything, because we have all been enamoured with the so-called green revolution of agriculture, a monoculture of one crop species with high energy subsidies. There are very interesting systems operating even today in the hill areas in terms of sustainable agriculture. I am not saying that they are sustainable any longer. Some of them in the remote areas may still be sustainable. But, it is necessary to keep our minds open to understand formal knowledge and the traditional ecological knowledge that has been responsible for creating these systems, which have the merit of being based on recycling of the resources internally available within the system rather than being dependent on external subsidy.

One other example is from a programme at my university called the Sustainable Soil Fertility Management Programme. It is an international programme. The tea garden people came to us that the yield of tea has started going down, the tea bush, which has a life span of fifty to sixty years, has over a period of time come down to 20 or 25 years. In other words, earlier they had to replace the tea bush every fifty years, which they were not willing to do, and now they are forced to replace it every 20 or 25 years because of land degradation. What is it that we could do?

We looked at the traditional knowledge that is available with the local communities, identified earthworm as an indicator species, a key-stone species within the eco system, and using that species we tried to manipulate the soil bio-diversity using organic residues. To cut a long story short, an in situ technology was designed for the tea gardeners by which the input of inorganic fertilizers came down anywhere between 30 to 50 per cent. This was a break-through, as it brought down the organic residue management within the system, acted as a buffering ability to reduce the input of fertilizers. This technology was eventually accepted and has spread all over the place. The tea garden people have adopted it to some extent, perhaps more so in China and in Sri Lanka also the tea people have adopted that technology.

There is a great deal of knowledge that is available within the system, which needs to be understood and scientifically validated and integrated. Take the case of vermi-culture as a technology which is being proposed by the NGO community. Actually, vermi-culture has limited value. The reason is, first, that vermi-culture is not standardized and hence some material is good, while the other is pretty bad. Second, vermi-culture material is usually based on exotic worms which, over a period of time, destroy the natural soil bio-diversity, making it unsustainable. Third, if all things are taken care of, vermi-culture material has got nutrients in such a fragile form that once the first rains come most of the nutrients get washed out of the system and are not available for the crops. These problems have to be understood and addressed.

For instance, one of the things we learnt from the inter-academy project between India, China and the United States is that in Haryana vermi-culture is being propagated but the farmers are not willing to accept it because of all the uncertainties associated with that technology.

What are the other existing possibilities? There are possibilities that we have been exploring, particularly from the point of view of the mountain societies, but that does not mean it is exclusive to the mountain societies. It is equally applicable to the people in the flatlands. What we have done in the flatlands is to follow this rule: if you want to go to the other side of the mountain, if I were to use a simile, create a tunnel and create a highway. That is what we have done with modern agriculture. It has created problems. The only way to ameliorate the problems is to go for other pathways that are available for agricultural development. One of them is to follow the ecological contour. Many of the agro-forestry systems come under that category. If you go to a tribal farmer in the north-east region, or even in Kumaon or Garhwal region, to give him these technologies, it may not be acceptable. The farmer has got a lot of traditional ecological knowledge. This knowledge has to be validated and we have to build upon that knowledge, step by step, in order to be able to make it acceptable to society. Once the farmer is empowered over the next five or ten years, let him make his own decisions as to what he wants to do, rather than trying to force something which has been time and again tried and rejected.

In the case of the Kumaon and Garhwal region, two agricultural scientists wrote a paper in 1920, suggesting the kinds of technologies that need to be give to the people there in order to improve their livelihood. In 1968, two other persons wrote a similar paper. In fact, between those forty years or so, there was not much change in agriculture and the system had only deteriorated. So, the people were not been given a viable technological alternative to what they have been doing for the last forty or fifty years.

The same applies to forestry. Recently, we did an analysis of bio-sphere reserves and it was realized that there is a big divide between what is ideal in terms of bio-sphere reserve management and in terms of what is actually happening on the ground by the forest managers, who are the bio-sphere reserve managers. How do we treat the gap? In order to bridge the gap we need to look beyond sericulture. We need to look into the ecological issues, socio-economic issues and cultural issues. And how do we go about doing that? One of the studies that we did was that traditional societies, the rural communities, retain socially selected species. In the central Himalayan region these are called 'panch', there are two or three species of oaks, which has got very important value in terms of determining the soil fertility, in terms of alternating the nutrient property of the system, in terms of improving the water balance within the soil and making water available during the drier seasons, in order to be able to do whatever kind of land use activities that they want to do, or contribute towards increased bio-diversity. The local people are dependent upon this bio-diversity for their various economic activities, resulting in agro-eco system, rehabilitation of agricultural development on eco-system rehabilitation.

Now, if you go into the root cause of the Chipko movement, it emerges that the Chipko movement did not take place because some contractors wanted to cut down the trees but because during the last hundred years we have systematically eliminated the 'panch', which is socially and culturally valued by the local community and which has got considerable ecological implications from the point of view of the stability of the eco-system as a whole.

When the G.B. Pant University was established, I did a variety of experiments and ended up with a shopping list of more than hundred from a whole variety of sources and then I said that let me go to the local community and ask them what their expectations are from the G.B. Pant Institute of Himalayan Environment and Development. They did not ask for a shopping list of hundred. They simply asked us to provide water during the dry season. And this is what we did by the rain water harvesting system right across the Himalayas, from the north-west to the north-east right up to Nagaland. And it did wonders. You can see the cascading effect in terms of development. People came to us and said that this is the kind of development that they wanted because by getting water, soil fertility had increased and they were able to grow the kinds of crops which they were not able to grow earlier. If you combine traditional knowledge and traditional technology, then the result is even better.

What is required then is a management strategy which is adaptive instead of being pre-determined and the management plan should enable adjustments to be made in managing the natural resources. The task of linking up natural resources management with sustainable livelihood of the local communities is a very difficult undertaking. To be able to do that, institutional arrangements play a very important role in terms of determining community participation.

17

Media for Ecological Security

N. Bhaskara Rao

Ecology as a Concern

Ecological security is viewed more as a talking concept rather than as a fundamental issue of societal concern or a way of life. It is confined to academics, NGOs and is a part of global politics. In the process, ecology is being perceived as a responsibility of the government, not so much of the people and civil society.

The culture, customs, rituals and traditions, which have sustained ecological security over the centuries, are themselves under threat as those virtues were never understood, so that they could be harnessed. In fact, they were looked down upon and viewed as not in sync with modernity and development endeavours. Today we live in an altogether a different culture, a 'mass culture' where lifestyles are sustained by the mass media, by media criteria and media judgment. It is all across, not just in politics, that such a mass culture has evolved and is being groomed. The agenda of a nation, the lifestyles of the people, are set by the mass media. That is why the pertinence of ecological security and media today. The fact that priority is not given to ecological issues is too well known and is too obvious. Worse, there is not even an understanding of the linkages with larger issues which have to do with sustaining the development process, quality of life and, of course, the peace and tranquility of a generation.

Short-term interests dominate, not so much the long-term concerns. Our planning, our policies, our public debates, all have a temporal outlook and are too seasonal. 'Me' and 'mine' concerns, rather than 'we' and 'us' dominate, not so much concern for the community. The 'either you or me' syndrome is how Vandana Shiva has called this phenomenon.

Respect and caring for the community has declined; patience and tolerance are no longer preferred virtues. Relationships matter and mould our very outlook, as our 'identities are not singular' and we are not 'one dimensional', as pointed out by Vandana Shiva, who believes an understanding of interconnections and interdependence is missing today. She also reminds us of the linkage between 'cultural diversity' and ecological security.

Saving was a virtue yesterday, today it is spending that gives one a social standing. Spend and spend more, by borrowing if necessary, as if there is 'no rainy days' any more. Saving is no longer a criterion. The ones who borrow are better off. This phenomenon is the antithesis of ecological security. That is why M.S. Swaminathan reminds us of Mahatma Gandhi's 'Needs vs. Greed' paradigm.

As Ashok Khosla has said, the 'premise that government will take care of everything', has become a fallacy and is deceptive. As a result of increased dependence on government, citizens have become passive; robust civil society is no longer a hallmark. It is the dependency syndrome that runs across the psyche today.

Voluntary and cooperative endeavours are no longer viewed as a virtue today. No single individual or group is seriously engaged in restraining excessive consumption patterns. Rituals and religions did this in the earlier years. If society itself is confused as to how to discriminate between the desirable and not so desirable, how then could the media be expected to do so?

The way the financial budget is prepared and hyped it is as if one is living from year to year. There is commitment and concern to come up with a balance sheet on ecological security as a 'budget for the decade'. After all, economics and ecology are often concerned with the same aspects although in a different context; that is, the resource availability, supply and demand, competition and the 'costs' involved. While corporations are expected to indicate 'risk' possibility, and cigarette packets must have obligatory advice on health risks, why should national policies not indicate future damage assessment or implications to ecological security?

Amrita Patel has referred to certain 'major links' that connect micro and macro factors involved in ecological security. The media has a special role in this regard. But forces and factors that drive and determine public priorities and mindsets and the very lifestyles need to be understood and addressed. The linkages between pattern of consumption, lifestyle and ecological security need to be explained. Behavioural change is what sustains lifestyles. We should be addressing not the woods at the cost of forest. Without such an understanding and a shift in values, only marginal changes, cosmetic ones can be expected. Mass communication channels are of course one such influencing factor and force. Since the change expected is attitudinal and behavioural, a linkage of media coverage with local-specific and ground-level activities is critical, in fact, essential.

The media plays varied roles; it sustains, enriches, endorses, enables and empowers. The mass media are change agents, they set the public agendas. In recognition of their special role, the mass media are described as the Fourth Estate and a Watchdog. But on behavioural change, the media are supportive, not a substitute, for action or implementation. In fact, where attitudinal and value change is involved, the mass medias' role is limited and such a role could be either way if not linked with civil society at the grassroots.

It is in fact a double-edged instrument. The influence or effect could be positive or negative. Which side drives fast or works more is what we need to be concerned about. The electronic media, particularly television in all its *avataars*, has changed the very scope and character of the media's role–even more in situations riddled with inequalities, imbalances and differences.

Mass Media Concerns

The dependence of media operations is based on profit-driven economics. The consumerist model of the mass media is one of priority being given to the 'deep pockets'; the community or society do not matter as much as the 'consumers'. That is why the media's best allies are consumerism, greed of the people, government and the divides in the society. The media is not concerned with the impact and implications of what is being presented today on the quality of life, lifestyles and value systems today, tomorrow, the day or year after.

How little ecology matters to the mass media is too evident, except perhaps when some dramatics are involved. Complex issues have less chance of figuring in the news than simple or dramatic ones. Newspapers spend hardly 10 per cent of their revenue for origination of news because complex issues call for more effort and expense.

Scare and scandal stand as priorities and are hyped rather than concern for a solution or resolution. This latter approach would require distinct discipline in journalistic outlook, skills and capabilities.

For the media government matters more than civil society and, of course, commerce and corporations matter even more. And government more often means politics and party politics at that. This is the typical 'common denomination' approach, for it is the numbers (viewers) that matter more than prompting of action or following issues up to their logical end. Trivialization, not serious insights or complexities–that is what television is all about. And ecological security would appear to be too complex.

Is public media a cause or the effect? Is TV the 'mother of all cynicisms' as some one described it recently? Vandana Shiva has termed it the 'negative culture'. Are we better informed as citizens today and also wiser and able to discriminate between good and bad? For, we are certainly better exposed to the media. Is the media a public utility, a public service or is it also a business enterprise in the conventional mould of profit maximization? Is that why it has become 'real estate'-concerned rather than remaining the conventional 'fourth' estate? Is it more of a 'marketing media' rather than 'mass media'?

To whom is it accountable? Should it be accountable at all? To whom should it be accountable? Should it be accountable to the viewers, the readers, the advertisers, the proprietors or to the government?

It is 'what sells' rather than 'what makes the difference' that is important. Equity concerns are only marginal. That is how it is that 'ratings' matter, not impact or implications of what is published or broadcast. That is why I said the country is in a 'TRP Trap', the ratings have misled the nation with wrong priorities and taken the media into a common denominator route, rather than to plurality and diversity. The new social realities flow from this illusionary phenomenon. Playing upon differences is more important, not conflict resolution, for conflict resolution calls for different kinds of journalistic concerns and capabilities.

There is an inherent hypocrisy involved in this. Take the example of a movie director professing peace while promoting gory tales; parents rudely criticizing children for rudeness; TV taking up occasional and isolated coverage on ecology. It is the same as George Bush sending food packets to Basra or Baghdad three weeks after the carpet bombing. That is why credibility and role modelling go together.

The more children see TV, the more they believe certain phenomena and the more they ape them, even years later when they grow old. This is the 'imitation effect' of the news media is as well as the entertainment media. Such an effect is even more when it is negative and associated with deviant behaviour. That is why more is not necessarily merrier.

While the need of the hour is an alliance of people, the modern media has often been attributed the effect of creating alienation. Numbness or unconcern is what the media is credited with promoting for rather than providing enlightenment or enrichment. If unrestrained consumerism is bad for ecology, as it stands the media could be said to be both the cause and effect of the decline in ecological security. On this, in fact, the media are not even passive or neutral. Preserving or conserving is not in the media's interest, going by its current priorities. Consumerism is the premise and preoccupation of the media, as if that is the sole means and end. That is why I say that despite all the potential, the mass media today are perhaps more a threat to ecological security than the contrary. Individually, journalists are as much concerned about the decaying ecology, for they have a lot more access to information on policies. But perhaps they are not as much concerned about its implications and impact. Even more, today they are helpless. That is what media culture is all about. I am afraid that we should not expect much change in the role of the media for a sustained support of ecological security.

But then the governments need to be blamed more for allowing and even encouraging unrestrained consumerism with their policies. The media cannot be blamed for helping markets or in promoting what is allowed and encouraged to be produced. If governments themselves remain insensitive to ecological security, what can be expected from the media? In fact, the media sees such situations as opportunities and takes advantage for itself.

Why do I say that the mass media is more of a threat today for ecological security? The Indian media scene has gone through a dramatic shift recently both in terms of content and control. While media content is more and more market driven, control has now shifted. Today advertising and market research in many ways determine the scope of the mass media.

Let us look at the basis for this statement. First, the share of advertising in the total revenue of the media has been on the increase from that of a 'supplementary' (25-30%) nature some decades ago, to that of a 'supportive' one (45-55%) in 2002. In fact, in the case of television channels, advertising has been a 'primary source' (50-70%) of their sustenance, 'determining' their priorities and preoccupations. Even in the case of some big newspapers, revenue from advertising constitutes as high as 60 per cent of total revenue. The recent boom in the media in India is often attributed to advertising. Advertising today sustains and steers the media although PR is now eroding into the role of advertising.

Second, advertising through newspapers and television today is mostly by multinationals and big corporations engaged in manufacturing consumer products. In fact, the top fifteen advertisers account for three-fourths of the advertising revenue of newspapers and television channels. The top brands being advertised in the media belong to these corporations. There has been a wave of foreign brands recently–all giving a big boost to the media as well as to consumerism in such a way that, as a country, we cannot reverse it even if we want to. And yet no one in the country seems to be bothered about this trend.

Third, the advertising agency business in the country has been getting concentrated in fewer and fewer hands during the last couple of years. The top five advertising agencies, with major holdings outside the country, account for well over half of advertising business in the country and this has been on the increase. Little over half of Indian advertising now is accounted for by overseas-based agencies, whose majority control is in the hands of foreigners. These agencies are now either answerable to private groups based abroad or to dollar-trading stock markets in London or New York.

Fourth, and not least, market research is a basis for proliferation of brands and consumerism as well as for the preoccupation and priorities of the media and the very scope and character of advertising. Until a few years ago India had about six or seven market research agencies owned mostly by Indians. Today, the top seven or eight market research agencies, accounting for more than two-thirds of research, have already been either taken over by a foreign corporate or these have acquired significant interest in them. In fact, with the recent mergers and acquisitions, a certain monopolistic trend is already evident in this sphere which has an annual turnover of over Rs.350 crores. And yet our media echoes them day in and day out. Together, they determine the priorities and preoccupations of the Indian mass media now.

More specifically, market research agencies are the ones which also conduct 'readership' surveys and 'rating' of television viewership and thereby directly influence advertising agencies as well as the media on their programme priorities. The point is that the methodology being followed for readership surveys and TV ratings is not without bias in favour of the sponsors and subscribers. (As one of those involved in launching India-specific readership and rating studies 25 years ago, I feel guilty for what is happening today, particularly the way the findings of these surveys are being used both by newspapers and TV channels.) The 'TRP trap', as I call the phenomenon, has larger and longer range implications for India than we seem to realize. The distortions are already evident today in our media scene. How can these distortions be expected to be corrected? Entertainment audiences also contain many who do not always patronize what they say they prefer. Television ratings are not a true reflection, but an illusion, a media illusion. But then, illusions have become part of modern life. Remote control now gives the illusion to TV viewers of the 'power to control'.

Fifth, with the media becoming more and more complex and also specialized, two 'new' mediating function have emerged since 2000 with serious consequences for the very nature and character of the Fourth Estate. Both these functions of media planning and public relations, in a way, encroach into the core prerogatives of media functionaries and their 'editorial commands'. And the fact that both these functions have become corporatised with foreign agencies having managing control, should cause even more concern in the country before it is too late. The media planners are the ones involved these days in buying wholesale space and time for advertising and selling the same retail on their own terms.

In the case of 'public relations', the scope of these 'experts' implies a certain undermining or interference in the functioning, particularly of reporters and editors, as the function of PR is to ensure coverage for a particular viewpoint or otherwise. The 'disinformation' being talked about recently is a part of this new phenomenon. Today, majority control of these PR corporations in India, some six or seven leading ones operating nationally, is with foreign agencies. In fact, some of these have entered India as a part of one or the other advertising agency with an existing majority foreign equity. The majority of these PR agencies mostly cater (directly or indirectly) to the interests of foreign corporations or their collaborators in India. Many Indian concerns, including some public utilities, now avail these PR agencies to make their presence in the media, as if it is a compulsion. At a time when the need is for more introspection within, the media has become touchy about any critical appraisal from outside.

Mindsets

The media is not an end in itself; it could at best be a means towards something. It could help sustain larger concerns and be supportive of a movement towards ecological security. But this assumes deliberate sharing of the concern by those in the media. Ecological security is to do with a way of life; it is a holistic concept, not an isolated one. It is not seasonal. It is not amenable to an 'event centered' approach, or even to a 'time-bound' campaign approach. But that also needs to get into the media. So, eco-security has remained on the agenda. Some celebrities in the USA last week targeted Citi Group for its environmental record by asking Citi Group credit-card holders to cut up their cards to stop support to projects that jeopardize endangered forests and drive global warning. This is a good example. Once this gets coverage, it is expected to prompt many others towards similar goals.

Mere awareness is not enough, credible concerns and behavioural change is what is needed, and for that, source credibility is an imperative. Different models of getting media attention, not any single one, need to be adopted. And even more, linkages with action or a follow up on the ground–at individual and community levels–need to be ensured. Generating larger concern is necessary to persuade governments to take effective action. The media could help towards this aim.

Take the campaign for CNG (compressed natural gas) and the difference it has made to Delhi's pollution levels. Continued media coverage led to such policy intervention. But the campaign on discouraging plastic packaging and plastic bags did not take off despite legal provisions. Revelations on the adverse effects of asbestos or DDT, for example, get good coverage in the media, as these originate outside the country and are based on studies by the WHO. But to what effect, since there is neither any follow up nor any local relevance of such coverage? Such findings need repositioning. Swajal's PIL (public interest litigation) in Uttaranchal–community awareness and participation in Garwal toxin–is yet another example. There are several such good cases but these have not become 'media stories'. The 'frightening' and 'forewarning' approach to highlight linkage is far more suitable for the media. So also the cost of not acting today on certain ecological security issues; it should be possible to present such issues to the media in terms of economics, business, industry and loss and gain concerns.

The recent Bottled Water Controversy (by the Centre for Science & Environment) is a good example of the scare approach to policy change. The 'Zoo scam' in Punjab made banner headlines, but the thrust was corruption, as the headlines screamed 'wildlife wardens loot crores'. There are so many such instances of death of endangered animals, and yet this has not led to a larger, national-level movement.

Sensitizing not just the media, but the society itself at large has to be a constant endeavour. The issues involved in ecological security– should also suit the media to keep up with ratings and such other competitive compulsions implied in its operation. For this, certain sensitivity programmes need to be organized for those in the media, based on analytical and research support, as also for the civil society groups. Many if not most of them are dedicated people concentrating on 'doing'. Different specialized services need to be devised to suit different media.

A positioning strategy for the movement for ecological security is required. Research on media effects has been limited, ad hoc and one-time, with no conclusive findings. These efforts have to be far more action-linked. Efforts to synthesize all such research for channelling the media more strategically is yet another activity that needs to be organized.

Beyond Mass Media

There are too many aspects involved in ecological security. These may be grouped into thirty parallel umbrella campaigns, each one adding up to the larger cause. The periodicals press and TV should be motivated to take up complex linkage issues. The 'Earth communication campaign' on the electronic media world-wide is a good example.

A national movement for ecological security with specific local actions and at the national level has to be far more visible. A common perspective is a prerequisite. This is what the media should help build first, a national alliance and advocacy programme, as suggested by Amrita Patel. The industry should be part of this effort.

A caucus of eminent personalities should write for the popular media, regionally and nationally. Periodicals should be motivated to carry regular features on larger and complex issues. An exclusive news and features agency (for mainline media) on issues involved in ecological security needs to be explored.

Is there an agenda for the media—for a concerned media with credible sources–on ecological security? Slogans like 'Restore', 'Rehabilitate', 'Recycle', 'Reuse', 'Reduce Consumption', around which traditional strategies were based, could become national movements and campaigns once again.

The print media can be used for agenda setting; the periodicals for the complex linkage dimensions. The cinema can reiterate the concerns, with regulator ads, special series, and special features. The radio can serve to remind, to network and for interactivity.

Public hearings and social audit (different from Environment audit) could also become a supportive media. The school system is a more reliable source for ecological security. The younger citizens are the best bet to address, involve and sustain. A lot more concerted effort is required to be taken up at this level. Colleges, universities, the departments of zoology, biology, environmental sciences, etc., should be more actively involved in local and regional level sensitization. They could be credible linkages with the media. The trade and industry associations and federations, etc., should be made more pro-active, but not in a Delhi-centric way. The media's role will emerge for and from these bodies based on their pro-ecological security initiatives.

In the middle of March of 2003 a unique charter on 'corporate responsibility for environmental protection' was released. It was a significant development, for it has voluntary initiatives for seventeen industry categories to ensure total and specific compliance with pollution control norms and for each category. There are specific time-bound actions. But this charter hardly received any media coverage (except in *The Hindu*), not even minimal coverage, for it was released by the Ministry of Environment and Forests, not by the industry groups like CII. The ministry is not everything. Disjointed efforts hardly make a difference nor would they add up to anything significant. Ecological issues should not be viewed as the concern of only the government. Eco-clubs, Environment Centres and a whole lot of paraphernalia being supported by government require a re-look and a repositioning.

It is better that all such resources be passed on to a national alliance outside the governmental setup, with eminent personalities involved, leaving periodic evaluation to the government. Legal provisions could be obligatory and enabling with provision for redressal. Several PILs are being filed across the country. The outcome of all such cases as well legal initiatives in the states and local bodies need to be kept track of and reprocessed for the mass media appropriately. Even more, provisions and implications of all such legal matters should be known to people at different levels. The media could play this role, but some one has to help it in this.

Forewarning (with long-term risks) & Frightening (with damage assessment) thrusts should be far more within the country at various levels and on various aspects involved in ecological security. Anil Agrawal's crusade from CSE–against industrial effluents, vehicle air pollution, pesticide in water, water harvesting–have demonstrated how research and analysis sustains advocacy and campaigns. Credible research, analysis, and monitoring support are essential for such efforts. Complacency that the environment is being protected and, as Amrita Patel has cautioned, the policy proclamations of government or politicians of a 'highly populist' nature could be deceptive even though they get media coverage much more easily.

In conclusion, let me state that, while recognizing the realities of media operations, the latter could be harnessed positively, but negative effects (however unintended they may be) also need to be moderated. All this is possible only if civil society is actively engaged at many levels. The double-edged character of the mass media needs to be remembered always when we think of ecological security and the complexities involved.

18

Accounting for Ecological Security

R. K. PACHAURI

The structure of my paper is that I first discuss the fallacies in National Income Accounting. I will then get into economic growth and its ecological impacts in India, and then a few ideas on how we might understand ecological security in all its dimensions, and dwelling briefly on the threat of climate change and then on how to really address the challenge.

It is getting increasingly apparent that conventional accounting systems are really not able to capture the true progress of a country because in these systems there is poor representation of the social and environmental capital of a country. This set of variables does not enter into the GDP stream at all. This does not enter into national income accounts. It certainly therefore fails to capture the welfare parameters, the quality of life and the income distribution within a country. Over-consumption is measured as economic progress in a country and, therefore, this actually perpetuates a system of excessive consumption.

There is a very interesting NGO by the name of Redefining Progress located in San Francisco and they bring out annually a set of indicators which according to them provide you a better picture of economic progress and they call it the Genuine Progress Indicator (GPI)—as opposed to the GDP, the gross domestic product. What their argument is I think carries a lot of conviction. You take, for instance, a country where people over-consume food; then they get fat. When they get fat, then they start going to gyms and health clubs. The income that the health clubs generate is added to the national income accounts. Then you also have health problems, so you go to a doctor. The amount of money that a doctor earns also enters into the national income accounts. So in the first place you create a problem which in no way adds to human welfare-if anything it takes away from human welfare, because obesity for instance has a lot of health implications that are harmful. Then to correct that you essentially create a set of activities which lead to an addition to the national income accounts. So there is something fallacious, something wrong with the GDP as a measure of progress.

If I can give an example closer to home, we had beautiful rivers that had pristine purity. Then we started dumping sewage and industrial wastes, chemicals and fertilizers and everything, so that water has become totally useless for any kind of economic activity and certainly for human consumption. Then we set up factories where water is cleaned and purified and all that goes into the national income accounts. And it shows up as economic progress, but in real fact it is not. So I think as far as GDP is concerned, it can give you some very erroneous indications of what economic progress is.

If we carry this argument further, then we can also estimate what is known as the footprint of human actions on the ecology of the world. I am reminded of what Mahatma Gandhi said when a particular British journalist asked him, "Gandhiji, would you not want Indian society to reach the same levels of prosperity that Britain has attained? "And Gandhiji thought for a moment and responded", well, it required Britain to conquer half this planet to reach their level of wealth and prosperity. How many planets will India have to conquer to reach the same level?"

The point is that through our over-consumptive activities and habits, we are imposing a huge ecological footprint on the earth which essentially strains the natural resources of the earth and thereby adds to the insecurity of human existence. This is what Redefining Progress has plotted in the context of two different components. There are carbon dioxide emissions which lead to climate change, and there are other environmental impacts which also become part of the ecological footprint. You can see that we have already crossed the threshold of the absorptive capacity of the earth to accept this huge footprint.

This is just a computation of different countries and the size of their ecological footprints. You can see that Canada has a population of 31.2 million, but the size of its footprint is 6.9. In the case of Bangladesh you have 134 million people; the footprint is 0.6, and so on. We really cannot change the system of national income accounts but it is important for those of us who work on these issues to at least come up with some alternative measures by which we can get a clear idea of what economic activities and human consumption are doing to the eco-systems of this earth.

Let me run through some of these which are proverbial and well-known facts. In order to provide food and basic needs, land degradation becomes an extremely important issue. I was born in the mountains in Nainital and I remember as a child we used to travel in the Terai region. All that area was occupied by forests. It has now been converted to agricultural land because perhaps there is no other way that we could have fed the population of this country. But in this struggle to provide food and basic needs—or what we know as basic needs—land degradation becomes certainly very important. If you look at the land in India, 27 per cent of the soil suffers from very severe soil erosion. 13 million hectares of irrigated land are now unfit for agriculture, largely because of excessive irrigation. An additional 125 million hectares are generally degraded. We know that the Ganga, the Brahmaputra and the Kosi rivers are among the 16 rivers worldwide, which have severe sediment loading. All of this is essentially the end product of the kind of lifestyles, the kinds of economic policies that we have pursued for a long period of time.

Impact of air pollution on climate, because this changes the hydrological cycle. (I am not talking about global climate change over here, but I am talking about local factors, like aerosols, like smoke going into the atmosphere, which certainly has an impact on precipitation locally).

If we look at sulphur dioxide emissions by fuel this is a reference case scenario for Asia. You see the enormous increase that we are likely to witness, say, by the year 2020. You look at the sources that lead to these sulphur dioxide emissions, there is coal, oil and other sources as well. So, obviously Asia with its rapid economic growth is likely to be threatened by large quantities of sulphur dioxide in the atmosphere. These, incidentally, can impact on security, because they will result in acid rain in different parts of Asia.

In fact, we have been involved in a major study that was mounted by the World Bank and the Asian Development Bank. The chances are—and in fact there is a high probability—that several parts of India will have high level of acidification of soil, which would make it very difficult for agriculture to prosper.

We know the problems of land use change, deforestation and contaminated water. We see that in our neighbourhood, in the river Jamuna, itself.

As far as water is concerned we have a case of physical scarcity which is growing. Per capita availability of water has declined from 6000 cubic meters per year in 1947 to 2300 cubic meters per year in 1997. That means that in the first fifty years of India's independence, we have reached a situation where the per capita availability of water became much lower. Over-exploitation of ground water in Rajasthan, Haryana, Punjab, Gujarat, ranges from 100 to 260 per cent. We carried out a detailed study in Mehsana district in Gujarat where the ground water table has sunk so low that people who were getting water to drink from the wells cannot possibly get it any more. So they have to walk long distances to be able to get water for drinking purposes from surface sources or shallower wells. By 2015, 36 per cent of the blocks in this country would be over-exploited for groundwater.

Of 80 districts in the Yamuna river basin the number of highly stressed is likely to increase from 20 in 1997 to 50 in 2047. That means, the area surrounding the Yamuna basin itself, more than 50 per cent of the area would be water stressed.

Today we know that water in major rivers is unfit for drinking or bathing. Sewage treatment capacity caters only to 10 per cent of present waste water or sewage water generated. Less than three-quarters of the municipal solid waste generated is collected; the rest is thrown into the sewers or burnt in the open. There is increased nitrate level in shallow ground water from excess of fertilizers, pesticides, chemicals. So there is also deterioration of water quality, quite apart from the physical reduction in availability.

We know what is happening with deforestation. Over the last fifty years forest cover has dwindled to less than 50 per cent of the area covered earlier, with land diverted to settlements, agriculture and just sheer felling for a variety of reasons including the demand of construction. Present dense forest cover is just under 13 per cent, against the desirable target of 33 per cent. It is laudable that the tenth Five Year plan for the first time has laid down certain targets to be met for afforestation. The point that I would like to make is that it is far more economically effective to invest in natural resources and their generation than merely investing in factories and other such assets. The threat of desertification exists in 52 per cent of the total land area which can lead to serious consequences.

Our estimate was that GDP loss due to environmental damage exceeds 10 per cent. This takes into account health effects, takes into account loss of production in agriculture, the loss of wealth and income in terms of forests where communities were able to thrive on a sustainable basis. 11 to 26 per cent of our agricultural output is lost due to soil degradation. The annual growth of forests—and this is I think where science and technology can make a lot of difference—is only 88 cubic meters as against 139 to 235 cubic meters which is possible under our climatic and geographical conditions. Twenty-three known species of animals are extinct, including the cheetah as well as several other plant species; 2.5 million people die prematurely each year due to air pollution. Water quality in most major rivers of India is far below acceptable levels.

Now what ensures security? All this background is not merely a case of preparing a scare scenario. We need to understand how each of these variables where you see degradation or damage to our natural resources actually impact on the security of human existence. First we must understand that security does not come from military or geo-political power, but it comes from providing the people in any society with basic subsistence level of well being and sustainable livelihood. Take the case of Bangladesh. We complain about the fact that refugees spill over our borders and settle down in different parts of our country. But in a country where you have cyclones, you have disasters on such a frequent and such a severe scale, you are really dealing with what you might call environmental insecurity. Therefore people have no choice, quite apart from the levels of poverty that exist over there, but to cross over and come into Indian territory. Therefore there are major social, cultural and human dimensions to a definition and an understanding of security.

When you have aggravated environmental stress, it exacerbates existing inequity simply because the poor are the worst affected as a result of environmental dimensions. A figure that a friend of mine who is Vice-President in the World Ban has come up with is that the poor depend to the extent of 33 per cent of the goods and services that they consume directly on the environment or the natural resources around them. We know that from observation—whether it is food, fodder or fuel, the poor have no real recourse but to go and rely on the natural resources existing around them. Therefore, if the quality of those natural resources declines, then to that extent their consumption, their livelihood also declines.

Dry areas today—one looks at a global view—are covering 40 per cent of the earth's surface. Soil degradation globally affects one billion people. 100 million are likely to be displaced due to soil degradation in the next 20 years. We know that in the case of sub-Saharan Africa where the social structure has completely broken down because of massive degradation of the soil. The fact is that people really have nowhere to go for subsistence living except move from one place to the other.

Finally, I would like to highlight the importance of climate change as it is going to impact on our ecosystems and the security of human existence. This comes from the third assessment report of the IPCC. As it happens, the worst impacts of climate change will fall disproportionately upon developing countries and poor persons within all countries. You could be a poor man sleeping on the streets of New York. Let us say you have a severe weather event—you may be living in the richest country in the world, but basically if you are poor you have no choice but to suffer the ill effects of that extreme weather event. So this exacerbates inequities and health status, and access to adequate food, clean water and other resources.

These are the impacts of climate change. You have problems of increase of temperature; a major disruption in the pattern of precipitation takes place, accompanied by sea level rise. This leads to health impacts where as a result weather-related mortality takes place. We have seen mortality on a large scale taking place in Andhra Pradesh this time and perhaps in other parts of the country which has probably not got properly recorded. You have had deaths, as Suresh Prabhu just mentioned, in a city like Paris. Their hospitals are full at this point of time; they are not able to cope with the large number of patients who are coming in there with heat-related problems and because of the heat wave. Infectious diseases will increase because with the disruption in the weather there are several types of organisms that would thrive. There would of course be air-quality related respiratory illnesses.

In the case of agriculture, crop yields are likely to go down and there would be much greater demand for irrigation that only exacerbates the water supply problem. Water supply will reduce because of precipitation changes. Water quality will change because of these imbalances in the supply of water.

I was looking at some data on water quality over the last six years. I find enormous fluctuation in that water quality. And that is largely because of the changes in flows that take place in different river systems. When you have large volumes of flow, then certainly there is reduction in the level of pollution per unit of water. When you have low levels of flow, then the density of pollution goes up. There will also be competition for water.

Coastal areas will suffer erosion. There will be inundation of coastal lands. Bangladesh is one of the most severely threatened countries as a result of that. The Maldives Islands, there is a danger that they might actually vanish. There is additional cost to protect coastal communities.

Species and natural areas are also likely to be affected, because of loss of habitat and species, and so on. Of course the cryo-sphere would also be affected, because we already know that our glaciers are receding; very rapidly, they are melting very fast.

In most developing countries, if you take any single developing country, the average sea level rise there by 2100 is projected at 50 cm. Most of the Maldive islands are at a height of one to two meters above sea level. You do not have to wait until they get completely inundated, but actually when you have storm surges, when there are cyclones, they will be far more severe if the sea is higher.

Fifteen to seventeen million people in Bangladesh and Vietnam would be exposed to one meter sea level rise. And small island states are in the danger of suffering submergence. The Himalayan glaciers, which are already receding, are likely to affect five hundred million people in South Asia. Initially you will get a larger flow of water because these glaciers are melting, but once they have reduced in size the flow will reduce and we won't get the kinds of water supply that we have become used to.

Agriculture is the largest consumer of water in the region, accounting for 86 per cent of water used in India. This is largely dependent on the monsoon. When the monsoon is affected, to that extent agriculture will also be impacted. Because of high temperatures there is yield deceleration of rice in Asia. For other reasons also, yields are actually on the decline, having come down from 2.8 per cent in 1980 to 1.1 per cent in 1990. The decrease is attributed primarily to water scarcity and indiscriminate and inefficient use of fertilizers and pesticides and reliance on narrow genetic material. All of this will get multiplied as a result of climate change.

As far as India is concerned, we are likely to see increases in inter-annual variability of daily precipitation; intensity of extreme rainfall events is likely to be higher with warmer atmosphere. And changes in monsoon will take place such that the north-western regions would receive less rain while monsoon would intensify over the north-east. There would be a disruption in the pattern of rainfall that we have experienced in the past.

This would have implications for food security. Experiments on rice in India report that high temperatures and reduced radiation caused sterility in rice production, reduction in yields such as any increase in dry production as a result of CO_2 fertilisation prove to be no advantage. You see there are two effects. Because of higher CO_2 in the atmosphere you would have faster plant growth, but at the same time if temperatures are high there is a heat effect which would actually reduce the yields of crops. This is particularly relevant in the case of wheat. So, let us say if wheat production is affected adversely, what are our farmers going to do who are at the moment dependent on wheat production? Well, either they get out of farming or they start producing other crops. So, there is a challenge for scientists to come up with strains that would be heat-resistant, that would be drought-resistant, so that farmers can continue to practice their professions. There is also a major science and technology agenda that we need to take in hand immediately because the results from some of these efforts will not come overnight, and will come over a long period of time.

I do not want to spend too much time on this. This is merely a distribution diagram which shows that you will get more extreme temperatures because there is going to be a shift in the distribution of temperatures from cold to hot, so the tail would move towards more record hot weather and you will probably get less cold weather. Now, friends in Russia often express delight that climate change would really do them good, the Siberian region can open up, but in actual fact the results could be totally the reverse, because of changes in precipitation levels. And this could lead to much heavier snowfall in the Siberian range in Russia and with that higher snowfall you would actually get colder weather on the ground and you would not really get any net warming. You see, we are dealing with a very complex system. There are no linear changes; there are no uniform changes that are going to take place.

Vagaries of the extremes—are we already feeling them? The number of disasters has increased significantly. The World Meteorological Organization in fact has estimated that the number of extreme events world-wide has doubled in the last ten years. We have had the case of heat waves in 2003 between April and June, in which

1,664 deaths took place in Andhra Pradesh. In fact, immediately the Cabinet in the state has set up a committee which they have asked me to chair. I am doing that to look at the factors behind this and what can be done to prevent these problems in future. There has been a significant increase in the frequencies since 1994 and the duration of the heat wave is lasting much longer. Suppose we were to have heat wave for three days and let us say a rickshaw puller—he might be able to take life easy for three days without going out into the sun and get baked in it. But if it lasts for 27 days, as it did in parts of Andhra this year, the poor man has no choice. He has to feed his family to earn a living. So he goes out into the open, he is exposed to very high temperatures, he gets dehydrated, one does not know whether he can get water to drink, so he succumbs and suffers the ill effects of that heat wave.

The recurrent droughts and desertification are already threatening the livelihood of 1.7 billion people who depend on land worldwide. This is the estimate from the World Meteorological Organization.

We need to understand this since the poor are the most vulnerable sections of society. What is poverty? First, it is the relationship of people to commodities and resources. You might ask what this means. If you go back in time 250 years, communities protected their forests, they had ownership of forests, and then a colonial power came and decided to nationalize all the forests. A large part of the forest wealth of the country was exported, and the people who depended on the forests and were essentially responsible for their sustainable upkeep were completely divested of this responsibility. Now we are trying to bring these together once again by programmes like Joint Forest Management. But essentially poverty is not merely related to income. Poverty is related to choices and it is related to the ability of the people to be able to decide their own destiny. And sustainability really means 'to sustain ability'. If you take away the ability of people to do what they see is in their best interests, then that is clearly not a sustainable situation. And the ability of people to retain control over their living conditions which is what I just referred to. There are differences between rural vs. urban problems. I won't go into this but I want to highlight the fact that the poor are the most deeply affected by any degradation that takes place in the stock of natural resources and in the entitlements to those natural resources. If you remove them from the entitlements that they have enjoyed for thousands of years, then to that extent you are also depriving them of their legitimate livelihood.

So what do we do in terms of interventions? We need to ensure that the poor have entitlements, have responsibility for maintaining those natural resources around them. Certainly there will be problems. This will not be a smooth transition but over a period of time you will be able to reach equilibrium. We need to build and sustain their abilities, so I think creating local capacity is vitally important. The property rights of communities over commons are extremely important. You need to have market access. Because you cannot possibly have the duality of development where the rich and the privileged continue to get the benefits and the poor are completely divorced from those benefits. We need rural enterprise for income and job creation so that people can attain income levels whereby they can invest in protecting the environment and natural resources.

You need an enabling system of devolution which translates into participatory governance at every level. You need to develop local institutions and their capacity and you need to create infrastructure in rural areas which includes connectivity in terms of communication, it means roads, transportation and other infrastructure so that the produce can be reached to the markets in order to ensure reasonable income, ensuring health care and education. And of course there is the central role of fuel and energy, because unless you have adequate supply of fuels and energy you cannot create a sustainable system at the decentralized level.

So what we need is to redefine property rights and the management structure for common resources, including property rights of management of water in particular. In several parts of the country this is working very well with Pani Panchayats and so on. The Joint Forest Management experience is very heartening and very encouraging.

Science and technology have a major role to play. We need goal-oriented, people friendly, renewable energy technologies. We have to reorient R&D for natural resource regeneration. Too much of our R&D is industry-oriented, too much is oriented towards goods and services the middle class is used to. One can understand this in the developed countries where the markets are established, where people have fairly large incomes. But in the case of a country like India where the bulk of the population lives in rural areas I think we need a complete reorientation of the R & D structure and focus on areas where you might be able to enhance the wealth of natural resources that exist.

We need technologies for sustainable water use. If you use drip irrigation, the efficiency would be about 95 per cent. If you use surface-water irrigation it is barely 40 to 45 per cent. So if we can use water efficiently even in the domestic sphere, it would make an enormous difference to availability of water.

The promise of bio-technology for bio-mass production has to be tapped and I think connectivity in information technology is also vitally important.

Just to show the kinds of distortions that exist in R & D, this gives you the picture for investments in research and development in major industrial countries. The bulk of research, say, in energy goes into nuclear; the rest goes into fossil fuels and a very small quantity into renewable energy research. In our country we really need a reversal of this. We need to be spending much more on decentralized forms of energy production which focus on renewable sources of energy.

Similar is the case of public investment in agricultural research. Look at the industrial countries. Despite the fact that they do not depend all that much on agricultural production, they are spending more and more on agricultural research. In the developing countries despite what we have done in the past we continue with a steady level of investment in this area.

I shall not go into this but this gives you the internal rates of return from R&D, from the use of agriculture bio-technology etc. Even in Sub-Saharan Africa the rates of return are 33 per cent. In the case of Asia and the Pacific it is even higher. There is some disconnect over here in our R&D policies. They obviously are not dictated by what might give us maximum economic benefits.

In national economic policies certainly we have to target equitable growth. We have to internalize environmental costs, which mean that those who are using the environment for their private purposes must necessarily have to pay for it. The social costs of the use of natural resources have to be internalized in the private costs and in the prices that the people pay. We need strong regulatory bodies and these have to be decentralized. State Pollution Control Boards are not the answer. We need a decentralized pollution control body . We have not moved in that direction at all. Unless the community is involved, unless the decentralized government is involved I do not think you would get the kinds of results that would be desirable. We must dismantle centralized bureaucracies and there has to be devolution of power.

Globally we need to promote markets that support traditional products so that those who are dispossessed, those who are poor have also the benefits of globalization. I think international economic assistance must focus on poverty reduction and regeneration of natural resources. In the case of climate change, we have to ensure means by which the most vulnerable are able to protect themselves, whether in early warning systems, and in the case of Bangladesh and the small island states you might need dykes to prevent the impact of sea level rise. And you of course need to regenerate natural resources.

As I come to the end I would like to remind everybody of what Mahatma Gandhi said: 'Be the change you want to see in the world'. All of us talk about these things but I think the time has come for us to practice them in reality to see that through our own lives, our own life styles we are able to translate this message into action. Otherwise the future generations would only be afflicted by all kinds of insecurity, the root cause of which would be environmental destruction and degradation.

Contributors

Dr Amrita Patel, Chairman, Foundation for Ecological Security & National Dairy Development Board.

Dr Ashok Khosla, President, Development Alternatives, New Delhi.

Dr D. K. Biswas, Former Chairman, Central Pollution Control Board.

Dr Erach Bharucha, Director, Institute of Environment Education & Research, Bharatiya Vidyapeeth Deemed University, Pune.

Shri Jairam Ramesh is presently Union Minister of State, Ministry of Commerce and Industry.

Justice Shri J. S. Verma, Former Chief Justice of India and Chairman, National Human Rights Commission.

Late Dr Kamla Chowdhry, an economic management specialist, headed the National Wastelands Development Board (1985-1988) and was Member of the World Bank's Advisory Committee on Environment and Sustainable Development.

Dr Karan Singh, Member of Parliament (Rajya Sabha) and President, People's Commission for Environment & Development.

Dr L. M. Singhvi, former Indian High Commissioner to the UK, and a leading constitutional expert.

Dr M.S. Swaminathan, Eminent Scientist & Chairman, M.S. Swaminathan Research Foundation, Chennai.

Dr N. Bhaskara Rao, Chairman, Centre for Media Studies, New Delhi.

Dr Najma Heptulla, Former Deputy Chairperson, Rajya Sabha.

Dr N. C. Saxena, IAS (Retd.) Former Member Secretary, Planning Commission.

Dr P. S. Ramakrishnan, Professor of Ecology, School of Environmental Sciences, Jawaharlal Nehru University, New Delhi.

Dr R. K. Pachauri, Director General, The Energy Research Institute (TERI) & Chairman, Intergovernmental Panel on Climate Change.

Shri R. Rajamani, IAS (Retd.) Former Secretary, Ministry of Environment & Forests.

Shri Shekhar Singh, Faculty Member, Indian Institute of Public Administration, and Director, Centre for Equity Studies, New Delhi.

Dr Vandana Shiva, Director, Navdanya and Research Foundation for Science, Technology & Ecology, New Delhi.

FOUNDATION FOR ECOLOGICAL SECURITY

PB No. 29, NDDB Campus
Anand-388001, Gujarat, India.
Website : www.fes.org.in

The Foundation for Ecological Security was set up in February 2001 and is registered under the Societies Registration Act XXI, 1860.

The mission of the Society is: 'To work towards the ecological restoration and conservation of land and water resources, in the uplands and in other eco-fragile, degraded and marginalized zones of the country and to set in place the processes of coordinated human effort and governance to this end'.

In order to do so, the Foundation collaborates and works with and through a range of democratic village institutions, their federal bodies, Civil Society Organizations, as well as governing bodies at the local, state as well as the national levels. The Foundation works with nearly one thousand villages in twenty-one districts spread across the seven states of Andhra Pradesh, Gujarat, Karnataka, Madhya Pradesh, Orissa, Rajasthan and Uttaranchal.

- The organization works in marginalized and ecologically fragile areas, and as far as possible with entire landscapes, and with all the interrelated communities within it, through a range of arrangements on their land and aquatic resources, whether Commons, Public or Private.
- The Foundation works to promote the stability of ecosystems through the protection and restoration of biological diversity, hydrological regimes and nutrient cycles.
- The Foundation works to assist and collaborate in the creation of a coherent perspective on forest and water related land-use policy, as well as a conducive legal and regulatory environment, and to disseminate knowledge and information through the media, and through dialogue with policy makers, legislators, bureaucrats, academicians and the public-at-large.
- The organization also undertakes, and collaborates in studies and research on all related dimensions to further the understanding of ecological processes and the biology of endemic species, as well as the various aspects of the political economy of the associated human communities.

• • •